UNTIL WE MEET AGAIN

Written By
RAMON A. BROOKS

Copyright © 2025 RAMON A. BROOKS
UNTIL WE MEET AGAIN

All rights reserved. No part of this book may be reproduced in any form or by electronic or mechanical means, including information storage and retrieval systems without permission in writing from the publisher, except by a reviewer who may quote brief passages in review.

First Edition 2025

Printed in the United States of America

This is a work of fiction. Names, characters, places, and incidents either are products of the author's imagination or are used fictitiously. Any similarity to actual events or locales or persons, living or dead, is entirely coincidental.

Dedication

I dedicate this book to my sandbox brother Boozer and my celly Chindo, both serving football numbers behind bars but y'all will be back.
I'M PRAYING FOR OUR FREEDOM.

Ramon A. Brooks contact info:
ramonbrooks9219@gmail.com
Facebook: Ramon A. Brooks

Chapter 1

Waking up from a bad dream, Baby J rushed to the bathroom holding himself to prevent him from wetting the bed. Well, wetting the pile of blankets his mother prepared for him every night. With his eyes barely opened, he began to release his bladder, spraying everywhere but his intended target. At 6:35 am, who could blame him?

Without shaking himself, he pulled up the pair of too little shorts his mother forced him to wear since they were too broke to afford so much as a bar of soap to hand wash their underwear with. Juan's mother, who used to be a very beautiful young lady, was now a hopeless dope fiend.

Big Juan, Cynthia's lover, and one of the biggest drug dealers in Chicago, made sure she didn't want for nothing, that's until he was sentenced to 23 years in prison that's a secret, Cynthia had no intentions on telling Juan Jr. Instead, she tried to forget the day that her life changed.

She was six months pregnant with Juan Jr. when the cops stormed in and took Big Juan into custody. All they left Cynthia with was the hope that one day he would come back to her and make everything alright again.

Juan's stomach started to growl intensely as he headed to his mother's room with his hopeless problem. *Knock! Knock! Knock!* his small light-yellow hands performed a beat on the bedroom door. *Knock before coming into mommy's room* is what she always told him.

Knock! Knock! Knock! He tapped again before sticking his hand in the hole in the door, pushing it open. His mother was laid across a pallet of her own, sound asleep.

"Mommy," he called as he shook her arm repeatedly. "Mommy," he called again. But his innocent voice was useless to his mother's heroin induced coma.

He could tell by the rubber band tied to her arm that mommy was off her medicine as she called it. Juan Jr did the only thing that he knew for sure would awaken his queen even though it was strictly prohibited. He pinched his mother's arm as hard as he could, causing her to jump. "SHIT! Baby J what the hell I tell you about doin; that shit?" She yelled while rubbing her fragile arm before playfully pinching him back.

"Ouch," he laughed as they traded pinch for pinch.

"What chu doin' up so early? What's wrong?"

"I'm hungry you said that you was gonna feed me yesterday," he sobbed

"Okay baby. Mommy finna go get you some noodles right now I promise. Just let mommy get five more minutes of sleep, okay?"

"Okay" he agreed knowing there was a very small chance that she would keep her promise.

Juan Jr was only 4 years old, but he was old enough to know that the only thing his mother cared about was her medicine. The only time he would eat was when one of his mother's friends came over to play "Hide N Seek" with them. Hide N Seek was Juan's favorite game.

All he had to do was hide in his secret hiding spot where no one could ever find him until the game was over and he would be rewarded a free meal along with a few snacks if he was lucky. He felt undefeated at this game. His young innocent mind could never imagine the *seeking* his mother was doing while he hid out in his secret spot.

Juan ran to look out the front window while waiting for his mother to wake up. He studied the block's everyday motion from the hand-to-hand transactions, to the game of cops and robbers, barely stopping at the shootouts that happened right in the middle of Springfield and Division Street. This was his daily routine in the middle of July. The hood was full of surprises.

Baby J's eyes lit up when he saw one of his mother's friends approaching their door. He ran to his mother's room full of excitement. "Ma!" He shook her much more aggressively then the first time he attempted to awake her. "Hmm," she replied with her eyes closed. Slob drooled down the crease of her lips.

"Your friend here to play Hide N Seek, wake up" he shook her harder with each push, but the mention of her dear friend caused her to snap back to reality, despite the extensive grade of dope she injected into her arm.

"Okay baby," she mumbled while attempting to collect herself. "Mommy finna count, you better go hide."

Chapter 2

Heaven
2 years later

"How was your first day at school, sweetie?"
Heaven's mother asked her as she watched her climb into the passenger seat of her mom's '98' Toyota Camry. Heaven had her headphones in her ear, so she didn't hear her mother Marrissa's question. Or at least she pretended like it. Staring at her daughter's distressed facial expression Marrissa knew that something was wrong. More than that, she knew exactly what the problem was so instead of cutting into her daughter she left the situation alone until Heaven was ready to talk. Heaven, relieved that her mother gave up on the small talk, buckled her seatbelt and turned the volume up on the car radio as her mother pulled into the busy Chicago traffic, heading home to the southside.

Pulling up to their home, Heaven spotted her best friends, April and Stacy, playing hopscotch on the ground across the street from her apartment. Suddenly, her mood changed as she eagerly unfastened her seatbelt while reaching for her door handle. Her mother grabbed her arm. "Now you know better, honey." Her voice was soft and sweet.

"I know," Heaven huffed harmlessly. "Change out of my school clothes before I go play."

She rolled her eyes playfully as she made her way to hug both of her friends before returning to change her clothes.

Her mother smiled as she watched her dash up the stairs of their apartment. She loved how Heaven's friends gave her so much life. They attended the same school but they were in 4th grade, a grade higher than Heaven, so they didn't see each other much during school hours.

Heaven got harassed daily. Rumors floated around but no one knew the truth about her lifestyle, they were all just guessing. No one knew her story. Not even her. Her friends on the block were the only two that showed her real love without questions. Despite Heaven being a mixture of Latina and Black and her parents being pure white their household was filled with love, there wasn't a thing Heaven wanted for, she was practically spoiled rotten.

She had a wardrobe her classmates could only dream of affording, which was only one of the reasons she was being teased. Heaven had way too much fire inside her to be bullied so every situation resulted in a detention, maybe even a parent teacher conference but this time Heaven was suspended for fighting.

She had bitten a plug out of Cherish's face. Cherish was her most jealous classmate, hands down. Before Heaven transferred into Juarez Elementary School last year, Cherish had her classmates on lock with her beauty but that clout was short lived the moment Heaven walked into Mrs. Coleman classroom. While Cherish was a pretty girl, Heaven was stunning. Being mixed gave her the advantage of having gorgeous eyes and extremely long hair that curled down to the middle of her back.

The little boys used to beg their parents for snack money just to give it to Cherish. Now they were drooling at Heavens feet with their pocket change, but she wasn't the least bit interested. However, Cherish wasn't too happy with becoming the second runner up, so she used every chance she got to make Heaven's life a living hell. This time Heaven was fed up and Cherish was on the receiving end of her built up rage.

"Oops ... scuse me," Cherish laughed as she purposely stepped on Heaven's brand-new Jordan's in the middle of the lunch line. Heaven let it slide. She could care less about the dirt mark that was left on her new shoes.

Mommy will just buy me a new pair tomorrow, she thought to herself as she stepped to the side, giving Cherish and her group of followers more than enough room to proceed, but she knew the show wouldn't stop there. However, she held her head high, appearing to be unfazed by the shoe incident, which made Cherish furious. After cutting Heaven in the lunch line, she turned around to pick a lil more.

"So, Heaven," she stood face to face holding one hand on her hip and the other hand on the wall, preventing Heaven from making an easy escape, "how you gone be black but yo momma nem white?" She giggled with the rest of her friends before continuing. "You must be a slave or someth—mn "

Before she got a chance to finish her sentence she was being dragged to the floor by her hair. This time Cherish had went a joke too far. Heaven began to pound away at her like Donkey Kong on the Gameboy color. Two of Cherish's friends attempted to pull Heaven off, but she wiggled out of their grips right before biting the girl.

Cherish screamed out in agony from the intense pain she was in. Heaven dug her teeth in refusing to let go

"Heaven, what has gotten into you today?" The principal asked as he handed her a napkin.

Instead of replying Heaven continued to breath harshly in an attempt to bring herself down from her enraged rollercoaster. After her breathing seemed to calm down a bit, principal Hobbs tried his approach again, this time a bit different.

"Tell me what happened," he commanded gently as he took a seat on the bench next to her, attempting to comfort her.

Tears began to fall from her eyes as she told the principal what went down. "Mr. Hobbs I'm tired of people," she paused to get a grip on her emotions, "picking on me and my family about our color." she continued. "What am I supposed to do? Sit here and let them people pick on me every day? This same thing has been going on since the second grade. I'm tired of her – ugh," she growled to prevent from using improper language that she so badly wanted to say.

"I understand your frustration, Heaven, I really do, but this type of behavior is unacceptable. You shouldn't allow anyone to make you as angry as I saw you just a few minutes ago. If I let you slide, then all the children at this school are going to run around thinking they can just punch and bite people and that's not okay with me."

Heaven began to cry harder. "But Mr. Hobbs, I've been taking this for so long and nobody ever gets in trouble, but me," she sobbed.

"That's not true, sweety. There's a zero tolerance for both bullying and fighting. I'm afraid she got exactly what she deserved, that girl is nothing but trouble and I hope she learned her lesson," he smirked before returning the serious gaze on his face, "But this is no way to start off the school year, so I'm going to give your mother a call and let her know you're both being suspended for three days," he said as he retrieved his cell phone from his waist clip.

He flipped his Motorola and pressed a few buttons before placing the phone to his ear. After being forwarded to her voicemail he closed his phone and replaced it in his clip. "I'm gonna try to call her again when I come off my break, meanwhile let me walk you to get your lunch –"

"I'm not hungry," she cut him off.

"I tell you what. I have Chinese food downstairs waiting on me, how about you join me?" he reached out his hand and Heaven accepted it with a smile. She always had a secret crush on him. This would be like her own little playdate in her mind.

Chapter 3

Cynthia

"Hurry up, boy, before we miss this damn bus!" Cynthia yelled over her shoulder as she pushed the baby stroller full speed. "Hold that bus!" She yelled even louder.

Baby J was too busy eating his snack he'd gotten from school to chase some CTA bus. It wasn't until she yelled his name that he realized his mother was fifteen feet away from him and nearly approaching the bus as the short Mexican held the door open for them. Baby J balled up his fist holding his PB&J cracker tightly and took off running as fast as his little legs would allow.

By the time he made it to the bus stop on the corner of Division and Monticello, the Mexican guy was helping Cynthia pull the stroller up the bus stairs. "Thank you," she said with a smile from the way the man just smiled and nodded she knew he didn't speak English.

She reached out her hand to help Baby J board the CTA bus before it pulled away from its stop at Cameron grammar school. Today had been Baby J's first day of school. Second grade had been fun judging by the Peanut Butter & Jelly cracker and the Pokémon stickers stuck to his face.

"Let yo brother get a piece of that before you eat it all."

"I got him one in my backpack," Baby J said as he pulled his backpack from over his shoulders and began searching for the zipper.

Mari, Baby J's baby brother at almost 2 years old, was already his best friend. He finally had someone to play with when mother wasn't paying him any attention. Sometimes she even left the two of them in the house alone while she ran the streets.

Within the last two years Cynthia managed to enroll Baby J into school, move into their three-bedroom section 8 apartment on the west side of Chicago, and get Snap Benefits for the three of them. But Cynthia couldn't resist that monkey crawling up her back, which caused her to risk it all every time she needed a fix. She would sell her food stamps, rent out her room to the D-boyz as a motel from time to time, or even use her spot as the dope fiend camp out just to get high as rent.

Baby J knew how selfish his mother could be so instead of eating his food at school. He learned how to sneak his breakfast and lunch home just to feed his little brother and him. *Ding!* Cynthia pulled the stop rope hanging above her head, indicating that she'd be exiting at Homan Street, which was the next stop. The bus driver eased on his brakes, coming to a complete stop before the doors on the front and back of the bus swung open with unison.

"You have reached Homan," the intercom announced.

"Come on, here go our other bus," Cynthia said as she took Baby J by the hand and pulled him to the rear exit.

Cynthia had been to her doctor's appointment three days ago and today she'd received a call from Doctor Hill, her primary doctor at Sacred Heart Hospital. All her test results had come back and just like any other time, Doctor Hill felt the need to discuss the follow up in person.

Doctor Hill had been Cynthia's family's doctor since before her mother pushed her out. Being twenty years her senior, he'd been there through the good, the bad, and the absolute worst. He'd witnessed her older sister beat cancer, her mother pass away from a heart attack, and her father overdose on the same drug that took over her life.

"Ms. Jones, right this way." Dr. Hill led Cynthia into a private room before closing the door behind them. "How's my little man doing?" Dr. Hill held out his hand for a shake and Baby J accepted. "That's my big boy," he said as he reached into his chest pocket and handed Baby J two popsicles.

"Give one to your little brother, you hear?"

"Okay," Baby J responded as he began to tear away at the wrapper of his popsicle.

Dr. Hill led Cynthia to the other side of the room where they'd have a little more privacy. He began shuffling through folders until he located the one with Cynthia's name written on it in black marker. He pulled the file out before starting his speech.

"Ms. Jones, I'm afraid I have some terrible news to share with you," he said sincerely as he removed his glasses and pinched the corner of his eyes to hold back the tears that threatened to fall before replacing his lenses over his grey eyes.

Then he guided her to a seat, with the news he was getting ready to drop on her, he felt a seat would be much needed. *How bad could it possibly be?* Cynthia thought as she took her seat.

"There's no easy way to say this," Dr. Hill said as he opened the folder. He withdrew a paper and handed it to her before continuing, "so I'm just gonna give it to you straight out…"

Cynthia noticed that she had been holding her breath the entire time and her legs began to shake uncontrollably. Dr. Hill placed his hand on her right shoulder for comfort.

"Ms. Jones, your test results came back …. and you tested positive for H.I.V," he finally announced.

His words took the breath out of them both. Cynthia held her stomach as she felt her morning breakfast finding its way back up the same way it went down. Dr. Hill rushed to grab the small trash can from the corner of the room to catch the vomit he was sure was coming. He placed the can in front of her and patted her back as she puked up everything without holding back. Dr. Hill didn't know what to say that would make her feel better. What could he say? That it would be okay? They both knew that would've been the greatest lie ever told. So instead of saying anything he just patted her back until she pulled herself together.

"I have a prescription here for you, with this medication you'll be able to survive for quite some time, it has its side effects so make sure to read the instructions." Dr. Hill placed the prescription in Cynthia's purse. "However, we both know that sooner or later this medication will become useless but no matter what, I want you to hang in there for as long as you possibly can for those two boys in there, ya' hear me?"

Cynthia nodded her head. Dr. Hill never liked giving his patients false hope, especially not Cynthia Jones. He'd sent her down this road before with both of her parents, since then he promised to be straight forward with her. She wouldn't have it any other way.

Baby J looked around the curtain to see his mother crying. He ran over to hold her hand. "It hurt, Ma?" he asked softly.

He thought she was getting a shot in her arm. *I know I cried when I got a shot,* he thought to himself as he tried to console her but he saw no needle and no Band-Aid on her arm. A look of confusion spread across his face. "Mommy's ok baby let's get out of here."

The bus ride home felt long and crowded as Cynthia's thoughts seemed to play a loud in her head. Her stop wasn't approaching quickly enough and she desperately needed to get a dose of the only thing that could fix her problems. "The next stop is Pulaski," she heard the intercom announce. With lightning speed she jumped up and shook Baby J from his sleep.

"Come on baby," she pulled his arm.

When the bus stopped, she exited and hurried across the street to the park where they sold drugs of all kinds. They called it *The One Stop Shop*. Division & Pulaski was always live, seven days a week. Shootouts happened daily, even as the kids swung back and forth on the swings. Cynthia was passing DJ's restaurant when she noticed the man she needed to see coming from the liquor store on the opposite side of the streets, with a pint of Remy Martin in his hand "Fresh!" She yelled out, holding one hand in the air waving it back and forth.

She became excited as he made his way across the street. She could feel the heroin running through her veins already. "Aye Boozer," Fresh, the big homie on the block, called one of the workers, "handle her real quick shorty," he demanded and kept it pushing.

When the younger boy ran over to make the sale, she looked at him in surprise. He couldn't have been no older than 11 years old. But she didn't come to judge, she just wanted her drugs and she would be on her way. She was reaching in her bra when she noticed a very familiar face accompanying the baby face drug dealer.

"Bizzy?" She called his name causing the boy to look up in confusion, "I know you ain't up her hustling. Boy were yo mama at?"

"Naw I ain't hustling, and who is you?" he shot back.

I haven't seen this baby in years of course he wasn't going to remember me, she thought. "You tryna shop or what?" Boozer snapped, breaking her from her train of thought.

She straightened out her bills and counted out fifty-six dollars. She pocketed five of them and handed him the rest "Can I get three for this fifty-two?"

He snatched the money and recounted it before digging into his boxers and retrieving a small sandwich bag from under his ball sack. He looked both ways before untying the bag and passing her the three dub bags of heroin. She usually only purchased one dime bag at a time and even then, she would come with eight dollars, so he didn't mind and he wasn't about to turn down this sale for nothing in the world. He handed her the product and jumped the fence dashing back through the playground in his school uniform.

"I only gave his ass fifty-one," Cynthia chuckled as she tucked the drugs she purchased in her bra and walked into the dollar store to purchase both kids a few snacks.

***

Baby J

Baby J helped his mother carry his baby brother's stroller up the porch stairs leading to their home. When they reached the top, he let go of the bottom and pushed open the first door which had already been unlocked.

Cynthia lost her house keys, so she kept a pocketknife to pick the lock on her front door. Once they stepped in, Baby J instantly dropped his backpack and unbuckled his brother from his stroller. It was playtime. "Go hide with yo brother, we finna play hide n seek," Cynthia said as she locked the front door and kicked off her two-year-old K-Swiss.

"But mama, ain't none of yo friends here to play," he opposed. He knew there would be no real game of hide n seek, just like he knew the needle his mom shot up her arm wasn't medication, but he played along for his mom's satisfaction.

"They on the way now, so go hide like I told you boy," she barked. She was in no mood for back talk. Not today.

Baby J grabbed his baby brother's hand and did as he was told. He knew he would be asleep by the time his mother came to find him or he'll find her sleeping with a rubber band tied around her arm. But he did hide his little brother. After about two minutes, Baby J tip-toed out of his room to sneak a peek at his mom.

Normally he would follow his mom's instructions, but after seeing her cry today at the hospital he became worried. He never saw his mom cry. He expected to find her in her own bedroom, but to his surprise she was in the bedroom she decorated for a girl. He found her, on her knees, holding a barbie doll while talking to this imaginary person.

"Mommy loves you, Miracle. I'll always love you," she sobbed.

This was not the first time Baby J caught his mother talking to this Miracle person. But every time he asked her who she was talking to, her response was nobody. He knew today wouldn't be any different.

"I hope you can forgive me; I was young and stupid back then. I cry every night, thinking about how you're doing or how beautiful you are," she cried.

Baby J wanted to comfort her so badly, but he knew he wasn't supposed to see this, so he just sat there, silently wiping the tears from his eyes. It hurt to see his mom hurt. Especially when he couldn't do nothing to fix her problems. At six years old, he did not know what pain or emotions were. He just knew his heart was throbbing and he didn't like the feeling. He watched his mom place the doll back into the doll house and before she could turn around, he snuck back into his hiding spot.

Baby J woke up holding his brother in his arms, still sound asleep. He didn't know how long they had been sleeping but it felt like forever. He laid his brother down and got up to go check on his mom. He knew the game had been over now.

His heart began to race as he held on his mother's doorknob for what seemed like minutes, before he twisted it, opening the door slightly. Peeking through the crack he created he can see his mom lying there asleep, alone. He pushed the door ajar and went to sit beside his mother. For the first time he noticed the white powdery substance his mom had been using. He also spotted a cigarette lighter, metal spoon, and a needle laying by her side. He went to remove the rubber band from around her arm when he noticed her skin colder than he ever felt. He skipped the shaking and went straight for the forbidden pinch. Each time he pinched harder and harder. Nothing!

"Mom!" he yelled loudly in her ear.

Nothing!

His heart started to pound; he thought he heard it beating through his chest. He cracked his knuckles as he began to cry. The next move would certainly bring him an ass whoopin'; when she woke up. He raised his hand high above his head and came down hard with an open hand across his mother's face.

Whack!

Nothing! He ran into the room next door and grabbed the barbie doll he'd seen his mom play with earlier and ran back to his mother's room.

"Miracle needs you mommy," he said softly, while dropping to his knees he held the doll close to her face.

After not getting the reaction he expected, he laid the doll on her chest and he laid beside her, pulling her arm around him. He needed to be held tightly like she would do when he had nightmares. He was searching for that warm loving, superhero hug from his mom, but today there would be no warmness, no hug, just cold motionless skin. He tucked his head beneath her arm and cried his poor little heart out. The sound of small footsteps caused him to pick his head up. That's when he noticed Mari, his baby brother, standing in the doorway with his sippy cup in his hand looking confused.

Baby J held out his arm, motioning Mari to join him. Mari held out his arm as he took step by step until he touched hands with his older brother. Baby J gave a gentle pull, bringing Mari to his knees before taking his spot on their mom's stomach. They all slept together but for Cynthia there would be no awakening.

Chapter 4

5 Years later
Heaven

Heaven was looking in the mirror, brushing her long curly hair into a ponytail, when she felt her cell phone vibrating inside her pants pocket. Knowing that it was her best friend calling to let her know that they were outside, she just let the phone ring as she finished getting ready for school. Once she finished fixing her hair Heaven rushed to her bedroom and grabbed her backpack before leaving out the door. When she made it outside, she saw her friends standing on the opposite side of the gate with frowns on their faces.

She took her headphones off to hear them talking their normal trash. "Bitch, you saw us calling that phone, yo' white ass gone get left next time," Stacy joked.

"Bitch you ain't got nowhere important to be, shut up," Heaven replied as she opened the gate and joined her friends on the sidewalk.

"I got a dick appointment." Stacy bent over and shook what her mama gave her.

"Trifling bitch, you're such a slut," Heaven laughed.

"I get it from my mama," Stacy remarked, which was nothing short of the truth.

Stacy's mom was a twenty-eight-year-old stripper with a banging body and she would use that banging body and her beautiful caramel face to get whatever she desired. Although she tried to keep her business away from home, the apple doesn't fall far from the tree, and like mother, like daughter.

The three girls walked up Ridgeland until they reached 68th Street on the east side of Chicago. They all sat on the bench at the bust stop and stripped out of their school clothes. The 8th graders only had a few weeks left school and today seemed to be the perfect Friday to ditch. The girls had met a group of teenagers from O block, a gang located on the southside. It had been two weeks since they met Blackboy, Tay B and Timo and the girls were already head over heels.

"Now you know you need to cover all that ass up," Heaven told Stacy when she noticed that Stacy had on a pair of her mother's Apple Bottom shorts revealing the whole bottom of her cheeks.

"Says who? Girl I'm grown."

"Girl, you ain't grown, you be having these grown ass men looking like they wanna rape us. Imma run and leave yo ass," April chimed in.

She didn't agree with Stacy's choice of clothing. She always drew too much attention. Not that April was jealous, she wasn't bad looking at all. She just enjoyed being a kid still. "Girl, fuck these grown men. All this is for my man," Stacy shot back as the bus approached.

The bus came to a stop and the doors opened. The girls stepped onto the bus and each of them paid their fare before walking towards the back of the bus. The bus driver stared through the rearview mirror and licked his lips at Stacy's cheeks.

"Hmph, hmph" an elderly lady cleared her throat, informing the driver that he's been caught red handed his expression quickly turned to a look of embarrassment as he pulled away from the stop.

The lady just shook her head in disgust. Even with her goodies on display, anyone could tell Stacy was an underage child seeking attention but that didn't give older men rights to violate her innocence. The stop string was pulled and the driver pulled to the next stop. When he saw the older lady walking to the front of the bus he tried his best not to make eye contact. The lady didn't let him off the hook that easily. "God bless you," she said and exited the bus.

***

Timo

"On BD you been acting different since you came back from Texas. Them Cartel mufucka's must scare you straight," Timo cracked on his homie Blackboy.

Blackboy grew up in the hood, but his mom moved him away after he was arrested for a stolen vehicle. A few years later Blackboy appeared in the hood with a lot more money than his friends had ever seen and a whole new attitude. He told the neighborhood stories of him catching a body, but no one believed him. Blackboy was known for his dramatic lies.

"Naw Skud, I just be laying low. The hood don't feel the same," Blackboy countered.

He was only ten when he left for Texas. He returned to Chicago when he was sixteen, so of course things had changed a little bit. "That's cuz this bitch bussing Skud. You gotta start getting some pussy," Timo and Tay B burst into laughter.

"You still ain't hit shorty yet?" Tay B asked, referring to Heaven.

"I ain't rushing her Skud. she ain't no Bop like Stacy, you fell in love with a eat," Blackboy joked, and him and Tay B shook hands, leaving Timo standing there speechless.

"That's why yo ass gone be a forty-year-old virgin, dick can't even get hard," Timo replied as he gripped his pipe. "On that car," Timo pointed out, Tay B and Blackboy follow suit.

A black Monte Carlo came cruising up the block in slow motion. Timo, the trigger happy one, had already drawn his piece.

"Man, that's an old ass lady yo ass too hot headed," Tay B the most laid back of the three pulled his shirt back over his Smith & Wesson.

He knew Timo's eagerness to blow his pipe would put them in a jam. He had been arrested just a few months ago for drawing his gun on an unmarked police car. Luckily, he dropped his weapon instantly or he would've become a memory that night.

"One day y'all bitch ass gone get caught lacking and y'all gone wish y'all had y'all shit out," Timo tucked his gun as he spotted three girls walking up the street. "Here come baby girl nem. Aye go grab some swishers folks," Timo told Blackboy.

"Nigga I ain't no muhfuckin store runner you better go get them yourself," Blackboy shot back.

Timo looked at Tay B and Tay B shot him a *don't even think about it* look "Y'all some hoes. Y'all ain't hitting my weed either."

"Stacy gone take it all anyway" Tay B countered.

Stacy was good for taking all Timo's weed along with his pocket change. She had his mind gone but he pretended like he had no real feelings for her in front of his guys.

"Y'all just mad I got the thickest bitch in the crowd!" he declared.

The boys laughed in unison as the girls strolled up the street. "Look what yo bitch be wearing skud, she looks like she strips," Tay B commented on Stacy's choice of fashion just before the girls came into ear shot range. Instead of replying Timo walked away and met Stacy halfway.

"Thirsty ass nigga," he heard Blackboy say.

Timo hugged Stacy and gripped a handful of her ass before reprimanding her outfit choice. "Boy, I'm grown. I wear what I want."

"You ain't gotta lie to me I know them school clothes folded nice and neatly in that book bag," Timo's words made Heaven and April laugh because they were true.

Like Timo, Stacy felt her friends were jealous of their relationship. In reality, Stacy was just a sucker for the crumbs Timo spoiled her with for blessing him with an opportunity to get his dick wet anytime and anyplace.

"Whatever, boy. Y'all got some weed?"

"Yeah, come walk with me to the store I need to grab some Swishers," Timo took Stacy by the hand, and they walked down the street.

Blackboy and Tay B gave their girls casual hugs and kicked off small talk. Blackboy created a little distance between him and Tay B. "I had a dream about you last night," he told Heaven.

"Aw yeah? And what was we doing?"

"It wasn't that kind of dream, like a wet dream. We was older and I had asked you to marry me... it felt so real though."

"Who knows? Maybe we'll live to see that day together as long as you're not like your friends. Well Tay B cool but I don't care much for Timo." Heaven spoke her mind, that's what Blackboy like about her, she was unfiltered.

"I can't even blame you. So did you eat this morning?" Blackboy asked.

"I ate cereal."

Blackboy went inside his pocket and pulled out a knot of twenties. He peeled off a few and stuck it into Heaven's front pocket of her jeans. "I don't care about your money, Dennis," Heaven said, calling Blackboy by his government name. "I'm not like my friend. I like you because you're sweet, not because you have money. My parents do a great job at making sure I don't want for nothing." She reached inside her pocket and returned his money.

Blackboy respected her for being so solid. Each second he spent with her made him realize she was the one for him.

"Well, how 'bout we go to the movies or some'in, just me and you?"

"Now you're talkin," Heaven smiled before planting a soft kiss on Blackboy's cheek.

Timo and Stacy made their way back from the store, both wearing sneaky grins on their faces. April turned her nose up at her best friend. She hated Stacy's whorish ways. April wasn't a virgin, but she had self-respect. It wasn't an easy score for Tay B and even after she let him smash. She never gave him control to hit it any time, any place. April had more discipline.

Heaven, on the other hand, had her legs all the way locked. *Clink! Clink!* She told Blackboy that she had no plans on losing her virginity any time soon. The moment she opened her legs would be the moment she opened her heart. Blackboy was fine with that. At least he knew she was looking for true love. He was willing to wait as long as she needed him to. Heaven, that's what Blackboy imagined it to feel like when he finally gets the chance to pop Heaven's cherry.

"Let's slide to auntie Linda crib," Timo suggested.

"Come on, it's hot as hell out hea," Tay B said as he grabbed April's hand and led the way to Timo's auntie Linda crib up the street.

Linda opened her doors for her nephew any time he knocked. She knew about his situation with his mother and her boyfriend, and she felt sorry for him. No child deserved to be abused and neglected. Little did she know Timo had more skeletons in his closet, but he'd rather take those secrets to the grave.

Timo knocked on his auntie door in a special rhythm *Thump! Thump! Thump! Thump! ... Thump! Thump!*

He waited a moment before knocking again. He knew his auntie could take her time answering the door. "It can't be nobody important cuz I'm not important," she would say.

Thump! Thump! The door swung open with uncontrollable force.

"Aw, hey nephew I ain't know who you was."

"Hey Te-Te, what chu doin?" Timo asked.

"Finna go to my friend's house for a minute. Y'all tryna chill out?"

"Yeah, we tryna chill for a lil but if that's cool with you."

"Oh hush," Auntie Linda joked.

"Hey Te-Te!" Blackboy and Tay B spoke.

"Hey, my babies y'all come on in here with these lil pretty ladies y'all got standing out there in all that hot sun." Linda stood clear of the doorway and let the kids step inside.

Despite the smell of crack smoke lingering in the air, the one-bedroom apartment was neat and clean. Timo always took out the trash and washed the dishes for his aunt whenever he camped out.

"Helloo." The girls waved as they made their way past Linda.

"Come on in, I won't bite unless you make me," Linda joked making the girls giggle. "Nephew, give yo' Te-Te a few dollars I need me a lil some'n to fix my attitude."

Blackboy reached in his pocket and peeled a twenty off his knot and handed it to her, "Here Te-Te."

"Aw thanks baby, I'm gone. If you need me, I'll be somewhere so damn high y'all might have to book a flight to find me, but I love y'all." Linda had no shame in her game about her drug habit. The girls thought she was quite funny as they watched her leave and close the door behind herself.

"She's so sweet," Heaven said.

Timo wasted no time emptying the contents of the blunt he was preparing to roll out into an ashtray. He threw Tay B another pack of Swishers and he did the same. They filled up each blunt with some pressure and twisted them up. Each blunt was flamed up and sat in rotation.

Heaven and April weren't smokers, so they just watched as each blunt passed them by. Stacy on the other hand was a chain smoker. She hung in there until every blunt went out each time they smoked.

Heaven and Blackboy took their seats on the couch next to Tay B and April while Stacy and Timo sat on the love seat on the opposite side of the living room.

After the second blunt went out Blackboy tapped out the session. He knew the smoke bothered Heaven, so he slowed his roll when she was around.

"Hold up." Timo removed Stacy from his lap and walked over to the stereo system his aunt had connected to her television. He turned on the radio and set the station to 107.5 WGCI. He blasted the music and took his spot back on the love seat, letting Stacy sit back on his lap. The boys rapped the lyrics to Lil Wayne's *Lollipop* like they were at a live concert. The song changed to Drake's *Night Off* and it became the girls turn to perform. Stacy started winding her hips on top of Timo's lap and he got excited instantly.

He removed his Glock from his waist so that she can feel his manhood rising. "Oooo, let me see that, bae," Stacy pleaded.

"You don't know nothing about this, lil mama."

"Boy, please! My daddy got all types of poles," she countered.

"Yo daddy ain't got this," Timo held the gun by its extended clip.

Stacy leaned forward and whispered, "I know what you ain't gone have if you don't let me see."

Timo gave into Stacy's demand, handing her his gun. The rest of the room began to look nervous, but no one said a word. They all just pretended like she wasn't even there. "Heaven take my picture," Stacy pulled out her cell phone and held it out for Heaven to grab.

"Bitch, take your own picture I'm not playing with you and that stupid ass gun."

"Stop being a hater, bitch. Come on," Stacy begged.

Heaven snatched the phone and quickly snapped a photo. "There you go." She held Stacy's phone back out.

"Stop playing and take a good one," Stacy said.

Heaven held the phone up to her face and prepared to take another photo. "Bitch, stop pointing that thing at me," she snapped at Stacy.

"Girlll ... I'm not gone shoot you, just take the damn picture." Stacy rolled her eyes.

"Bitch, take this picture and get out my face before you blow me." Heaven held the camera phone up as Stacy rehearsed her poses.

She threw up the peace sign with her left hand and poked her juicy lips out. In her right hand Stacy had the Glock pointed at herself to show Heaven it was harmless. Heaven took the photo. Stacy took her phone to check out the photo, deleted it, and handed the phone back. "Take one more, bestie." Stacy licked her lips and posed in the same position.

Heaven focused on the angle. Stacy bit her bottom lip like a thug. "Savage bitch!" she said as Heaven snapped the photo.

Boom!

A gunshot echoed throughout the small apartment. The room went silent as Stacy's body hit the floor with the smoking gun still in her right hand. Everyone thought she was joking until a pool of blood formed around her head, as she laid motionless. April rushed to her side and fell to her knees screaming for help.

"What the fuck skud?" Tay B said to Timo as if he's the one who pulled the trigger.

"Damn I fucked up." Timo gripped at his dreads with both hands.

"We gotta call the police Skud," Blackboy said.

"Nigga, I'm on probation and my fingerprints on that strap, dick head."

"Well, we can't just leave the bitch."

"Watch yo mouth," April barked at Blackboy.

"I gotta get out of here." Heaven started to panic. She just witnessed her friend put a bullet in her own head. That moment will forever hunt her. She rushed out the back door and April followed right behind her. The boys didn't know what to do. They couldn't hold the gurls hostage just because their friend had taken her own life. Had Timo not been young and uneducated he would've called the police and reported the accidental suicide, but he was too nervous.

"Blackboy, go talk to them. Make sure they don't say shit while we figure something out," Timo demanded.

Blackboy rushed out the back door in an attempt to catch them.

Chapter 5

Detective Mason

"Eleven-twenty-three to dispatch," Detective Mason called over the radio.

"Go for dispatch," a voice boomed through the car speakers.

"In response to the shots fired call— we're on location everything's clear."

"Ten-four." Detective Mason and Detective Diaz were riding around the neighborhood looking for some trouble to get into when dispatch came through the radio and reported a possible gun shot on 65th and King Drive.

Detective Diaz was taking a sip from his Dunkin Donuts coffee when he spotted two young females wandering up the street like they had lost their best friend. Little did he know that's exactly what had occurred. "Hey partner, check this out," Diaz pointed. "Something seems to be wrong with those young ladies, why don't we check on 'em?"

"I'll tell you why. Because we're detectives not babysitters that's why you have to stop chasing behind the small shit and go for the big fish. It's drug dealers and killers running the streets and you rather waste our precious time trying to wipe away some little whore's tears who probably just had a bad break up."

Detective Diaz hated his partner's attitude. He didn't give a care for nothing in the world except his next paycheck. Diaz's wife also hated Mason's guts. She always told her husband that she got a funny feeling from Detective Mason. "He reminds me of Denzel Washington when he played in the movie Training Day," she would joke about how crooked he seemed.

"Like this motherfucker right here" Detective Mason pointed to Blackboy. "this motherfucker got trouble written all over him," he added.

Blackboy was so busy trying to catch up with the two girls, he barely noticed the boys in blue stalking him like prey. Blackboy finally looked over his shoulders and noticed the squad car come to a complete stop.

"Fuck," he whispered.

He knew he was caught slipping but he tried to play it cool-- so much for a poker face. Blackboy noticed the passenger side window rolling down. "Aye you, come over here" Detective Diaz called.

"Wassup?" Blackboy called over his shoulder. He knew it would be a dumb idea to walk over to a cop car with his pipe on him. Blackboy noticed the reverse lights come on and the police car sped back in full speed. He was about to ditch his gun in the bushes, but it was too late.

The doors flew open with lightning speed as Blackboy turned around and took off running.

***

"Let me go see what this dumb ass nigga out there doing" Tay B said as he stood up from the couch he'd been sitting on and headed out the back door. He barely made it out the door when he spotted Blackboy along with a vehicle he knew all too well.

"Tsss," he mumbled under his breath as he realized Blackboy was slipping bad but the thought of the dead girl laying on their front room floor erased the thought of him wanting to yell heads up to his friend. He took a step back and pulled the door closed behind him before peeking through the side window.

He watched as the two cops emerged from their vehicle and chased Blackboy through a vacant lot until they were out of sight. "Dumb ass nigga," he whispered to himself as he locked the door before placing the two by four piece of wood across the door for extra security, then heading back inside to warn Timo.

Timo grabbed Stacy's hand gently. rubbing it as tears began to form in the corners of his eyes. He wouldn't show it in front of his boys, but he was more hurt then scared. He and Stacy had a thing going on that no one would understand. "Why you do this to me baby?" he cried, taking his thumb and caressing her caramel-complected cheek bone which was becoming colder by the minute.

As he went to pull the carpet over her body, he noticed something sticking out of her front pocket. He reaches to retrieve the small object and after laying his eyes on it he begins to sob even harder. "Nooo! This can't be happening. God whyyy?" he cried as his hand went from rubbing her face, to her stomach.

Stacy had a positive pregnancy test in her pocket and though Timo never had thoughts of being a father, he would've taken on the responsibility proudly. He leaned forward, kissing her stomach repeatedly.

"Aye, the jakes chasing Blackboy folks, we gotta do something about this body before they end up kicking the door in again," Tay B yelled catching him off guard, causing him to jump.

Timo quickly put the pregnancy test in his pocket and wiped the tears from his eyes. He looked up and Tay B saw the pain written across his face. Tay B grabbed his hand and pulled him up.

"This wasn't your fault, bro. I know you were falling in love, my boy, you can't get shit past me. We gone get through this but for now we gotta put our heads together and come up with a plan," Tay B said as he embraced his best friend, keeping him from falling.

Timo was no longer hiding his pain as he let his tears fall freely and his cries echoed throughout the house.

"Come on let's go see what's up with Blackboy, you know he got his heat on him," Tay B said as he reached in his waistband and withdrew his gun before walking into the bedroom to hide it. "Come on," he ordered as he walked out the front door this time, remembering the directions the detectives had chased Blackboy.

When they reached the sidewalk, they heard tires screeching as more police cars came speeding up the street, surrounding Blackboy who was now handcuffed with his face against the ground. Tay B spotted the plastic bag officer Mason was holding in the air containing a black object and instantly knew what the bag held inside. Timo was so lost in his thoughts, the situation unfolding before him failed to register as he stared blankly.

"Gotcho black ass. You thought you can outrun Mad Mason?" Detective Mason barked as he snatched Blackboy up from the ground roughly. "Imma make an example out cho lil ass today, boy," he yelled as he pulled the boy by his forearm causing the handcuffs to saw away at his skin, cutting through the boy's flesh.

"Arghhh," Blackboy yelled out in agony. "These fucking cuffs too tight," he spat as he attempted to snatch away from the officer's grip out of frustration.

"Shut the fuck up before I squeeze these cuffs so tight it stops your blood circulation."

"What the fuck happened to you?" another officer asked Detective Mason. Noticing his uniform covered in dirt, he became concerned.

"This lil son of a bitch made me trip over a garbage can in the alley over there." Detective Mason nodded his head in the direction where he slipped and fell.

The other officer burst out in laughter until they noticed his nostrils flare up. The crowd grew quiet until the neighbors began to appear from the left and right. Some were still in their pajamas cursing at the cops. "You ain't gotta handle him like that he just a kid, you inconsiderate ass pig," a woman yelled as she stepped in the street and got a closer view.

"Ma'am, back the fuck up before it be *you* in these cuffs next," Detective Mason cursed back but the small woman wouldn't be scared off so easily.

"Bitch please! I wish you would lay a finger on me. I'll own you and that dirty ass police station you work for," she snapped. "Now try me if you think it's sweet." She rolled her eyes.

"Let's get the fuck out of here before I shoot that crackhead bitch." Detective Mason grabbed Blackboy's shirt and shoved him into the back seat of the squad car and slammed the door. Tay B and Timo disappeared unnoticed as the patrol cars pulled away.

"Man, we got to move this body. You know Blackboy gone panic and fold first chance he get," Tay B said as he paced back and forth. He peeked through the blinds as if he was expecting the cops to return any second.

"Just go get some gloves and some bleach, I got a plan," Timo ordered, never taking his eyes off the corpse that lay before him.

"Say less, I'll be right back." Tay B stormed out of the apartment after retrieving his gun from the bedroom.

"I love you, lil mama. I swear to God I do," Timo cried as he placed his hand over Stacy's eyes, closing them from the world.

***

Tay B put the yellow cleaning gloves along with the Clorox on the counter. "Ring this up for me Skud," he demanded as he tossed a ten-dollar bill across the counter.

"Four-sixty-two!" the Arabian clerk said as he shoved the bill inside the register and counted the boy's change.

Tay B bagged his items and raced up the street as his mind replayed the incident repeatedly like a rerun on television.

"Here, I got everything, what's the pla–" Tay B started to ask but realized he was talking to himself.

There were no signs of Timo. No signs of Stacy. Tay B raced through the whole house searching but became hopeless. "What the fuck!" he cursed to himself as he returned his phone to dial his homeboy's number. Immediately after pressing the green phone icon, he heard his friend's voicemail. He tried several times but had no luck.

Man, where the fuck you go??? Hit my line back. He texted and left the apartment.

***

Ciara

"What about these right here nephew?" Ci-Ci pointed to a pair of white and red shell toe Adidas she spotted in Footlocker while shopping for Baby J a few outfits at North Riverside Mall for the summer. Ci-Ci aka Ciara was Cynthia's older sister and even though Baby J never knew she existed, she knew everything about him.

She had promised to never come near her sister and her screwed up family again but she couldn't see herself leaving the last of her bloodline hanging. After the incident with Miracle==mn Cynthia's first child—mn Ciara separated herself from her sister and in a way, she felt she was to blame for her sister's overdose and sudden death. She'd been in touch with the family doctor and knew about every doctor's appointment her sister attended.

UNTIL WE MEET AGAIN | RAMON A. BROOKS

The doctor had informed her about her sister's drug abuse issues, along with her newfound disease. But she turned the other cheek even though she knew she should've swallowed her pride and been there to support her sister when she needed her the most. Cynthia had been there every step of the way when Ciara was on her deathbed fighting cancer. While she appreciated her sister for being there when she needed her the most, she hated her for crossing her and sleeping with her husband Juan Alverez. They both expected her to spend her last days in the hospital bed and used that time to get to know each other sexually, physically, and emotionally. What made matters worse is the fact that Cynthia gave Juan what Ciara couldn't— a child.

***

When Dr. Hill called Cynthia and Juan to the hospital they'd thought the worst and came storming into the hospital room holding hands but were caught off guard by the sight of Ciara sitting there smiling from ear to ear. That joyful moment was short-lived as Ciara noticed her lover and her baby sister embracing each other a bit too tightly for her liking. She didn't need confirmation, the look in their eyes answered all of Ciara's questions.

"I'm guessing this wasn't the news you two expected," Ciara said softly as tears began to dance down her honey brown cheeks, falling one drop after another until they created a small, wet stain on her hospital gown.

Cynthia released her hand from Juan's grasp and rushed to her sister's bedside. "Sister I'm sorry," she cried as she attempted to hug her sister but was shoved with the force of a NFL middle linebacker.

"Don't give me that fake ass cry. You're only sorry I'm still alive. All our life, you've had all the love and all the attention, not once have I tried to take that from you. But it seems like you've only been living to take my dreams and turn them into nightmares." Ciara was now crying uncontrollably.

She was broken beyond measure. Juan and her sister were the only reasons she fought a long, stressful fight to overcome her sickness, and now that she'd lost them both she silently wished she had died.

"You never cared about no one but yourself. Our parents' only wish was that me and you remain close. Don't ever let a person, place or thing come between us," she repeated her mother's words.

"But I see you forgot the rules," Ciara said through clenched teeth.

She wanted to hop up and go across her sister's head with the first thing she could get her hands on but the tubes and machines she was connected to prevented that.

"I take it you've heard the great news," Dr. Hill said as he entered the room holding medical charts. He looked up and noticed the distress in all of their facial expressions. "Oh ... uh, I'll give you guys a few more minutes."

"No, it's fine, they were just leaving," Ciara said, cutting Dr. Hill's sentence short as she stared daggers through her husband's eyes.

Juan was speechless. Truth was, he loved Ciara with all his heart. Little did she know, he only started the affair with her sister because she resembled his lover so much. In a way, he felt like he was going for the next best thing, but he wouldn't admit that sickening truth to Ciara. He just held his head low in shame as he made his exit, but Cynthia didn't follow. She would give her sister that much respect for what it's worth.

"Dr. Hill, do you mind telling me what's going on here?" Cynthia asked but her eyes never left her sister's gaze.

She would accept the burning sensation she felt when their gazes met. She knew she deserved every moment of hatred her older sister felt towards her, but she couldn't conceal the fear she felt when their eyes locked.

"Sure thing, darling. Well, after the first test results came back, we thought there must've been a computer error. So, we carefully ran all those tests again before sharing the news with Mrs. Alvarez. But after the second lab results came back it confirmed that these machines here are very much accurate," He smiled before continuing. "It also confirmed a miracle, your sister no longer has cancer and is expected to make a full recovery. Our God is a great God." he praised before leaving the two ladies there drowning in their own tears. As the news sunk in, they cried tears of both pain and joy.

***

"Them decent but I like these," Baby J said, holding a single black and blue Air Jordan number 6. He noticed his auntie was staring at him with that uncomfortable look again. "Hello." He waved the shoe past her face, breaking her from trance.

"Oh, I'm sorry, nephew. Just can't believe how big you're getting on me," she lied.

The truth was she couldn't believe how much he resembled his father—from his baby face features, to his long curly hair, which he wore in a ponytail. Even his masculine body structure and massive height all came from his papa. "You like 'em?" he asked, ignoring her apology.

"Yeah, these are nice too but why do you like Jordan's so much?"

"He's my favorite player. One day I'm gonna play just like him," Baby J said, dribbling an imaginary basketball before pretending to take a 3-point shot.

"No, one day you're gonna play *better,*" she smiled as she grabbed both shoes and placed them on the counter. "Excuse me," she called for the young men at the register, "Do you have these in a size 8?"

"Let me check." He grabbed both shoes and scanned the barcodes on each of them. "Yes, we do, would you like me to get them for you?"

"Yes please," she replied with her beautiful smile on display, causing the young man to feel butterflies in the pit of his stomach.

His high yellow skin was now turning red as he tried his best to hold his composure. His mind was telling him to run but his feet wouldn't move. "Aye, let me get them number 6's in a size 9, while you're back there," a voice called out. Baby J turned around to see who the words belonged to.

His mood went from joy to pure hatred the moment his hazel eyes landed on a familiar face he would never forget "My bad, lil dude, I ain't try to cut you," the boy threw his hands up in surrender. He took a step back as he and Baby J had a stare down.

"He sholl don't like nobody cutting him in line for his shoes," Ciara joked to make light of the situation. She'd never seen Baby J act like this before and was clueless to his reason.

The face Baby J was staring at was the same face he seen in his dreams, night after night. The face had become more mature as it had gone through puberty but undoubtedly, that was the same face that sold his mother heroin 5 years ago and killed her. He was staring his mother's killer directly in the eyes and his heart burned with hatred.

Though he was only a few months shy of 12-years-old, the look in his eyes caused Boozer to feel uneasy. "Here, let me pay for that," Boozer said as he peeled off a few hundred-dollar bills and placed them on the counter. "Keep the change," he told the young man at the register as he grabbed his bag and turned to leave.

"Do you need your receipt?" the guy called but was ignored as Boozer and his friend left the store.

"Now what was that about?" Ciara asked as she reached for the bags on top of the counter. Her question went unanswered as Baby J's expression went black. He was so deep in his thoughts, he heard nothing at all.

The images of his mother invaded his mind. The feeling of her cold skin against his as he lay under her with his little brother in his arms. A single tear escaped from his left eye, slowly making its way down his cheek. He didn't realize he was crying until he felt a soft hand wipe across his cheekbone, bringing him back to reality.

"Who was that boy? And what did he do to you?" Ciara asked. Now she was more furious than concerned.

"He was the one who sold my mama drugs. He killed her."

Those words caused Ciara's heart to drop. She felt like she was trying to breathe with a sock stuffed in her mouth and glass stuck in her windpipe. It took her a while to collect herself but when she did, she felt just as angry as Baby J. "Can you go get two different pairs of shoes? My nephew don't want anything that boy has to offer," she demanded as she dug into her purse and retrieved her credit card.

"Yes, ma'am," the boy replied nervously. *This woman throwing orders around is a far cry from the woman I spoke with a few minutes ago,* he thought as he disappeared into the back of the store.

Chapter 6

Heaven

Heaven took a deep breath and held it for a second before relieving. Her anxiety was getting the best of her as she searched for her house key, her hands trembled uncontrollably. Just as she was about to insert her house key into the keyhole, the door came swinging open and Heaven was in total shock as she stood face to face with Mr. Hobbs. Judging by the look on his face, she can tell that he was just as surprised to see her.

What is he doing here? Was he here to tell my mom I didn't show up for class? What the fuck am I gonna say? Her mind raced as she asked herself all these questions inside her head.

"Hey honey, I thought you were going out with your friends after school, me and Mr. Hobbs was just talking about you skipping a grade so that you'll graduate with your friends, right?" Marissa nudged Mr. Hobbs with her elbow.

"Uh, yeah ... you definitely have the intelligence to graduate this year, Heaven, but I bet you already knew that," he said as he gave her a playful push.

"Really? So, I get to graduate with April and S–" her excitement was replaced with sorrow as reality set in.

Thoughts of Stacy came rushing back at once. "Yes, and Stacy," her mom finished her sentence, but she noticed Heaven's sudden shift in energy. "What's wrong, honey?

Aren't you excited? After all, this is what you wanted, right?" Marissa sensed that something was wrong.

"Yeah, I'm excited, I just have a headache. I need some rest," Heaven replied as she pushed past her mother and Mr. Hobbs and walked straight to her room before closing the door.

She heard a few whispers before hearing the front door being shut, followed by the sound of the shower running. Heaven stripped free of all her clothing and fell onto her bed, where she balled up into a fetal position and cried herself to sleep.

***

Blackboy

Detective Mason held Blackboy inside an interrogation room at the police station on 111th Street where he roughed him up for hours before processing and charging him with felony possession of a firearm. He tried breaking him a deal, offering him his freedom by making the gun disappear in exchange for some useful information on the murders piling up across the city, along with the spreading of ecstasy pills, cocaine, and heroin.

All Detective Mason wanted was a name, he assured Blackboy as he placed several sheets of paper on the table in front of him. Staring down at the familiar faces, both suspects, and victims, as the faces appeared to be staring back, the 17-year-old boy had no words for the man in blue.

By Dennis (Blackboy) Coleman just having a birthday, he was processed and charged as an adult. Blackboy thought he would fall asleep for a couple of hours and wake up to the sound of keys opening his cell, leading him to his freedom but instead he was awakened to the sound of the night shift officer beating on the cells with a baton.

"Alright gentlemen! Off your ass and on your feet. If you have to use the shitter, I advise you to do so now because once these cuffs are on, you'll be pissing handcuffed to the guy next to you. These cuffs will not be coming off until you reach the county jail," he warned.

"Aye CO, where I'm going?" Blackboy asked, apparently confused.

"What's your name?" The tall brown skin Will Smith-look-alike officer asked.

"Dennis Coleman," he answered,

"Let's see, Dennis Coleman... Denis Coleman," the officer repeated as his eyes roamed down the sheet of paper he held in his hand. "Coleman, you're going to 26th and California," he confirmed.

"I'm a minor, why the fuck they got me going to the county?"

"How old are you?"

"I'm 17," Blackboy countered with confidence.

"Well, Mr. Coleman, looks like you're a man today. Grab your mattress, throw it over there with the rest, and cuff up. Brown!" the officer called the next name on his list and a short, well-built older man stepped out and cuffed up with Blackboy, who held his head down in defeat.

"Pick yo head up youngsta, life ain't over." Blackboy looked up. "Your body only does what your brain allows it to do, then the soul follows suit. So, if your mind thinks it's being defeated, your body will show signs of defeat, causing the soul to vanish. A body feels no life without soul, for it is just existing, not living." The well-built Denzel Washington looking man dropped countless jewels on Blackboy as the young man tried to understand the meaning behind his words.

"Remember those words, young blood. Mind, body, and soul."

"Mind, body, and soul," Blackboy repeated and held his head high as if he were accepting an award instead of a gun charge.

After the last guy was cuffed, the officer did a count check before packing the men into the back of the police truck AKA the Meat Wagon. After what seemed like hours, they reached the Cook County Department of Corrections. Blackboy felt butterflies in his stomach as they were being unloaded from the vehicle, and uncuffed, but his head remained high. "Mind, body and soul," he repeated to himself again as he stepped into the garage of the big brown building.

***

Heaven

Heaven felt her cell phone vibrate as she was listening to her music on her MP3 player. She removed the pink sheets from over her naked body and located her iPhone lying face down beneath her right leg. She grabbed it and entered her password before the phone unlocked. Heaven saw that she had a red dot sitting at the top, right hand corner off her message icon, notifying her that she had unread messages. She pressed the icon, revealing her messages.

She saw that they were all from her best friend April.

Are you ok? This doesn't feel right, maybe we should tell someone

Another message read: *Call me. I'm coming over!*

Just as she was about to reply, another message popped up across her screen that made Heaven drop her iPhone onto the bed. Fear took over her body as she quickly removed her headphones from her ears, letting them fall into her lap. She took a deep breath as she retrieved her cell phone. As she exhaled, she flipped the phone around so the screen would be visible again.

She didn't notice her breathing had stopped momentarily as she read the message across the screen. *Bitch, open the door.*

It wasn't the message that had her shaken up. It was the sender. The contact read *'B3ST!E ST@CY'* with a red heart emoji. Heaven removed the sheets from her toes and stood up from her queen-sized bed. She quickly pulled the handle on the top drawer of her clothing dresser, shoving her hand inside, she pulled out the first pair of pajamas her hand landed on.

After slipping on her pink pajama shorts and a matching tank top, she slipped on a pair of house shoes and ran for the door. Her heartbeat sped up intensely as she fumbled with the locks on the front door. *This has to be some sort of trick*, she thought, as she finally got the doorknob to twist. She pulled on the door, feeling a small breeze of wind as the door opened.

Stacy stood there smiling. "Bitch, why do you have on PJ's? You must've been sleep still?" she asked, staring at Heaven with a look of confusion as Heaven shared the same stare.

"This can't be real," Heaven whispered as she closed the distance between Stacy them.

She placed her left hand on Stacy's cheekbone, rubbing her face soft and slow as she expected her hand to roam straight through the figure before her like she'd seen plenty of times in the ghost movies she had watched. But to her surprise, she felt real flesh. Despite the sun shining bright in the sky on a beautiful day, Stacy's skin felt as cold as December as she grabbed Heaven's hand, removing it from her face.

As she turned her head slightly, Heaven noticed the hole in the side of her head where the bullet had made its entrance. Heaven took a step back with both hands covering her mouth.

"What's wrong with you?" Stacy asked but Heaven was in too much of a shock to respond. "Heaven ... Heaven," Stacy called out but received no reply. She grabbed Heaven by the shoulders and began to shake her "Heaven ... Heaven." This time it was her mother's voice she heard as she jumped up from her sleep, shaking uncontrollably. "Heaven, it's me, sweetie. It's okay," Marissa assured.

As she embraced her daughter, she felt Heaven's body tense as sweat began to form all over her forehead. Heaven took in her surroundings, trying to gain control of her thoughts and emotions. Her mother rocked her back and forth like she was a newborn baby until she was sure that her daughter was back to normal. "Are you okay?" Heaven nodded but didn't say a word. "Stacy's mom called looking for her, she says she hasn't talked to her since you guys left for school. Have you talked to her?"

"Um ... I," Heaven paused to think of a lie but came up with nothing.

"You what?" Marissa looked her straight in her eyes, searching for an answer.

"I haven't seen her since school," Heaven lied.

"School?" Marissa repeated. She gave Heaven a strange look that made her feel uncomfortable.

"Yes, we went to school together and I ... I seen her once in the restroom and that's it. I came straight home from school because I wasn't feeling good."

"Well, Stacy's mom called the school after she failed to reach her and was told that Stacy never showed up to class," Marissa countered.

Heaven's heart dropped. She began to feel suffocated. Her mom had her backed into a tight space with no way out. Panic took over her as she began to bite her nails, tears fell from both of her eyes, soaking up into her pink sheets.

"Heaven," her mother wiped away her tears, but they were replaced instantly, "I'm gonna need you to tell me the truth, don't let Stacy's actions get you in trouble. Her mom is worried sick so if she's at some boy's house you need to speak up," her mother warned.

Heaven shook her head as she began to cry harder and harder. "No, what? Speak up," Marissa pressured her daughter, backing her further and further into the corner until Heaven felt like she was in a small box instead of her bedroom.

With her tank top pulled over her eyes, catching her tears, she finally opened her mouth, and the truth came spilling out. "She's dead mom! Stacy's deeead!" she cried.

Marissa looked at her daughter like she was speaking a foreign language. She heard her loud and clear, but her ears must've been deceiving her. "Heaven, what did you just say?" Heaven began to rock herself back and forth in an attempt to calm her nerves, but it was useless. "Honey, calm down. Tell me what happened. I can't help if you're leaving me in the blind."

Marissa felt tears form in the corners of her eyes before falling down her cheek. Heaven took a deep breath, then began to explain the entire story from the bus ride to the moment they ran out of the house and came home. Marissa couldn't believe her ears, now she was shaking just as bad as her daughter as she tried to take it all in. "Heaven, we have to go to the police, someone's daughter is out there probably being eaten by rats by now. Why didn't you let me know right away, instead of taking matters into your own hands?" she asked.

With her mother's mind made up, Heaven thought she was going straight to prison. Marissa sighed, "Get dressed, I'm going to give Tiny a call and we're going to the station to get this cleared up right away."

"Yes ma'am," Heaven replied reluctantly before snatching the sheet from over her body with attitude.

She grabbed her phone and texted April. *I told my mom. I couldn't take it anymore.* After a few seconds had passed a text came back through.

April: *me too, her momma wouldn't stop calling.*

Heaven: *What did your mom say?*

April: *She wants me to tell the damn police everything. What about yours?*

Heaven: *Same here, we're about to head out. I'll see you in a bit.*

April: *Ok. Love U*

Love u more, Heaven replied before placing her phone on the dresser while she got dressed. At the station, Tiny didn't want to believe a word she was hearing. Her daughter couldn't be dead. *Life doesn't work that way,* she thought as she broke down.

"Do any of these faces look familiar to you?" the tall dark detective asked Heaven.

"Yes," she sniffled.

She had been crying since they left home, non-stop. "Can you point to 'em?"

Heaven stared at the photos for what seemed like minutes before placing her finger on three different photos out of the twelve, Detective Mason presented to her. "Do you know any of their names?"

"This is Tay B ..., his name is Timo, and ..." she paused when she got to Blackboy's photo.

"And?" Detective Mason asked. "Do you know his name?"

"No," she lied, "I just seen him around before."

Detective Mason knew she was only giving him half the truth, her friend April had already given him all the information he needed. "Your friend said that you and this guy had sort of a thing going on, is that true?"

"Um ... well," she hesitated before deciding that she'll give him the whole truth seeing that her lies had gotten her nowhere, "yeah, we kinda talked."

"So, do you know this guy's name?"

"His name is Blackboy."

"What about his real name?"

"His real name is Dennis," Heaven answered with her head hanging low.

She liked Blackboy, he was different from the other two, who seemed to be in their relationships only for the sex. She had already witnessed him being shoved into the back of a police car by this same detective just yesterday. She didn't want to bring him any more trouble. *I'm more of the blame than anyone*, she thought. *If I hadn't accepted to take that stupid ass picture, Stacy would've given Timo his gun back and she would still be alive right now.*

Her tears started to flow all over again, replacing the ones that had dried up. "Can you take this penand circle each of their pictures?" Detective Mason asked.

After Heaven did as she was told, he snatched the piece of paper up from the table and left the room. Detective Diaz sat behind the two-way mirror trying to figure out where did he remember the girl's face from. When his partner came storming into the room,

"Aye partner, you remember the little bastard we had to chase down yesterday? The one that made me bust my ass and thought it was funny?" Detective Mason asked.

Detective Diaz pretended like he was trying to recap yesterday's events but of course he remembered. He laughed and joked about it all the way home and told the story to his wife. Of course she got a kick out of it, she didn't quite favor Detective Mason. She believed he was a dirty cop, trying to pollute her husband's mind.

"This little bastard," Detective Mason slammed the paper down with his finger on the picture of Blackboy.

"Aw, yeah, that guy. What about him?"

"The young lady confirmed that he was at the scene of the crime when it all went down. It happened right over there where we caught him at, maybe that was the gunshot the neighbors reported, we should run ballistics on the gun we recovered, it could be the murder weapon."

As Mason refreshed his memory, lightbulbs lit up in Detective Diaz's head.

"Oh shit, Mason, remember the two young ladies I tried to check on yesterday? That's *them*, asshole. If you'd let me do my job we could've had this case cracked by now. I thought this was a suicide anyhow, what's he got to do with this?"

"They said it was a suicide, but who knows? Maybe the boys threatened the poor little girls and made them say their friend accidentally shot herself. As far as we know, this can be a homicide but we're gonna find out. Call Sergeant Fox and tell him we need search warrants for this address, until we find her body we won't know a thing," Detective Mason ordered as he collected the papers and made his exit.

Chapter 7

Ciara

Ciara rolled over to the sound of her cell phone ringing. Without reading the caller ID she pressed the answer button before placing the phone to her ear ."Hello," she said in a raspy voice with her eyes still shut.

"Hello, this is a collect call from..."

Click!

She hung up the call before the operator could finish her sentence. She already knew who the caller was; she had been declining his calls and shredding his letters since he went to prison. After Juan broke her heart and left her in the hospital on her last breaths, she vowed to never speak another word to him or her baby sister. She threw the phone on the bed and pulled the covers from over her naked frame.

At the age of 39, Ciara looked absolutely stunning. Her smooth almond-colored skin shines even in the dark. Her long, wavy hair stopped just half an inch from the middle of her back. Without any underwear, her body had the perfect hourglass shape. With her pretty brown eyes, and deep dimples to complement her gorgeous face, she'd give the Young Money rapper Nicki Minaj a run for her money.

Ciara rolled out of bed and threw on her robe before stepping into the bathroom and running her some bath water. She ran her fingers through the water as she adjusted the temperature until she was satisfied it was warm enough.

Then she stepped back into her room, opened her drawer and retrieved her vibrating dildo. She pressed the power button to make sure the battery wasn't dead. When she felt the toy come to life in her hand, her pussy began to throb as she imagined the magic the toy worked on her body.

She turned the toy off and quickly made her way to the bathroom where she let her robe fall to the floor as she locked the door before stepping into the hot bath. She sat under the steaming water, letting the heat settle on her skin. She threw her head back and closed her eyes, resting her head on the tub while the hot water caressed her body and soul. She threw her left leg up, letting her footrest on the side of the tub, then she powered the toy back on. With her right hand, she reached down, spreading her pussy lips. She used her thumb to pull back the hood, revealing her pretty pink clit. The head of the toy made its way to his target, making her gasp on contact.

"Uughh ... Shhh," she moaned, pressing harder with the toy "Mhmn ... yesss ... oh my god ... yesss." Her eyes began to roll to the back of her head as the vibrator worked its magic.

She could feel her juices pouring out, mixing in with the bath water. She wiggled the toy up and down with the motion of a tongue, flicking across her clit. She felt like screaming as her orgasm reached its peak, she squirted all over the dildo. Cream came bursting out of her pussy as her body went limp for a moment before she rose up and turned the water off.

Ciara wasn't finished yet; she wanted to be penetrated by the toy now. She took the dildo by the base and stuck the suction part to the back of the shower wall. She turned around and placed one hand on the sink and the other hand on the window sill beside the tub. She backed up until she felt the toy rub against her ass cheeks then she took the hand from the window seal and placed it around the head of the black 9-inch dildo, guiding it inside her walls.

She replaced her hand on the window seal and bent over, easing back until the full 9 inches filled her insides. She backed her ass up on the dildo, making her ass cheeks smack the wall. She placed her left foot outside the tub to gain better control as she rode the rubber dick like it was the real deal. "Fuck me ... ah yesss!" she said just above a whisper, she didn't want to awaken her nephew.

She bit her bottom lip as her thrusts sped up smacking her ass against the wall with more force, bringing her to another breathtaking orgasm. After she came, she rolled her hips in a circle, savoring the moment. She stood up and turned around, turned on by the sight of her juices dripping from the dildo she bent down and took the toy into her mouth, deep throating the whole 9 inches, tasting her sweet juices. She wanted the rubber dick to be her boy toy, Josh, but dealing with a married man, she had to sit back until it was her turn.

At first she felt bad about dealing with a married man until one day she told herself, *if my own sister can fuck my husband and have kids with him, why should I feel sorry for the next bitch?* Since that day she's been fucking the white boy's brains out. She can tell he wasn't happy at home anyhow. Every time they'd fuck, he'd roll over and vent to her about him believing his wife has been cheating on him. She would have to suck his dick to get him to shut the hell up with his girl problems.

Ciara grabbed her sponge from the shower head and soaped it up with her dove body wash before turning the shower on and freshening up. She was drying off when she heard her doorbell ring. Ciara grabbed her robe off the bathroom floor and wrapped it around herself. As she went to answer the door, she spotted Baby J coming from his bedroom, heading towards the bathroom. She walked to the front door and looked through the peephole, seeing who it was, she rolled her eyes before undoing the three locks. "Who gave you permission to pop up at my house unannounced, at this time in the morning?" she snapped.

"I called you twice, but ya' phone went to voicemail," Josh answered as he pushed past her like he'd been invited in.

"So that gives you permission to just pop up?"

"No, but I was in the area, and I figured you missed this," he grabbed his dick, "just as much as I missed this." He reached for her juice box, but she grabbed his hand.

"Well, you're about five minutes too late," she stated as she relived the episode, she had in her bathroom with her toy a few minutes ago. "Plus, my nephew woke—" Just as the words left her mouth, she remembered leaving the dildo stuck to the wall.

Oh shit, he's gonna be so mad, she covered her mouth with embarrassment written across her face.

"I'm gonna throw that damn toy away the first chance I get."

"You wouldn't have to if you brought *this* toy around more often," Ciara said as she grabbed his dick which grew in her hand. "Somebody ain't been getting laid lately," she teased.

"I'm trying to right now," he replied, trying to close the distance between them but Ciara kept her arm extended, preventing him from doing so.

"Maybe later, I have to take my nephew to basketball practice," she told him before kissing him on his lips and pushing him back out the door, locking it as Baby J came out of the bathroom. To her surprise he kept it pushing, right back to his room to finish getting dressed.

Maybe he didn't notice this time, she thought as she hurried to collect her toy and put it away.

Baby J put his brand new Jordans in his gym bag and zipped it up. Suddenly he became weary thinking about his baby brother. It's been five long years since he'd seen Jamari, but his face was embedded in Baby J's mind. Even though he was much older, that same 1 year old was who he would see every time he thought of his best friend.

The day his aunt Ciara came to adopt him from the foster home he asked her about his baby brother. Baby J remembered the day like it was yesterday.

"Excuse me, I believe my other nephew is here somewhere, am I allowed to sign for him as well?" she asked the female social worker.

"I can certainly check for you, what's his name?"

"Um well I don't quite ..."

"His name Jamari," Baby J chimed in.

"Aww, he's so cute. Let's see" she started typing on a computer. "Do you know what date he was admitted? Because nothings coming up under that name."

"They came here on the same day." Ciara began to get frustrated.

"Let's see." The social worker began typing away at the keyboard again.

"Oh, I see. It looks like he was adopted out a week ago."

"Is there a way I can get his foster parents' information? My sister passed away and I'm sure she wouldn't want her children to be separated."

"I'm sorry to hear that, but I'm afraid we can't share that type of information for it is confidential," the lady said apologetically.

"Confidential my ass, he's my nephew," Ciara snapped.

"Ma'am, I understand your frustration I really do, but once the children are adopted out it's out of our control, it says here that the child has been here for over three months. Had you come to adopt him when you came for his brother you would've certainly been able to do so."

"Had I known he existed, don't you think I would have?" Ciara rolled her eyes at the social worker.

She looked down at Baby J's face, which revealed a look of defeat and deception. His brother was the only person he grew to love besides his mom. "It's okay baby, we're gonna find your brother if that's the last thing I do, you hear me?" she placed her hand under his chin, lifting his head up.

He nodded his head, but his emotions remained on display. Ciara took the ink pen taped to the desk and finished signing the papers before tossing the pen back aggressively and walking out the office. Baby J turned around and gave the social worker one last stare. Her eyes met his gaze, and she saw pure hatred in the little boy's eyes. She felt like she was having a stare down with the devil. Baby J disappeared on the opposite side of the door, leaving her shaking as sweat started to form around her forehead.

She walked from around her desk and hurried to lock her office door in fear of the mad woman and evil child returning. Once she locked the door she placed her back on it, finally taking a moment to exhale, she hadn't realized she'd been holding her breath the entire time.

"Come on, big boy, you ready?" Ciara asked, catching him by surprise, causing him to jump just a little as he quickly wiped away the evidence from the lonely tear that managed to creep down his cheek.

"Yeah," he answered, grabbing his gym bag and pushing past her.

He was starting to believe Ciara had given up on finding his baby brother, she never mentioned his name unless Baby J asked about him. It's been that way for the past three years. *Out of sight, out of mind.*

Ciara followed behind him, locking each lock before stepping out into the sun. She inserted her key into the mailbox hole, twisting it then pulling, the mailbox came open and mail came spilling out. She grabbed a handful, tossing it inside her brown coach bag before reaching for the rest. Once she retrieved it all she closed the mailbox back, locking it. "How long has it been since I checked the mail?" she asked herself as she tried to remember on the way to her vehicle.

She hit the unlock button on her remote, unlocking the white 2005 BMW. Baby J opened the rear passenger door, throwing his gym bag on the backseat before closing it and jumping into the front seat. As Ciara was climbing into the driver's seat, her phone rang. After sitting her coach bag on the rear seat, she reached in and grabbed her cell. Noticing the number that appeared on the front screen, she quickly answered, "Wassup girl?"

Chapter 8

Detective Mason

Bang! Bang! Bang!
"Police, open up!" Detective Mason yelled as he hammered on the front door of apartment 1B, with his gloved fist, followed by a dozen cops.

As he was about to give the door another bang, it came swinging open "Now why in the hell y'all beating on my door like y'all the police," Linda spat. Too high to open her eyes, she stood there nodding.

Crack smoke invaded the cops' nostrils instantly, causing them to throw their hands up to cover their noses as they pushed past the frail lady, who appeared to be in her mid-thirties. "Let me see your hands, ma'am," a short redneck officer approached her with his weapon in hand.

"Was that supposed to be a joke?" Linda opened her eyes, finally realizing what was occurring.

It wasn't until the cop closed the distance between them, that he realized both her hands had been severed at the wrist. Linda used to be a pretty good-looking prostitute, making a living turning tricks for Devious, her drug dealing, psychopathic pimp. Until one night he came home and caught her stealing from the stash of crack he had hidden inside the floor of his bedroom. Devious took a butcher knife and chopped away at her wrist until it became completely detached, repeating his offense with the other hand before making her watch him feed both hands to Lady and Jabba, his 80 pound Pitbull terriers.

"What the hell do y'all want? Devious ain't here," she spat as the drugs took her back in time, making her believe Devious was still a part of her life. Just as she did any other time, she hit the crack pipe, she became delusional.

"Ma'am, we have a search warrant," Detective Mason waved the papers across Linda's face.

To his surprise, she reached out with both arms and clamped the papers with her wrists, snatching it from his hands. She pinned the search warrant up against the wall, reading over it as the officers ransacked the apartment. "Don't no Timothy Atkins stay here, so whatever my nephew done did, I advise you to go fuck up his apartment," she slurred as the crack made its way to home base in her system.

The officers ignored her as they continued to search for evidence. So far, they had no luck, finding any signs of suicide or homicide as they turned over couch by couch. Detective Mason was fixing the couch he had flipped over when he spotted something interesting. He bent down and picked up the pregnancy test, reading the two pink lines he knew whoever the test belonged to was pregnant. "This yours?" he asked Linda.

She looked up and replied, "If that ain't a crack pipe then hell naw that ain't mines."

"Someone bag this up," Mason held the stick in the air, awaiting someone to grab it and bag it as evidence. "So, if your nephew doesn't stay here, where do he stay?" He turned his attention back to Linda.

"He stays with his mama." She looked at Detective Mason like he was dumb.

"And where does his mom live?"

"She lives with him," she answered sarcastically.

She could feel the steam rising from the Detective's skin as her remarks began to frustrate him. "And do you have any idea where that is?" he asked calmly, trying to hold on to the last bit of his composure.

"You wouldn't believe me if I told you."

"Yea? Why don't you try me?" he said sternly.

She looked up, staring him right in his eyes and said, "They stay together."

"Let's see how funny this be when I walk you ass out of here in handcuffs."

Linda threw both her arms up. "I'd like to see you try."

The whole room burst into laughter causing Detective Mason's nostrils to flare up. He felt himself losing control of his acerbic temper as he headed for the front door. "Talkin to that woman is like talking to a brick wall," he spat as he made his exit.

Detective Diaz tailed his partner to their vehicle, anticipating Mason's abrupt attitude from failing to recover the information he intended to find. Detective Diaz hated to be on the receiving end of his partner's dysfunctional temperament, so he remained silent the entire ride back to the precinct. "Test the pregnancy test for prints. We may not get much but it's worth a try," demanded Detective Mason.

His badge read *Detective,* but his attitude yelled Lieutenant asshole. Of course, he could've accompanied his former partner Lieutenant Frazier at the precinct barking orders, but he loved the field work and the props it came with like planting guns on gang members or sticking his married dick in prostitutes from time to time. While Mason sat back barking orders Diaz had his eyes glued to his computer screen, looking up possible addresses on Timothy 'Timo' Atkins.

The run-in with Linda was a dead end. After busting a sweat, he finally caught a break. "Bingo," he whispered as he clicked his computer mouse a couple times before reaching for pen and pad.

He felt a presence looming over his head as he jotted his information down in his notes. He looked up to see Mason reading the information on the computer screen. Detective Diaz managed to find mug shots of Timo's mom along with a few recent addresses. Diaz wrote down the most recent one, which was reported from a recent court appearance containing fraud charges. "Good job, chicken shit," taunted Mason as he snatched up the pad from his partner's desk. "Let's roll out."

He walked away and left Diaz there with his ink pen in his hand. Sometimes Diaz hated when his partner barked orders like he was his pet, but he was afraid to stand up to the tall and well-built black guy so just like any other time he jumped up and followed the leader.

Chapter 9

Blackboy

Blackboy was in line waiting to dress into his D.O.C. uniform and bag all his personal property when he heard his name being yelled by a correctional officer, "Dennis Coleman, where you at?"

"I'm right here." He raised his hand like he was in a classroom.

"Well bring ya ass, sir," demanded the C.O.

A quizzical look spread across Blackboy's face as he stepped out of line and followed the chubby 'George Lopez' looking officer.

"Where am I going C.O.?"

"Home unless you wanna stay here."

Blackboys eyes lit up like a Christmas tree. He hadn't even received his phone call; *this must be some kind of mistake* he thought. But that didn't stop him from power walking behind the C.O.

He smelled like yesterday and was eager to shower. He was uncomfortable being tossed from bullpen to bullpen with dope sick fiends who'd been having bowel movements along with sweaty drug dealers, murderers, and sockless thieves with terrible foot odors. He told himself he'd never come to the county again.

"Stand in line and wait for your name to be called."

Blackboy's eyes roamed around as he stood in line with the rest of the men who were going home. His eyes landed back on the old man from the station and he smiled. The old man winked and returned the love. "Coleman, step up," barked the C.O. sitting behind the desk.

Blackboy stepped up and took a seat on the opposite side of the desk. "What's your full name and date of birth?"

"Dennis Coleman, May 17th, 1992," replied Blackboy.

"What's your charge?"

"I got a gun charge."

The CO looked up from his paper and stared at Blackboy for a brief second before continuing. "Who posted your bail?"

Suddenly Blackboy became discontented. *Bail?* He thought to himself. He had no idea who posted his bail. "Um … Tefanie Coleman," he guessed his mom would be his only hope but then again, she didn't want nothing to do with him publicly.

She loved her only child with all her heart, but his ambition of a hustler and her safety drew a fine line between them. "Nope," the C.O. answered flatly.

Blackboy hung his head low in defeat. *If my mom didn't bond me out, then who did?* he wondered to himself. "Does Ciara Jones ring a bell?"

"Yea, that's my auntie," Blackboy lied. Truth was, he didn't have a clue who Ciara Jones was. All he knew was he was desperate to get home.

The C.O. shot him an untrusting look. "Sign here. You're young, I advise you to pick yourself up before the streets swallow you whole. Here!" The C.O. handed him a copy of his bail papers and told him to step back in line. "Davis," he called the next man in line, effectively dismissing him.

Blackboy expected a limo to be awaiting him once he made his way out the county since his bail was paid by an unknown individual. *Maybe it's the cartel, bonding me out to make me a rich man for staying solid under pressure,* his undeveloped mind thought. Standing outside the county, he looked both ways in search of an explanation. *No limo,* he ruled that theory out as he began to walk towards the bus stop.

"Aye young blood, you need a ride?" Blackboy looked to his right to see the old man from the station hanging out the passenger seat of a black tinted Mercedes-Benz.

Who the hell is this nigga? Blackboy wondered as he raced towards the nice car. He heard the locks click as he pulled the door handle. He climbed into the backseat as the car joined the evening traffic.

"Where ya' heading, young blood?" the old cat asked a question he already knew the answer to.

"I'm going south, but you can drop me off at the pink line."

"I'm headed south I can get you closer than that," the man insisted.

"Aight, good lookin," Blackboy agreed.

He paid no mind to the fine woman in the driver seat; he just wanted to go home. The woman pulled the car into traffic and headed towards the expressway. Blackboy nodded to 'Lil Wayne' lyrics until he fell into a deep sleep. He hadn't noticed the older man, and his companion pull masks over their faces as the anesthesia pumped through the rear ventilation system. Once Blackboy was out like a light the driver turned the A/C off and rolled the window down to let the fresh air circulate as they headed towards the opposite directions of where Blackboy resided.

Chapter 10

Timo

Yesterday's tragedy repeated itself inside Timo's mind as he sat in his mom's basement holding Stacy's hand while rubbing her belly. Tears ran down his face like a waterfall as he continued to turn up the half-filled bottle of Remy V.S.O.P he'd taken from his mother's bedroom while she was asleep. What was left of his sanity slowly slipped away as the bottle neared empty. He closed his eyes for a moment to try to get a grip on his conscience but the voices he was hearing were telling him that he was doing the right thing.

When his eyes opened, they landed right on the gun that took his lover's life over 24 hours ago. It felt like the gun was calling his name as the brown liquor took control of his young innocent mind. Timo let Stacy's ice-cold hand slip from his grasp and reached to grab the piece. His hand trembled uncontrollably as he held the nine in his palm. He took his free hand and placed it on Stacy's belly, rubbing it back and forth. Flashbacks of Stacy accidentally squeezing the trigger, played in Timo's mind over and over again.

Timo had sweat dripping from his forehead as he raised the gun to his head, breathing heavily as his finger caressed the trigger. Meeting Stacy was his breakthrough from the unworthy life he lived. Timo never had love in his own home. His mother used to sit around drinking while his stepfather abused and sexually assaulted him each and every day until he was old enough to defend himself.

While he was no longer a victim of rape, those demons from his childhood would forever stick with him. Even now, at 16 years old Timo still had nightmares of the gruesome actions he endured in as a helpless child. Too embarrassed to share his problems with the world, Timo kept all his deep, dark secrets bottled up. *What do I got to live for? Nobody would ever love a nigga like me anyway,* Timo cried to himself. His eyes were wide open but all he saw was darkness as his memories drove him over the edge. "It's me and you forever baby," he said to Stacy before making his crossover to the other side.

BOOM!

Timo felt nothing as his mind went blank. Lights out.

***

Detective Diaz

Detective Mason pushed his squad car to 60 mph up Garfield Boulevard, trying to reach his destination in record time. Sweat beads formed at the top of his forehead as his adrenaline pumped, causing the pits of his grey detective shirt to dampen. Diaz held on to his door handle with his feet pressed firmly against the floor. He hated his partners driving just as much as he disliked his attitude, but like any other time. He said nothing about it.

Detective Mason made a hard right turn on Prairie St., causing Diaz to shift in his seat so hard he damn near shared the driver seat with Mason. With eight blue and white tailing them, Mason threw the vehicle in park and jumped out with the speed of a cheetah. Gun in hand, he approached the two-story apartment building matching the address his partner had written down. Mason was about to give the door a hard knock, when something caught his attention. He noticed a pattern of what appeared to be dried up blood stains, on the ground leading to the back of the apartment building. His brows furrowed as he held up one finger, signaling the others to wait for his instructions.

He and his team followed the trail of blood, which led them to a black door at the rear of the building. He placed his ear to the door, listening for the sound of movement, voices, or any signs of existence on the other side of the black door. After a few seconds of total silence, he finally made the announcements.

Bang! Bang! Bang!

"Police, open up!" He raised his gun, aiming it at the door, as the others followed suit.

With his Glock still drawn he inched closer to the door, listening for sounds again. Once he was satisfied with his instincts, he looked at his partner and nodded towards the door. Diaz took two steps back, and one step forward, with a big boot to the door, taking it off the hinges. Mason, along with the rest, swarmed the place like roaches when the lights came on. *"Police!"* Mason yelled, swinging his flashlight and Glock from left to right as they searched the entire first floor of the vacant apartment.

While searching, Diaz spotted a hint of light coming from beneath a door in the kitchen. He tapped Mason's arm and pointed his flashlight in the direction the light was showing from. Without warning! Big, bad Mason rushed and snatched the door open with aggression. A stale smell smacked him in the face as he made his way down the flight of stairs that led to a basement. Mason damn near lost his footing as he stumbled over a pile of stilettos scattered across the floor. Mason kicked the heels aside, making a clear path for the other officers.

It's so hard to say goodbye ... to yesterday, BOYZ II MEN bled through the 36 inch speaker sitting against the wall.

An intense smell hit Diaz's nose as they crept towards the rear of the basement with their guns drawn. Diaz was first to spot the set of legs sprawled out across the floor as he turned the corner. "Holy, shit!" Diaz couldn't believe his eyes as he stared down at the two corpses, one matching the missing victim, Stacy Lomax and the other undoubtably, Timothy 'Timo' Atkins.

They both laid there motionless, in a pool of their own blood. Diaz couldn't take staring at the gruesome scene any longer. He stepped back and let Mason take charge. Not every day do you find a set of teenagers lying in cold blood, right... wrong.

Growing up in Chicago, Diaz has witnessed plenty of teenagers lose their lives across the city, but this scene was much different. This scene wasn't the ordinary street beef homicide. According to Stacy's friends, Diaz was now staring at a double suicide. He noticed that Timo was holding Stacy's hand, with a lone tear drop running from his left eye that hasn't even dried yet. Meaning Timo had taken his own life just moments before they arrived.

"Call the ambulance, I think this one has a pulse," yelled Mason from the other room. Diaz quickly pulled himself together to check out the scenery. He kneeled beside both victims and checked for a pulse. *This motherfucker here is trippin*, he thought to himself as he failed to discover the pulse his partner had found but he grabbed his walkie talkie and called it in anyway.

He took one more look at the victims and dropped his head low in his chest as the track in the background repeated itself. *If we get to see tomorrow, I hope it's worth the wait.*

Moments later, the paramedics came rushing into the apartment. Diaz watched as they carefully placed one of the bodies onto a stretcher before throwing a white sheet over the other. *It's so hard to say goodbye ... to yesterdayyy,* The track went on in the background as the investigators stepped on the scene.

Chapter 11

Heaven

Breaking News, flashed across Heaven's TV screen at 9:00 pm as her eyes zoomed in on the photos of her best friend and Timothy as the news reporter announced today's tragedy.

"Two teenagers were found in a basement on the southside of Chicago, with bullet holes in each of their heads. Investigators seem to believe there has been a double suicide commitment after a couple of teenagers reported a fatal incident just yesterday morning," The reporter's voice became inaudible as Heaven went into shock over the updated news she just discovered.

Just a few minutes ago, her friend April had called her phone to share the rumor of Timo shooting himself in the head. Heaven jumped out of bed and turned her TV to the news channel. The photos of her best friend caused tears to run down her cheeks. Heaven didn't realize she was crying until her mom entered her room unannounced and used the remote to power the TV off.

Marrissa sat beside her daughter and held her tight until she was assured her only child was okay. "Heaven, honey, I know it's gonna be hard to live with the fact that one of your closest friends has left you here. We can't question God, but one thing I do know is that sweet little girl didn't deserve to leave this Earth that way." Heaven was speechless, her mother's attempt to comfort her only made her break down harder than ever before. "It's okay honey, I'm here. Let it all out so your heart can heal," said Marrissa.

She held Heaven for two hours until her daughter cried herself to sleep in her arms. The next morning, Heaven woke up to the smell of breakfast lingering in the air. She stretched and yawned before climbing out of bed. She didn't remember falling asleep the night before. All she knew was that her mother never left her side. Heaven slipped on her pink slippers and followed the smell to the kitchen.

"Good morning, sunshine. I made your favorite, blueberry pancakes, turkey bacon, and sunny side up eggs for my favorite person in the whole entire world."

For the first time in a long time, Marrissa saw that beautiful smile spread across her daughter's face. That alone warmed her heart. "Sweety, I've been thinking about your situation, and I'd be lying if I told you I'm okay with this," Marrissa admitted.

"I'd be lying too," agreed Heaven.

"What do you think about relocating? I just want you to start fresh. I know this healing process will need an extensive amount of time and prayer."

"I want to finish this school year, and graduate with my friends like we agreed, Mommy."

"Okay, if that's what you want, I'll support your wishes. But the moment you walk across that stage, we're out of here— deal?"

"Deal!" Heaven pounded her mother's fist before sharing a hug.

"Honey, there's one more thing I'd like to discuss with you."

Heaven, still in her mother's embrace, looked her mother straight in the eyes. "I'm listening," she stated flatly.

Heaven knew when her mom was going through something. She sensed it the moment she entered the kitchen, but her personal problems prevented her from acknowledging her mother's grievance. "Me and J — your dad — are getting a divorce. It's for the best that we both take some time to figure out what we really want."

"Whose idea was this? Are you leaving my dad for principal Hobbs?" barked Heaven, her world came crumbling down all over again.

Fuck what have I done? Marrissa cursed herself before responding. "No honey, what made you say that?"

"Mommy, I'm a big girl please don't lie to me. Daddy hasn't been home for the past three days, and I've been hearing that front door close every morning around the same time."

Heaven's statement caught her mother completely off guard. "The next time you decide to make my favorite breakfast, at least let me enjoy it before you spoil my appetite." Heaven lifted from her chair and stomped back to her room before slamming her room door.

"Shit!" Cursed Marrissa. *Too early ... I knew I should've waited,* she thought to herself as she grabbed her cell phone and sent a text.

"She knows."

A few short seconds later, her phone vibrated and a text from an unknown number flashed across the screen.

"How did she find out?" Marrissa read the text before replying.

"She's growing up. She's not a little girl anymore."

"What are we going to do?"

"We're gonna stick to the plan unless you're getting cold feet." Marrissa texted back, feeling that her plan of escape would backfire and leave her cold and lonely. Just as she was about to sit her cell phone down on the kitchen counter a text came through.

"Never in a million years. I know where I wanna be. I luv u."

Marrissa couldn't stop herself from smiling inside and out as she replied. *"I love you too."* Before sitting her phone

back down. "Now I have a beef to settle," she said in a low tone as she made her way to Heaven's room door.
KNOCK! KNOCK! KNOCK!

***

2 Weeks Later

Heaven stared at herself in the bathroom mirror. Her natural hair flowed down her back in a feather wrap. She was absolutely flawless on the outside, but on the inside, she was broken into a thousand little pieces. Today she was set to walk across the same stage her best friend Stacy was supposed to strut across, but fate just had other plans.

Heaven's nights had been reckless since the day her friend put a bullet into her own skull. "We're running late, honey. Are you ready to go, beautiful?" Josh, Heaven's dad, asked from the doorway.

"Yeah, I'll be out in a second." Heaven thumbed away the lonely teardrop that trickled down her face.

Her father felt ashamed that he hasn't been much support when his daughter needed him the most. He allowed he and Marrissa's break up to interfere with him being the father Heaven needed him to be. Little did he know, his little girl was growing up and seeing things more clearly now. The love she had for him was slowly but surely slipping away, just as much as her mother's had.

"Okay, I'll go get the car started." He hung his head low and walked straight past Marrissa on the way out the door without saying a word.

Josh hadn't slept in his own home in two weeks and Marrissa became accustomed to sleeping alone. At least, Josh assumed she was sleeping alone. Just as sure as he found someone to spice up his life, Marrissa's heart was in another place as well and she felt optimistic about her next move. Heaven thought her mom's decision was selfish, but she would later find out that it had always been about her.

The 8th graders took their spot on the stage before singing in sync with the Kirk Franklin song, *Imagine Me,* that blasted through the auditorium speakers. Stacy's had funeral taken place yesterday and her mother was now at her graduation to accept her diploma in her absence. The school principal ordered a large copy of Stacy's graduation picture and sat it in a seat as a show of sympathy and respect for the grieving mother. Heaven tried her best to keep from making eye contact with Tiny, Stacy's mom. Her guilty conscience got the best of her as sweat began to pour down her face like rain drops. The entire room became mute except for the sound of Stacy's beautiful voice, singing the lyrics to the song better than any of the students could.

Heaven looked to her left and there Stacy was, singing her heart out with a bullet wound in the right side of her head. Heaven squeezed her eyes shut to prevent herself from crying. *Pull it together, Heaven. You got this*, she told herself as she took a deep breath, holding it in, then exhaling. When Heaven's eyes opened, the first thing they saw was a pair of eyes, staring daggers into her soul. Those eyes belonged to nobody other than the infamous Tiny.

"I'm so sorry," Heaven mumbled as her hand rose to her heart.

Heaven was torn beyond belief but Tiny lost her only daughter so no tears would be enough to repay that debt. Heaven was way past her limit and Marrissa noticed it but was too late. As she tried to comfort her; Heaven took off running off the stage and out of the auditorium. Marrissa shared a brief stare with Mr. Hobbs before chasing after her daughter. Josh caught the connection, but he remained silent.

He knew his wife's heart belonged to someone else. He just didn't know who. Josh loved his family, but the strings Marrissa used to tug on his heart had loosened and his feelings were slowly slipping away. He and Marrissa had only been dating a few months when she showed up to his doorstep with a newborn baby, babbling about starting a family. At first, he thought Marrissa had been smoking crack, but her sweet talking along with her ethereal sex game convinced him to think they were in love, which made him agree to adopting the infant.

Still to this day, only two people alive know the truth about Marrissa's love story, and Josh wasn't one of 'em. When Marrissa made it out the main entrance of the school, she spotted Heaven sitting on the curb crying her poor heart out. Marrissa knew this day would be her daughter's breaking point. For sixteen nights straight she'd had to wake her daughter up from her horrific nightmares. Some nights she even slept in Heaven's bed with her just to keep the demons away. She offered Heaven the easy route, moving away and transferring schools but this is what Heaven wanted.

"This is what Stacy would've wanted," was the response every time her mom put the topic on the table.

Marrissa walked up and sat right beside her daughter, and held her just like any other time, only this time the pain hit too close to home as Marrissa felt tears of her own surface then fall, one after the other. Heaven didn't know how long they sat there crying but by the time they were done the graduation had ended and the families came spilling out of the main entrance. Marrissa lifted Heaven up by her waist and walked her back inside to collect her certificates. The two were in total shock when their eyes landed on Mr. Hobbs and Josh having a heated discussion. Marrissa cleared her throat to let her presence be known. Josh quickly dropped the finger he had pointed at Mr. Hobbs' face to his side in an attempt to appear as if nothing was going on, but no one was fooled by this performance.

He said one last thing to the principal before walking towards his family. Once he reached them, he held Heaven in his arms and told her, "Sweetie, I'm sorry these last couple of weeks have been hell for you. I really wish I can take all your pain and place it on my shoulders." Tears began to fall down Josh's face now as he searched for the right words to say. "No matter where you are, no matter what you do I'll always love you. From Day One I've loved you. Sometimes I may have slacked at showing it, but you'll always be the best thing that ever happened to me," Josh might've been talking to his daughter, but his words were piercing right through his wife's heart.

    Marrissa took a deep breath and let her eyes close trying to prevent from shedding tears. Epic failure! The waterfall slipped right through the cracks of her eyelids. Principal Hobbs pinched the bridge of his nose. Tears were forming in his eyes as they met Marrissa's. He was a man with a heart just like any other human and even though he was on the winning team in this situation he had his own skeletons to deal with at home. Josh took his arm from around Heaven and wiped Marrissa's tears away. "You take care." He spoke softly before turning around and nodding towards Mr. Hobbs. Mr. Hobbs returned the gesture and Josh walked out leaving the trio in the auditorium, alone.

    Marrissa and Heaven held hands as they made their way to their vehicle. Heaven felt the hairs on the back of her neck stand up. She felt butterflies in the pit of her stomach. *Why is my world falling apart?* she wondered as she crossed the street with her head in her chest. Heaven heard her mother's alarm as she let her hand slip from her grasp. Just as Heaven was making her way to the passenger side, a car came speeding up the street at NASCAR's speed.

    "Heavennn!" Marrissa yelled to the top of her lungs.

    She tried her best to react, but her legs wouldn't move. All she could do was watch as the scene unfolded. The dark blue BMW came crashing into Heaven, knocking her out of her pink heels as her body flew across the street like a rag doll. The driver of the BMW never took their foot off the gas as the car disappeared from the scene. "Noooo!" cried

Marrissa as she ran full speed across the street. She rushed to Heaven's side and scooped her into her arms. "Honey, talk to me, pleaseee!"

The blood from Heaven's head quickly filled up Marrissa's pink and white dress. "Someone call an ambulance!" yelled Marrissa as pedestrians started to gather around.

Heaven's eyes were rolled to the back of her head. Her arms and legs were visibly broken. Marrissa rocked her child back and forth while tears from her eyes splashed on Heaven's face.

"What the hell happened?" someone asked as the crowd grew larger.

"Somebody came speeding up the street and knocked that poor baby all the way across the street," a witness responded.

"And they didn't bother to stop?"

"Nope, looks like they were gunning right for the kid Mr. Hobbs."

Principal Hobbs stepped out of the main entrance of the school with a look of confusion written across his face all he could see was a huge crowd. But the screaming he heard was undoubtedly Marrissa's cries. He wasted no time jogging to the scene to see what had occurred. The crowd was so thick Mr. Hobbs had to push and shove just to make an entrance. The moment his eyes landed on his favorite student his heart shattered into tiny little pieces.

He covered his mouth with his hands as he bit his bottom lip to try to keep from crying. But his pride was no match for his heart. He kneeled beside Marrissa and grabbed a hold of Heaven's hand. He cupped her hand inside his and squeezed tightly unintentionally. Heaven's entire body was covered in blood. Mr. Hobbs could see her bones broken in several spots. That alone made him break down hard. The crowd started to open as the sound of an ambulance sirens became evident.

It seemed like the sound was moving without the vehicle as the sirens grew louder the vehicle took its sweet time making an appearance. Everyone took a few steps back as the ambulance finally made a left turn and parked directly in front of the school. The doors swung open, and the paramedics rushed to the scene with a stretcher in hand. One of the paramedics checked Heaven's arm for a pulse, when he failed at getting one, he placed two fingers to her neck. "She's still alive! Let's get her to a hospital" he demanded as he placed an oxygen mask over Heaven's face to help her breath.

Mr. Hobbs pried Heaven from her mother's arms so the paramedics can do their job. "Let's go sweetheart, it's gonna be okay," he assured.

She wanted to believe him, but reality just didn't seem that way. "Are you the child's parents?"

"Yes," Mr. Hobbs answered as they stepped inside the back of the ambulance without invitation. The sirens came back to life as the doors slammed shut and the ambulance rushed off the scene.

***

Blackboy

Blackboy had been held captive in a dark room for 2 weeks and had yet to figure out what the hell was going on. All he could remember was catching a ride home and waking up in a dark basement soaking wet from buckets of water being poured on him. His hands were tied behind his back, and he was stripped of his clothing. Surprisingly he hadn't suffered any real injuries; the only thing that was bruised was his pride.

How the hell did I let somebody kidnap me? Like a kid falling for a stranger with candy, he thought to himself. At first, he thought it was some sick joke. He played the tough guy role for the first few hours. But his mask had been broken after those hours became days and he no longer knew how long he'd been captivated.

Blackboy was alerted by the sounds of locks clicking above his head, followed by footsteps. From the pattern of the steps, he could tell there were multiple bodies approaching the basement. Quickly, he struggled to sit up straight and back up against the wall. Sick of being someone's play toy, Blackboy decided to speak up and find out why the hell someone would want to bond him out and kidnap a useless piece of shit like himself. The same old man that had offered him the ride came into view along with the woman who drove the black Benz.

"Aye look, whatever funny shit y'all tryna pull, I'm not the one for it. If y'all looking for a muhfucka to sex traffic it's plenty ho's out *hea* for the job but this ain't that," Blackboy spoke with his chest out.

The woman couldn't help herself as she laughed at Blackboy's twisted ideas. "No bullshit, y'all on the wrong shit right now. I got betta shit to do with my time than to be in somebody junkie ass basement, folks. Y'all ass trippin," spat Blackboy.

He became visibly irritated, but no one was intimidated by his demeanor. "Is that right? Blackboy heard a familiar voice boom from the doorway and became horrified.

His heart felt like it was going to pop out of his chest. He looked in the direction where the voice came from, hoping that the face didn't match the monster he heard. Blackboy's heart rate sped up more with every step the person took.

My life is over, he thought to himself as a lone tear threatened to fall from his left eye suddenly. He felt a rough hand beneath his chin, squeezing his jaws so tight it felt like his jawbone was on the verge of breaking. Blackboy shut his eyes, sucking in the pain his abductor was causing. When his eyes opened, he was staring the monster right in his eyes.

The evil grin spread across his face made Blackboy's stomach weak.

"Somebody's surprised to see me."

***

Ciara

Tiffany, Blackboy's mom, sat on Ciara's sofa biting her nails until her fingers bled. It's been two weeks since she'd sent Ciara to bond her son out of jail and she hasn't heard from him since. She called the Cook County jail countless times even after the superintendent assured her that he'd been released. They even gave her a copy of his bond receipt with Ciara's name on it. She instructed Ciara to wait outside until she spotted Blackboy and give him a ride home, but the long day Ciara faced, running Baby J from destination to destination, had her stomach growling so she decided to make a quick run across the street to Popeyes while Blackboy processed out.

She could've sworn she'd seen someone that matched the description that Tiffany had given her walking out of the main entrance when she was eating her 2 piece chicken combo. She jumped up with a piece of chicken still in hand and ran towards the side exit which leads her directly towards the county jail. As she strutted across the street a CTA bus came to a halt right in front of her, blocking her view as the pedestrians loaded onto the bus while others made their exits.

The bus driver released his foot off the brake just as Ciara attempted to walk around the bus. She became frustrated as she waited on the bus driver to get the hell out of her way. "Finally," Ciara mumbled under her breath as the bus passed the green light. The figure that Ciara had been watching had disappeared. The only thing she saw was a black Benz pulling away from the curb into the night's traffic.

"I fucked up big time. I promise, friend, I only went into the restaurant for five minutes. Next thing you know a shitload of mothafuckers come running out the damn place," said Ciara as she tried to plead her case.

She took full responsibility for her actions. She knew she should've stayed and waited for Blackboy to appear like she was instructed. She should've known something serious had to be going on from the way Tiffany had been acting. She never seen her friend so shaken up in her life. Tiffany wouldn't give her much information to feed off of, all she kept saying was, "I just been through a lot of shit and I think it might be time to flush the toilet."

Tiffany hadn't been able to sit down since she got the call from an old friend saying that her son was just arrested. She tried her very best to wean him away from the street life that he hungered for, hoping that keeps them off the radar of a very powerful person. When Tiffany ran away from Texas, she knew Chicago wouldn't be her best option but it was the only choice she had at the moment.

Just as she was trying to repel herself from thinking about her past, her phone vibrated in her lap, a text message alert popped up on her phone screen from an unknown number, her hands trembled as she struggled to enter her passcode to unlock her phone. Ciara had no idea why her friend was so shaken up. Tiffany opened the message and the sight before her eyes nearly made her stop breathing as she stared at the photo. Tears began to trickle down her light brown cheeks.

"What is it?" asked Ciara.

Tiffany took a deep breath before unfolding the truth about her past. "Friend, I haven't been completely honest with you about my past. There's a reason why I left Texas, I'm just gone tell you the truth." She wiped her tears away and took Ciara back to the day it all went down.

Tiffany was cruising the Texas streets with Chindo, her lover and best friend. Chindo had the coke game on lock and since the day he had to put his own right-hand man in a casket, for turning state, he vowed to never trust another nigga. So, till this day it was just him and Tiffany making all the moves. Together like Bonnie and Clyde.

Chindo and Tiffany met at a mall in Dallas where she was a salesperson at the Gucci store which happens to be Chindo's choice of designer for the day. He had been out shopping for some all-white attire for a yacht party with his Columbian plug, Matto. Just like any other drug deal the night would start off with naked women and heavy liquor while Chindo tested endless lines of top-of-the-line cocaine. Then it would end with the women escorting Chindo to a 5-star hotel to hit him off with a happy ending and a heavy supply of coke.

The moment Chindo stepped inside of the Gucci store, Tiffany hazel brown eyes sucked him right in. He'd shopped at the store a thousand times but never have he seen a pair of eyes so mesmerizing.

She appeared to be a mixture of Black and Asian the way her eyes slanted. No lashes, no makeup, she was a natural ten plus tax. Chindo couldn't help himself from coming at her after she rang up his items and bagged them. Chindo invited her to his event. At first, she rejected his invitation but he wouldn't leave the store until he got her to agree. Since that night they've been inseparable. Chindo promised her that if she had to quit her job she would be set for life, staying with him. Chindo spoiled Tiffany and took care of her son like he was one of his own. Tiffany became so attached to Chindo she almost forgot the real reason she was dealing with him in the first place.

As Tiffany pulled into the driveway of their massive mansion, she pressed a button on her remote unlocking the security gate. Her and her lover had just left another party drunk, and high off coke with a trunk full of white gurl, Chindo was lit. He was ready to rip Tiffany out of her Dolce and Gabbana two-piece since they'd left the party. He'd been playing with her pussy the whole ride home; her juice box was dripping wet.

Tiffany deaded the engine on her Range Rover and hit the locks. Chindo removed his hand from inside her panties and rubbed them all over his face before sucking his fingers.

Tiffany was hot and ready to strip out of her clothes right in the driveway. With Chindo on her heels Tiffany rushed to unlock the door to their home. She struggled for a moment before she finally found the correct key. "Got it," she said as she inserted the key before twisting it to the left, unlocking the top lock, then the bottom.

Chindo stepped inside the house behind her, his hands were back feeling her up while his lips locked on her neck causing her knees to buckle. "Shiiitt! Let's go to the room baby," Tiffany moaned.

Chindo reached in his waistband and pulled his gold Desert Eagle out and sat it on their living room table before rushing to their master bedroom. Chindo left a trail of clothes in his wake as they approached the stairs, by the time they made it to the bedroom, Chindo was completely naked. He helped Tiffany remove the little pieces of clothing she did have on before picking her 150-pound frame up with no problem.

"I want to taste this sweet pussy baby," he said as he lifted her above his head by her thighs lining her freshly waxed pussy with his tongue like a bullseye.

Tiffany wrapped her legs around his head as he held her in the air by her ass cheeks while he ate the pussy like it was his last meal. His tongue hit all the right spots, making Tiffany's body shake uncontrollably as she felt her orgasm building up from the tip of her toes. "Ahh, shit!" she cried out.

That let Chindo know she was about to bring Niagara Falls into their bedroom tonight. He gently laid her on top of the California king sized bed and with both hands Chindo raised Tiffany's legs high above her head before going back in for the kill. "Mhmm ... yesss. Uhhh," Tiffany purred as she reached her peak. "Fuuck!" she yelled as she exploded in Chindo's mouth.

Now she was running from the tongue like he knew she would, but Chindo pulled her back each time. Once he felt Tiffany was about to reach another orgasm, Chindo started planting soft kisses on her kitty. First the left side then the right side then finally her clit received all the love one man can give. Tiffany never felt so good in her entire life. What the fuck am I doing? she thought to herself as tears began to build up in her eyes. I done fell in love with the enemy ... No, he's not the enemy. That no good son of a bitch in that closet is, she thought just as the closet door began to open.

Chindo grabbed and teased Tiffany's juice box before inserting his 8 inches into her womanhood filling her up inside. He felt her body tense up as her super soaker started to dry up.

"What's wrong baby?" he asked as he looked into her eyes, watching her tears fall. Through her pupils, Chindo saw a shadow close-in behind him like a thief in the night.

"Why?" his eyes asked the question without his lips moving. Suddenly he felt the unmistakable feeling of cold steel pressing up against the back of his head.

"Don't do nun you gone regret, Migo. You know what time it is," The menacing voice echoed through the room.

Chindo now felt disgusted by the woman he'd fallen in love with. The horn tattoo above his left eyebrow seemed to have grown outside his head as the love inside his eyes quickly turned to hate. "Baby I'm sorry," Tiffany sobbed. If she could've turned back the hands of time, she would've done things differently but it was too late.

Weezy, Tiffany's slime ball ass baby daddy had been forcing her to set up every nigga that had a dollar sign behind is name. Many times, she had disagreed but all that's ever gotten her was an ass whooping for hours on end. Tiffany had gotten used to taking down the marks with Weezy so she'd stop complaining and went with the flow to save herself from the damage, but this mark was different.

Chindo was out of these small-time hustlers league it had taken Tiffany nearly a year to find out where he lay his head and another two years to get the drop on his stash. She thought about pulling out a long time ago, but she knew she was being watched closely and Weezy wouldn't hesitate to kill her if she got in the way of his paper. Weezy only cared about two things in life. That's money and money.

Weezy snatched Chindo up by his chains. "Point me to the stash so we can get this shit over with. So, I can go home, and you can finish fucking this no good piece of pussy that got down on you." Weezy threw the low blow at Tiffany while staring her directly in her hazel brown eyes with a sinister grin spread across his face.

She knew he was devastated by the fact that she was giving Chindo the pussy and was having fun doing so. Weezy had seen her have sex with their marks before but never had he seen her so in the mood to do so, not even with him.

Weezy followed closely behind Chindo as he led him into the basement where the built-in safe was hidden behind a large painting of himself on a yacht, drinking beer. Chindo removed the painting before twisting the knob left then right, then left again before they all heard a click!

Chindo pulled on the door of the safe, revealing the hidden treasure that made Weezy's dick hard instantly. "This is everything, just take it all and leave my fucking home," spat Chindo as he stepped aside. He was more disappointed than scared.

He trusted Tiffany with his life like he did with no other woman and now he was paying for it, literally. "My pleasure," were the last words Chindo heard.

Bang!

Fire spat from the barrel of Weezy's Glock 9 as the bullet entered the side of Chindo's skull. Tiffany rushed to Chindo's side screaming and hollering. "Nooo!"

She picked his head up and caressed his wound. "You sick bastard. You could've took the fucking money and left, you didn't have to kill him," she sobbed as she rocked back and forth with Chindo's blood spreading over her naked body.

"You righ,t I could've taken the bread and dipped," said Weezy with his banger now pointed at Tiffany's head. "But what the fuck do I look like giving a nigga a chance to get back at me? Or worse, what I look like leaving the bitch who fell in love with him alive to tell the story?"

Those words caught Tiffany by surprise as she stared up, looking straight into the barrel of his 9. She could've sworn she saw a red eye staring back at her as she tried her best to swallow. Tiffany saw a wicked grin spread across Weezy's face that made her stomach ache. She shut her eyes tightly saying a prayer in her mind as tears slipped through the cracks of her eyelids.

BANG!

This time the bang seemed louder as Tiffany's body jumped from the sound alone. *At least it was painless* she thought to herself as she made her transition to the other side. *Where's the white light? Where's the grim reaper? Are any of those tales real?* she wondered, then another loud bang caused her to jump again.

This time she opened her eyes to see Weezy standing there, holding his chest as blood filled his white Gucci shirt, turning it maroon. Tiffany spotted another large hole in Weezy's back as he turned to face his shooter. Tiffany's eyes followed Weezy's stare all the way to the doorway where Blackboy was standing there holding Chindo's Desert Eagle with both hands. He slowly walked towards his father with the smoking cannon still aimed right at his torso.

Weezy's Glock fell from his hands as he fell to his knees, then flat on his stomach. Blackboy dropped the gun and rushed to his mom's side. "It's okay, ma, he can't hurt us no more," Blackboy assured.

Tiffany stared at Chindo lifeless body as tears of regret began to trickle down her distraught face. The man who was supposed to have been an easy lick became the man of her dreams. Had she met him under different circumstances, Tiffany would've ridden off into the sunset with the love of her life. Her sorrow was replaced with anger as her eyes landed on Weezy's slumped body. He appeared to be staring back at her as blood continued to spill from his gunshot wounds.

Next, Tiffany's eyes landed on the opened safe filled with drugs and money. She began to collect her thoughts as she scooped herself from the floor with Blackboy on her tail, Tiffany rushed upstairs and entered the supply closet attached to the kitchen. Once she found what she needed she raced back to the basement.

"Here, fill this up baby!" She handed Blackboy a trash bag and filled another one up herself.

After taking all the loot Blackboy reached for one of the many bundles that piled up inside the safe. "Leave it," Tiffany demanded.

Blackboy looked at her like she was insane. After a brief stare down, he yielded. Tiffany tied both bags in a knot before throwing them over her shoulder. After cleaning Chindo's other stash in the bedroom for another 2.5 million she grabbed the pants Chindo had taken off and began searching until she located her car keys. Once she found them, she threw on her clothes and called the only person she could depend on ...

Ciara sat back and took in all the information her best friend had dropped on her with a dubious expression written on her face. Tiffany had told her that she hit the lottery and wanted to return to Chicago to bask in her richness, but Ciara wasn't sold by her story. However, she went with the flow for the time being because like they say what's done in the dark shall come to light. Tiffany moved back to the city and paid her way through school like she'd always dreamed of and became a teacher by day and a broker by night.

She owned properties all over the city that she flipped to clean up Chindo's dirty dead presidents. Even though she had hopeful dreams she had a feeling that one day her past would come back to haunt her, but that day has come way too soon and her hell bent child was the cause for their cover being blown.

"Let's just go to the police station," Ciara started to suggest but was cut off right away.

"No, he'll kill my baby with no hesitation!" cried Tiffany.

"So, what else can we do? What do you think he wants from you?"

"Maybe the money, maybe my life. Who knows." Tiffany shrugged. "I just hope he doesn't kill my baby. He's all I have."

Just as words came from her mouth another text came through Tiffany's phone and her hands trembled as she struggled to unlock it. She became dizzy as her eyes roamed over the message.

"Meet us back in Texas or he's dead …"

Chapter 12

Marrissa

Marrissa stood next to Heaven's bed and watched as the nurses changed the bandages on her daughter's wounds. Heaven had been brain dead for two weeks and her chance of survival was slim to none. The impact from the BMW had broken over 20 bones in Heaven's body which caused her to wear a full body cask. Even though Heaven's body failed to show any signs of improvement, Marrissa refused to pull the plug on her daughter. "God has a better plan for her," Marrissa told the doctors every time they placed the topic on the table.

But deep inside she only hoped the words she delivered were true. Heaven was hardly recognizable with all the cuts and bruises over her face. Police had tracked down the BMW but was unable to identify the driver since the car had been reported stolen. When they located the vehicle, it had been set on fire burning to ashes any chances of finding a fingerprint. Local detectives had stopped by at least four times this week, trying to figure out who would have the motive to do such things.

The first person that came to Marrissa's mind was Tiny, Stacy's mother. She'd noticed the look on her face as she mugged her daughter at the graduation. The detectives marked Tiny down as a person of interest and picked her up for questioning but without any solid evidence they were forced to let her go free. Plus, the school cameras showed Tiny pulling off in a maroon Nissan Altima after graduation ended. So that ruled Tiny out as a suspect. She even sent her remorse along with flowers to Heaven's room.

Josh had stopped by once when he first heard about the incident, but he hadn't been back since. Principal Hobbs on the other hand hasn't left Marrissa's side as she dealt with the tragedy.

With restless eyes, Marrissa stared at her daughter as she lay there motionless. "Hey honey, if you can hear me, just want to let you know that I love you, and I'll never give up on you no matter what." She rubbed cast ond Heaven's the arm as gently as she could.

"Since the moment I laid eyes on you, so innocent ... so sweet." Tears formed in the corners of Marrissa's eyes as she continued to vent. "I knew you were a gift from God, straight from the Heavens above." Marrissa smiled as she remembered the first time she'd seen Heaven open her beautiful eyes. "The day I took you home I didn't know what it took to be a mother, but I promised you that I would give it my all and up – " Marrissa became overwhelmed as she tried to express her feelings.

"Up until two weeks ago I thought I was doing a damn good job. God couldn't have put you in my life for us to go through hell together. He's not that cruel," she cried as the nurses made a quiet exit, leaving them alone.

Marrissa didn't acknowledge their presence to begin with. In her eyes it was just her and her baby girl. Those nurses wouldn't understand the pain her heart feels as a mother and a best friend. No one would understand the picture she had to paint so her daughter didn't have to suffer the lifestyle of an orphan child.

"All I ever wanted was for you to have a regular life, sweety, like any other child."

Mr. Hobbs placed his hand on Marrissa's shoulder for support. He was the only person in the world that understood exactly what she'd been through. Marrissa felt nothing, she just kept on talking to her precious little Heaven. It wasn't until she heard his voice say "We're gonna get through this baby," that she snapped out of her trance.

Her mood went from sorrow to hot as fire and she snapped. "Just get the hell out of here. You're the reason everything is the way it is. You're nothing but a selfish inconsiderate pussy, too much of a coward to hold yourself accountable for your own actions. She didn't need you thirteen years ago and she damn sure don't need you now. You had all the time in the world to step up and be the father she needed but you abandoned her like some unfinished project," she snapped, catching Mr. Hobbs AKA Karim off guard.

He looked dumbfounded as he took his medicine without batting an eye. He knew this moment would unfold. He just hoped he would be better prepared. *Now would be the time*, He thought to himself as Marrissa continued to throw stones at a glass house, breaking his heart into tiny pieces. "I never expected it to be like this," Karim admitted.

One lonely tear built up in the corner of his right eye then slid down his handsome honey brown face. "I knew this moment would surface sooner or later, but since it happens to be now. Let's get it all off our chest because I don't ever wanna have to relive this day again."

Another tear fell from Karim's eye. *He cries*, Marrissa thought to herself as she fell into his arms. She didn't mean to explode the way she did but thirteen years of built-up emotions would blow a house down. Those words were long overdue.

A pair of eyes watched from a distance as Karim poured his heart out. "If I could go back in time and repair the damage that I've caused, I would. I'll take full responsibility for my actions. We both knew how much pain my secrets have caused over the years. I wake up living in regret every day. I – ... We were young, I had no idea that life would turn out this way. I was living in the moment Marrissa, I'm sorry. Every day I pray for my daughter's recovery so that I can make things right with her," Karim cried.

The pair of eyes in the dark grew wide with rage at the mention of Heaven's name. "That little bitch should be dead by now," the intruder whispered to themself as they sat in the shadows lurking.

Karim turned around, expecting to see someone standing there but all he saw was the back of the nurse's scrubs as they disappeared from his sight. Karim broke free from Marrissa's embrace and rushed towards the doorway of the room. Looking out the room both ways, he saw no one except the nurse sitting at her desk typing on her computer. She looked up and spoke "Hi, do you need anything?" she asked.

"Nothing. I ... I could've sworn I heard someone talking." Karim became lost in his thoughts.

Even from behind that nurses walk looks too familiar. *I know I'm not tripping*, he thought as he closed the door behind him. He wanted to believe his mind was playing tricks on him, but his nose worked perfectly fine and the scent he inhaled was unmistakably real. "Imma go grab something to eat, you want something?" Karim asked Marrissa.

"Um, I'll have a Ceasar salad."

"You and these damn salads, you need to put some meat on them damn bones," Karim joked as he grabbed his wallet and car keys from inside Marrissa's purse.

"I'm meaty where it counts." Marrissa winked at Karim.

His eyes roamed down to her pussy as he bit his bottom lip. "You're right about that." Karim closed the distance between him and Marrissa before sliding his hand inside her blue jean shorts.

His middle finger found its way to the entrance of her water park. "Mmm, don't start nothing you can't finish," Marrissa moaned as she grinded her hips, dripping her juices all over Karim's hand. Karim pulled her into the private restroom attached to their room.

"Karim, what if we get caught?"

"What if we don't?" he countered as he closed the restroom door before unfastening Marrissa's pants, pulling them down to her ankles.

Marrissa bent over the toilet as Karim pulled his dick out. She held one hand on the toilet and spread her ass cheeks with the other. Karim spread her other cheek as he slid his dick inside her walls, deep and slow. Marrissa let a moan escape her mouth as Karim went as deep as he could before pulling back slowly. His dick became drenched with her juices. Her cream made his dick look like a glazed long john from Dunkin Donuts as he hit her g-spot. It took everything in Marrissa not to scream like she would normally do. Her sex cries always put Karim in overdrive.

Karim let go of Marrissa's ass and gripped her waist with both hands pounding her insides out like they were in the privacy of their own home instead of a hospital restroom. Marrissa held both hands on the toilet. Tears came from her eyes as she fought back her cries of ecstasy. Karim was digging her out from behind.

Marrissa tightened her pussy muscles around his dick and almost made his knees buckle. Her pussy was already a bomb so when she tightened her pussy muscles it felt like she had a little hand inside her vagina, jagging Karim off as he stuffed her walls. Ten hard thrusts later, Karim and Marrissa were exploding together, mixing their love potions together. Karim pumped every drip of his seed inside Marrissa's walls before pulling out.

Marrissa seemed to be stuck in the same position, so Karim helped her stand up straight. Her legs wobbled as she tried to make her way to the sink where they both wiped themselves off before fixing themselves and joining Heaven in the other room. Marrissa hadn't realized it but that was exactly what she needed. Karim had lifted so much weight off her shoulders in just five minutes. "I'll be back. Imma go get this salad for my baby." Karim smiled before disappearing, leaving Marrissa sitting there blushing.

She turned her attention back to Heaven. Marrissa traced Heaven's jawline with her thumb. "The last couple of weeks have been so hard for me, staring at you lying here and I can't do anything to help you. I pray three times a day. Sometimes more." Marrissa had fallen right back in her feelings.

It was impossible to pretend that everything was okay when her daughter was a vegetable. "God has to have a better future for us, honey. This can't be the end; I went through hell so that you'll live a decent life." Tears began to fall again.

Marrissa had cried so much in the past two weeks that her eyes seemed to have permanent bags under them. The pair of eyes in the shadows sat watching as Marrissa broke down. *I'm the one who's been through hell and it's all because of that little bitch,* the figure thought silently. "She has to die," she said to herself as she disappeared.

A short moment later, the power went out inside the room, causing Heaven's life support machines to beep out of control. The noise made Marrissa jump out of her skin. She jumped up from her seat and ran to grab help, meanwhile the intruder emerged from the shadows and crept over to Heaven's bedside. The woman pulled down her hospital mask, revealing her identity to an unconscious Heaven. "You ruined my life. You made it impossible to live the happy life I deserve." Tears began to form in the women's eyes as she started her assault by clipping the wires to Heaven's life support machines before reaching into her jacket pocket and retrieving a needle. "If I have to lose the man I love no one will have him." The woman placed her thumb on the back of the needle and applied pressure, causing the liquid inside to squirt out the tip of the needle and hit the floor. The floor began to smoke as the battery acid burned through.

The woman grabbed Heaven's IV cord as she stared the motionless child over, one last time. "See you in hell," she said as the needle made its way into Heaven's IV.

Suddenly a group of nurses came swarming the place, causing the woman to jump. The needle fell from her hand and rolled under Heaven's bed. "There's no power coming from these machines, someone call the technician," a blond haired nurse who appeared to be in her late thirties barked orders like she owned the place. "You, check the fuse box, make sure a fuse hasn't blown."

"Sure," the intruder replied as she pulled her mask back over her face before turning around to face the crowd. She walked straight past them until she came face to face with Marrissa who was busy trying to keep an eye on her daughter. Suddenly that same familiar scent that Karim had smelled invaded Marrissa's nostrils as she turned around to see the nurse walking full speed towards the elevators.

"Excuse me!" Marrissa called out but the nurse just kept pushing the elevator call button. The doors opened and the woman stepped onto the elevator as Marrissa attempted to catch up. "Excuse me!" Marrissa yelled again, this time the nurse turned around and stared at Marrissa just as the doors were closing. Marrissa couldn't get a clean visual of the woman's face, but her fragrance was disturbingly familiar.

The woman exited the elevator on the main floor. She stripped free of her wig and uniform after she exited out the main entrance. She stuffed the belongings into a nearby dumpster and made a clean getaway. "Until we meet again, sweetheart."

***

Ciara

"Do you know yo' mama's favorite color?" Ciara asked Baby J as they strolled up the toys & gifts aisle of Walmart searching for gifts to take to his mom's gravesite for her birthday.

"If I had to take a guess, I would say yellow," Baby J replied as he tugged at the newly grown strings of hair on his chin.

"And why do you say yellow?" Ciara challenged him.

"I know she loved her yellow dress more than any dress in the world, and her fingernails were always polished yellow, and she loves that little thing right there." Baby J pointed to a stuffed Tweety bird.

"Okay sir, you know yo' mama's favorite color, dang!" Ci-Ci joked.

She picked up the largest Tweety Bird she could find and collected a few dozen sunflowers. Baby J kneeled and picked up another teddy bear, this one was much smaller but meant just as much value to him. "So, you want both?" Ci-Ci asked.

"This one is for Mari, since he's not here to pick his own gift," Baby J said flatly, as the mood quickly changed.

Ci-Ci felt guilt building up in her heart. She hadn't been trying hard enough to find Baby J's little brother. Truth was, she didn't know where to begin. It'd been years since she'd adopted Baby J from the foster home. For all she knew, his baby brother could be somewhere in another state by now, but that didn't stop Baby J from missing him. "Well in that case, why don't you grab one more gift," Ci-Ci insisted with a smile, in an attempt to lighten the mood.

"For who?" Baby J asked in confusion.

"Let's just say I know one more very special person who wouldn't mind giving your mama a birthday gift." Ciara grabbed another stuffed animal and headed towards the register to check out.

"Is it my daddy?" Baby J's question caught his auntie by surprise.

"Wh ... Huh?"

Baby J figured a cat had gotten her tongue, so he proceeded. "I've been reading the letters he's been writing you. I thought they were for me since they had my name on all of 'em. How come you never told me about him? What's he in prison for?"

Ci-Ci sighed. "Nephew, it's a very long story but it's not what you think. When you're old enough to understand I promise we'll sit down and have this talk but for now let's just enjoy your mom's birthday, okay?"

Baby J weighed his options and decided to drop the conversation for the sake of his mother's birthday. But he was hurt by his aunt's life changing secrets. Baby J never knew he had a father up until a few months ago. He read his name on an envelope in the trash can. He took the letter in his bedroom and read it, since then he'd been intercepting all of his aunt's mail.

All his father's letters were filled with remorse. Some were filled with regret and others mentioned memories of his father and his auntie being one. *How could she do my mom like this?* he asked himself each time he opened up a new letter. He didn't know the long story behind his dad's letters, but he hoped to one day find out.

Ci-Ci grabbed all the items and placed them on the counter before reaching in her purse for her credit card. After swiping her card, she was given a receipt. "Thank you for shopping at Walmart, have a nice day," the cashier said with a smile that could light up a room.

Instead of retrieving her things and leaving, Ci-Ci stood there looking dumbfounded at the young lady before her. She wanted to run out of the store, but her legs wouldn't move. The face she was staring at was a face she hadn't seen in thirteen long years, yet her features were unmistakable. "I'm sorry, did you forget something?" the soft voice asked as Ci-Ci stared at her name tag, confirming what she already knew.

"Oh no, I'm sorry sweetheart, have a nice day." Ciara took her things and rushed out of the store.

She hit a button on her car remote, unlocking the doors. A seat was much needed at the moment. Baby J thought his aunt was acting very strange, but he had no idea why. Instead of asking a question that would come with no answer he sat in silence the entire ride.

When they made it to his mother's grave, Baby J set up the balloons they picked up along the way and saw the sunflowers beside his mother's tombstone while Ci-Ci sat back daydreaming about her encounter at the supermarket.

Since they'd arrived Baby J tried to make small talk, but the woman was in her own little world. "Who sat this here?" Baby J asked, holding a small stuffed Tweety Bird in his right hand.

Ciara could tell by its condition that the stuffed animal had been sitting there for some time. It was covered in mud and soaked by the rain. "I'm not sure," Ci-Ci responded.

They hadn't been to visit his mother's grave site since Mother's Day and all the gifts they placed around her tombstone were stolen or had been blown away by the wind. Even though Ci-Ci couldn't confirm it. She had the slightest idea of who might've paid her sister a visit. "Maybe the wind blew it," she said.

Baby J shot her a disbelieving look and continued to decorate his mom's grave. He began to think about how life would have been had she still been alive. He probably wouldn't have met his auntie Ciara who seemed to be cool, but his little brother wouldn't have been taken away from him and that's the most important thing that had crossed his mind.

Ciara lit a candle on the cake that she purchased for her sister and together they sang happy birthday. "Now close your eyes and make a wish." Ciara held the cake closer to her nephew's face,

Baby J squeezed his eyes closed and made his wish. Just as he was about to blow the candle out, a gust of wind whistled past his ear and blew the candle out. Baby J opened his eyes with a slight smile. He felt like that small gust of wind came just in time. It was the first week of August, the

3rd to be exact and with the humid 85° weather, Baby J hadn't felt a wind that strong all day. *Mama gone answer this wish for me, I can feel it*, he thought to himself.

Curious, Ciara asked, "So what chu wish for, nephew?"

"It's a secret." Baby J smiled.

That alone lit up his aunt's day. She smiled as she swiped the cake with two fingers. "Oh yeah, secret this." She wiped cake across Baby J's face before taking off across the cemetery, throwing the cake until he was down to the last piece then the two of them split the remains. "Let's go see your grandparents," Ciara said as they walked across the graveyard until they reached a spot where her parents were buried side by side. Ciara planted red roses next to each of their graves. Baby J was busy thinking about his wish and whether it would come true or not.

Ciara took the top off her water bottle and poured it over her parents' tombstones before taking a few napkins from her Coach purse and wiping the dust from around their names so she could read them clearly. Carrie Lee Jones and Vincent Donnell Jones laid to rest only six months apart. While Ciara loved her parents equally, she'd always been a daddy's girl.

Growing up she always went to her old man for everything. Her sister Cynthia was their mother's favorite. The two would sit in the room and sing all the old jams from the Temptations to Gladys Knight, stopping just short of Erika Badu. "So, this is what it comes to huh? Just me and nephew out here all alone." Ciara began to pour her feelings out.

"Don't forget about Mari," Baby J chimed in.

"Of course, and Mari. I bet you two know exactly where he is. Can y'all tell him we miss him and show him his way back home?" Ciara became distressed. Demons from her past had caught up with her and there was no way she could hide from them.

While searching for more letters from his father, Baby J stumbled across a bottle of pills sitting on top of his aunt's dresser. Of course he didn't know what the pills were for, but he did know they were quite different from the Tylenol she would take for her headaches.

Out of curiosity, he wrote down the name on the front of the bottle, then he went to school and googled the name Cyclophosphamide, and a review of heart cancer medications popped up on the screen. A picture of the same exact bottle appeared on the left side of the screen.

Baby J's heart shattered. His aunt had given him an insight into her journey and what she had to go through, leaving out the details about his mom sleeping with her husband while she was on her deathbed and creating him and his sister. He thought that chapter of her life was over but from the looks of things God has had a change of heart. Baby J's only wish was to reunite with his baby brother before death snatched up his aunt.

Ciara wrapped up her conversation with her parents, then her and Baby J went to get a bite to eat. After devouring a ribeye steak, the two of them took it to the nest where they showered before getting ready for bed. Baby J played on his PlayStation until he fell asleep. Ciara picked up her phone and dialed Josh's number. After the second ring he answered. "Hey, sweetheart, how are you?"

"Could be better but later for that. Come spend the night with me, I don't feel like sleeping alone."

"Sure, I'll be there in about twenty minutes," Josh said avidly.

He'd never been invited to spend a night with Ciara before. He rushed to get his things together; he knew how quickly she could change her mind and pull out her dildo to get the job done.

Before she knew it, Josh was calling her cell phone. She let it ring a few times before she answered. "Hello?"

"I'm outside, sweetheart."

Ciara ended the call and let Josh in.

Chapter 13

Marrissa

It's been six long months since Heaven was hit by some lunatic with no heart. Although her brain managed to show some type of functional improvement, Heaven remained in a coma with slim chances of pulling through. Marrissa and Karim would take turns watching over her while the other went home to freshen up. Since the last time they'd left her unattended someone cut the plugs to her life support machines they vowed to never leave her alone again.

Marrissa was sitting in a chair beside Heaven's bed when she heard a soft knock on the door followed by a twist of the doorknob. A small Filipina nurse came peeking in with a suspicious smile on her face. Marrissa didn't have a clue why she was receiving this euphoric energy from the nurse, but her gut forced her to return the smile.

"Hi, Ms. Hamilton. How are you feeling today?" The nurse spoke politely.

"I'm still holding in there, thanks for asking."

"Well keep holding because I have wonderful news." The nurse opened the folder she held in the pit of her left arm and began thumbing through papers until her eye caught what she was seeking.

Marrissa hadn't noticed that she'd been holding her breath since the nurse entered the room with that life changing smile. The nurse sat two sheets of paper on the desk next to Heaven's bed. "You see this here? This is the cat scan results from last week. As you can see, Heaven's brain was showing little to no signs of communication." The nurse pointed to the nearly flat lines that waved across the sheet of paper.

Marrissa had no idea what the nurse was talking about, but she nodded her head in agreement. The nurse then pointed to the other sheet of paper. "And these are the results from this morning's cat scan." Marrissa looked at the now wavy lines. "This shows that Heaven's brain is still unconscious, but it appears to be quite functional, which means she probably can hear us right now."

The nurse smiled. Marrissa's eyes shot to her daughter as she lay there appearing asleep rather than comatose. "I know she hasn't awakened yet but count your blessings because this is a complete miracle." With that, the nurse left the room, letting her words linger in the air.

"Which means she probably can hear us right now." The nurse's voice replayed in Marrissa's head. As she approached her daughter's bedside. Heaven's body was now visible apart from her ribcage which had taken the worst damage so she remained in a body brace until the doctors were sure that her body would continue to heal without it.

"I gave Santa my Christmas lis,t honey," Marrissa took her daughter's hand into her own as her tears made their appearance in the corner of her eyes. Finally, her tears would be happy tears, after all the pain she let pour from her soul. "I told him that the gift I want doesn't have to be wrapped, and what do ya know? These bandages have been magically removing themselves from the best gift a mom can ask for." A smile spread across Marrissa's face. Her daughter wasn't awake yet, but she knew deep down that any day … any second, her daughter could open those beautiful eyes and life would take its course back on the right track.

Marrissa picked up her phone to call Karim and fill him in on the good news. Then she dialed Josh's number but received no answer, in fact she hadn't heard from him in the past three months. Marrissa thought about sending him a text but she second that thought. She placed her phone back into her purse and began to have a heartfelt talk with the most important person in her life, hoping that Heaven could hear every word.

Chapter 14

Tiffany

Breakfast was served to Tiffany in the form of heroin. Her eyes stared at the needle greedily as it made its way to her on a silver platter, a small payback for her deception to a very important man. Since she was strung out on the drug, she seemed to forget her purpose for returning to Texas. Now all she searched for were two things— high, and higher.

Blackboy, her only child, became no more than a memory as she abused the liquid substance. What started out as a drug induced abduction became an amenable decision as she became addicted to the feeling of heroin flowing through her veins. Heaven on earth is what it reminded her of as she lay there, high as downtown's rent with dick stuffed in every hole of her body. It wasn't until she became sober that she realized she was on the wrong mission. She made her way back to Texas for a different reason, but what was it? *Only if I can stay sober long enough to figure this shit out*, she thought to herself as her mouth began to water. *Wishful thinking.*

The needle injected its dose of pain reliever into the crease of her vagina, where her abductor demanded she stick the needle. Forty pounds lighter, her beauty faded away and she became a skeleton of who she once was.

Another day another dick, she thought as the man in front of her began to unzip his pants. Chapo, Chindo's younger brother, sat back and watched the show. He couldn't believe she thought that she would get away with robbing and killing his brother. Chindo had hidden cameras installed throughout the entire house. Even the bathrooms. The only person that should need privacy in my home is me, is what he told Chapo each and every time he asked him why he had cameras in the bathroom. Chapo would rather take a piss outside before he becomes a victim of one of his brother's sick jokes.

The first thing Chapo did when he received the news about his brother's murder was locate his phone where he had all the footage from the cameras stored.

He listened and watched as the whole thing unfolded. Tiffany's punishment would undoubtedly be death. But Blackboy on the other hand would be rewarded for his loyalty. He played no part in Chindo's murder, in fact, the story his mother made him believe was a far cry from the truth that was unveiled as Chapo replayed the video for him. Blackboy had no clue that his mother had played a part in his father's act of greed.

For all he knew, Weezy became jealous of her newfound love and came to put an end to all of their lives. He felt like he had taken a dagger to the back by the hands of his own mother. Chapo made him believe that she wanted nothing to do with him. In fact, he had no idea that his mother was in his very own basement being a lab-rat for a drug operation he now helped manifest. Chapo didn't torture the innocent kid, he plugged him with the key to the city and helped the seventeen-year-old boy become a man, all while killing his mother slowly in the process.

Chapo exited the basement after witnessing Tiffany get slutted out by three of his goons, locking the 3 dead bolt locks behind him.

Entering the kitchen, he saw Blackboy standing at the stove where he left him, with a white surgical mask on. "How much have you cooked up so far?" asked Chapo as he watched Blackboy break down pure cocaine, turning it into crack.

"I finished a whole brick and I'm halfway done with this one right here."

"And just how much do you think you will make off each white girl, when selling it cracked?" A look of confusion spread across Blackboy's face. He shook his head.

"I never seen so much crack in my life," Blackboy admitted. Chapo smiled, he enjoyed turning the nickel and dime hustler out. He threw Blackboy a brown paper bag.

"Bag that and meet me in the car. I'm gonna show you something," Chapo said as he grabbed his set of car keys from the kitchen counter and left Blackboy standing there.

Once Chapo was out of sight, Blackboy quickly bagged the crack before making his way to the door where Chapo had appeared from. Chapo had warned him not to ever step foot into the basement but that only made him more eager to go inside. His mind was telling him to stop but his gut kept leading him towards the door. Blackboy placed his hand on the first lock. He took a deep breath before preparing to turn the lock. He slid the lock to the left. 'Click! *One down, two to go*, Blackboy thought as his hand touched the second steel lock. Slide, click! *Two down.* His hand started to sweat as he began to slide the last lock.

HOOONK! HOOONK!

The sound of Chapo's horn roared, nearly making Blackboy piss his pants as he jumped back from the door. After collecting himself, he grabbed the brown paper bag and headed out the door in record time. Blackboy sat in silence, nodding his head to Sean Paul's *Gimme the Light* while Chapo smoked a big blunt of cocaine laced Kush as he cruised the Texas streets.

After nearly a forty-minute drive, Chapo finally pulled up to a spot where a mixture of Black people and Latino folks hung out. They seemed to have a live dice game going on, but it was short lived as the crowd noticed Chapo's red BMW and began to disperse with the exception of two young Mexicans that appeared to be in their late teenage years.

Both sported diamonds from their earlobes to their wrists. Blackboy instantly became fascinated by their appearance. He pictured himself rocking the iced-out chains and fresh Jordans every day like a real D-boy. Chapo rolled his passenger window down and nodded on cue, the two youngins approached the vehicle. They climbed in the back seat and greeted Chapo "What's going on, Pa?"

"What's up is you fuckin knuckleheads throwing craps in front of the spot again," Chapo spat before converting his conversation to Spanish, like he always did when he was pissed.

His two sons sat there with their heads in their chest. After giving them a piece of his mind Chapo grabbed the brown bag from Blackboy's lap and tossed it into the backseat. "When it's all gone, give the profit to my new lieutenant here. He's gonna stick around and make sure you two fuck=ups don't do anything else stupid."

The two goons burst into laughter. "You're kidding right?" Milo, the oldest of the two, spoked up.

"Do you see a smile on my face you little —" he went back to cursing in Spanish. The boys removed themselves from the vehicle so quick, Blackboy didn't realize they were gone until he heard the doors slam.

"What are you waiting on?" Blackboy realized Chapo was speaking to him.

He quickly grabbed the door handle, nervously pulling it trying to escape Chapo's presence. He'd seen him mad before and wanted no parts of his venom. Chapo shook his head as he hit the unlock button on his door. "Now open it." Blackboy pulled the handle and exited the vehicle, joining Chapo's sons on the sidewalk. Chapo sped off, leaving all three of the young boys confused.

Chapter 15

Ciara

Ciara had butterflies in her stomach as she sat in the visiting room of Mount Sterling Correctional facility, waiting on Big Juan to appear. She drove four long hours to see him face to face. It'd been fourteen long years since she saw his face in person. She made a promise not to ever cross paths with the man who broke her heart again. But now she has decided to pop up and settle their differences. She wanted to trade apologies.

Ciara was about to get up from her seat to grab a drink from the vending machine when she spotted Juan being escorted into the visiting room by a CO. She quickly fell back into her seat before he spotted her, trying to collect herself. Juan couldn't believe his eyes as he stared at the beauty before him. Ciara's heart rate increased more and more the closer he stepped in her direction. Juan was caught off guard himself.

He had written to Ciara at least a hundred times in the past three years, begging her to come see him but never in a million years did he expect to see her sitting there looking as beautiful as the day she was born. Juan took his seat at the opposite end of the table. Ciara felt the urge to cry so she pinched the bridge of her nose. Juan reached across the table and took her free hand in his. *Pull it together, you got this*, she thought to herself as she took a deep breath. They sat in silence for what seemed like an eternity before Juan finally decided to break the ice. "After all this time you still give a nigga butterflies."

Ciara stared into his eyes to see if she still felt the same way and she did. "Them butterflies couldn't keep you from making yo' way in my sister's bed," she shot the low blow.

Juan expected the conversation to go left so he swallowed what she dished out, until she was satisfied with her shots fired. After thirty minutes of going back and forth about Juan's deception, Ciara finally decided to get to the point of why she really paid him a surprise visit.

"Do you think fourteen years was enough time to pay for what you did?" Ciara asked, looking Juan directly in his grey eyes.

"Ci-Ci, I didn't rape my fuck–. I didn't rape my daughter, baby. You know that ain't me–."

"Don't call me *baby*, I'm not yo' baby," she spat. "And I'm not talking about what you did to Miracle. I know you didn't rape her." Juan looked at Ciara like she had grown an extra head. "I'm talking about what you did to *me*." Ciara kept talking but Juan didn't hear a word after *"I know you didn't rape her."*

His head started spinning from the possibilities that came to his mind behind the words she said. *Either she got to the bottom of this madness or this bitch had me set up the whole time,* Juan thought to himself. Sweat started forming at the top of his bald head as he felt himself overheating like a '92 box Chevy. "What the fuck you mean, you know I didn't rape her?" Juan shot her a questionable look.

Ciara was unfazed by his fiery gaze. She felt like he deserved everything that had come to him. He had broken her heart to the point of no return and at the time she wanted to end everything he stood for. Even her sister and niece.

It wasn't until she saw Miracle again that she began to feel ashamed. Her past had come back to haunt her once again but this time she would try to make amends. She came to settle their differences. "You didn't answer my question," she snapped.

"Of course, it was enough fucking time, I went bald in this shit hole, Ci-Ci," yelled Juan, causing other visitors along with the COs to stare but he could care less about the attention. He wanted a clear understanding of what Ciara was trying to imply.

"I heard they approved your request for an appeal. I'm considering taking the stand for you and withdrawing my statement. But the question is: are you ready to be the man I thought you were?"

"Ci-Ci, a statement won't make a difference, they found semen, my semen in my own daughter's underwear. On top of that, she'd been penetrated by some fuckin' scumbag under my roof and I can't think of one person that could be capable of doing all this."

"Well, I can." Ciara stared at Juan with tears in her eyes.

Life had stuck it to her hard. Cancer had found its way back into her life and this time she didn't have half the fight she had before. She just wanted to repent for her merciless acts before she stepped through those pearly white gates of heaven. Fourteen years ago, she was hungry for revenge for what Juan and her little sister had done to her, and since Miracle was the product of their infidelity she became a target as well.

"What do you mean, you can?" asked Juan with his nostrils flaring up. He had spent fourteen long years in prison behind some sick lie and her his ex-wife was dropping bombs on him.

"Juan, you and my sister broke my heart more than anything I ever felt. It hurt worse than losing my father and you know how much I loved him."

Juan just listened without saying a word. He felt no sympathy for Ciara, knowing that she was getting ready to drop an explosive right in his lap. Ciara continued, "I expected you to be a man and make things right after I found out about you and my lil sister but, instead, you stayed with her and built a family. Do you know how many nights I sat outside y'all bedroom window? Listening to you fuck her how you use to fuck me? How many times I followed y'all to mall after mall? Watching you spoil her how you used to spoil me. But one thing that I watched you do that was unfamiliar ..." Ciara paused. Closing her eyes did nothing to stop her tears as her heart caused a rainstorm. "I watched y'all create a family. My family." Now she was beginning to pull strings on his heart. He felt something for her, he just didn't know what. "I know you're just as careless as you were fourteen years ago about my feelings. So, I'm gonna get to the point of why I came here, and you can be a free man." Ciara took a deep breath then sighed. "I raped Miracle. "

Juan went deaf as his mind exploded with rage. His eyes began to burn as the fought back his tears. He wanted to rip her limb from limb, but he couldn't move a muscle. Juan dropped his head into his buff chest and chewed on his bottom lip until he drew blood. Ciara knew that the words that came from her mouth would crush Juan the same way he had crushed her years ago.

Fourteen years later, she finally felt satisfied yet remorseful for what she had done. She felt that she had finally evened the score but now it was time for her to make her bed. "Give me one good reason why I shouldn't end your miserable little life, right here, right now." Juan stared at her with the eyes of Satan. The gray she once saw was now red with fire. She stared him directly in the eyes. No fear, no emotions.

"Because I'm already dying." She got up and left Juan sitting there in his thoughts.

The information she piled on top of him was enough to sink a ship. The CO that had strip-searched him called out his name three times but Juan heard nothing. "Mr. Alvarez," he called one final time before he decided to walk over and help the big guy up.

Juan had been one of his favorite inmates during his bid but even Calary knew not to push him when he was this far gone. Calary was about 245 pounds of muscle, favoring the wrestler Big Show. He stood neck and neck with Juan. "Come on, big fella, visitation's over." He pulled Juan up by the arm. Big Juan didn't resist. He stood straight until Calary let his arm go then Juan collapsed.

***

Baby J

"Man fuck these niggas/I'm scared of errthing but these niggas/I take the gun and gun butt these niggas/Take the knife off the AK and cut these niggas." Baby J and his friends from school shook the floor of his house party geeking to Lil Wayne's *Steady Mobbin* song. Ciara promised him she would let him throw a house party for his birthday if he kept his grades up. Not that she needed to bribe him.

Baby J had the best grades out of his crowd. Even though he ditched school from time to time just to get high with Vonny and Danky. He never let it get out of hand. His love for basketball wouldn't let him slip. Baby J wore his long curly hair in designed braids by Danky's mom. He rocked a fitted True Religion fit with the latest leather Pelle to match. Screw in diamond earrings shined from each earlobe with an icy JoJo watch to accompany his wrist. He and his friends all sported the new Gore Tex boots which was the trend throughout the neighborhood. Baby J was one of the popular kids at his school, so the entire 7th and 8th grade made it to his party including the kids who had dropped out to sell drugs.

His aunt Ci-Ci laid down the rules, *No drinking, No smoking, and No girls behind closed doors.* Other than that, she would give her maturing nephew his privacy.

Vonny decided to slow it down a bit so he and his crew can show the girls what they're made of on the dance floor. Besides his friends, no one had seen Baby J in action.

This is the moment everybody's been waiting for, especially Porshia. His crush he had been eyeing since 5th grade.

"This here is on some truthful shit/it seems like everything I do you're used to it/and I hate hearing stories about who you've been wit'/so that's why I gotta hide/what I'm feeling inside/so you still think I'm confident and down," Drake poured from the surround sounds as they locked eyes.

Baby J watched Porshia's friends whisper something in her ear before pushing her to the middle of the floor. He heard stories about her being the G.O.A.T at belly rolling but now it was time to put her money where her mouth is.

Baby J took off his Pelle coat and tossed it to his homie Danky before meeting her in the middle of the floor. Porshia tied her t-shirt in a knot so that her belly would be visible while she did her thang. Baby J stared as she rolled her body in a circle with her hazel brown eyes locked on him. He didn't realize that she had him biting his bottom lip, but it did something to her insides.

Neither of them had lost their virginity yet but the looks in their eyes said they were ready to. Porshia was a yellow bone with a beauty mark over her lip that made all the boys want a taste when she smiled. The small gap between her two front teeth added flavor to her already beautiful smile. Baby J got tired of just watching. He had to show her that she'd met her match. He put his shirt into his mouth and did a smooth glide until he closed the distance between them. It seemed like he was sliding on ice. From that one slick move, Porshia knew she was in trouble, but he wanted to tease her first.

Baby J had moves like he was a grown man with bedroom experience. Porshia tried to keep up until they both had worked up a sweat. They danced the whole track together until Jamie Foxx's voice bombed through the speakers. *"There's so much sh*t I wanna do to you/(you, you, you) first you gotta step into this room/(room, room, room) look into my eyes imma look right into yours/cut the lights out but don't you close the door/tonight I'm gonna make my hallway echo you/(you, you) I pull my shirt off, pull yo' jeans down/ew baby take yo' time, now turn around/as our bodies catch the mirror and we grinding to this song/imma do ya' all night long."*

Before he knew it, Baby J had Porshia by the hand, leading her to his bedroom. Porshia didn't care who watched them, she wanted this moment to last forever. Baby J led her into the room and locked the doors. They can still hear Jamie jamming from the living room. "That's it, here we go, put our love in the air/if the curtains are open. I don't care let 'em stare." Porshia pushed Baby J onto the bed and climbed on top of him. She planted a single kiss on his lips that made his soldier stand at attention.

She leaned in for another one, and another one until their tongues eventually started a wrestling match. Baby J came up for air while trying to unfasten Porshia's pants. She grabbed his hand and led it back up to her breast each time he attempted. "What's wrong?" asked Baby J.

"I'm not ready to do this, but I do want to be yo' girlfriend," replied Porshia.

Baby J went for her buckle again with the same results. "It'll be worth it, I promise."

"I know it will, because I'm not giving you none until I know for sure that you love me. I'm a virgin, I'm not like my friends, Juan." Porshia climbed off him and pulled him up.

She could see the bulge in his True Religion jeans and could tell he was packing. She wanted to feel him inside of her, but she wanted it to be special when she lost her v-card.

Not just some one-night stand. She wanted to know all about his past. What makes him happy? What makes him sad? Baby J was surprised to hear that she was a virgin. The Porshia he knew from school wasn't the same Porshia in his bedroom. The Porshia from school made it seem like she was a pro in the bedroom which was why Baby J was hesitant to shoot his shot. He didn't want to embarrass himself.

"Okay. We can take all the time in the world." Baby J pulled her close and kissed her again.

"So does this mean you're my boyfriend?" Porshia looked into Baby J's eyes and saw fireworks.

"I'm whatever you want me to be, baby."

"Well let's go back in there to party before yo' auntie snap on us, bae." Porshia smiled as she took Baby J's hand and put it inside her pants giving him a sneak peak of what's in store for him if he played his cards right. As they were opening the door they can see shadows rushing away. Porshia knew that her friends would be thirsty to hear them having sex. She looked at Baby J and they both laughed.

The party came to an end right before midnight. The school kids who had parents that love them made it home in time for curfew. Baby J stayed home and helped his aunt Ci-Ci clean. Once he took out the trash, he called Porshia and spent the rest of his night talking on the phone until they fell asleep.

Chapter 16

Heaven

Marrissa sat by Heaven's bedside reading a book about time travel. She always wondered what life would be like if she could just go back and undo things. Had she not started letting Heaven catch the bus to school she would've prevented her from being involved with all this madness her life has encountered in the past nine months. Everyday Marrissa prayed for a change. Every day she wished for a fresh start. If she had things her way, Josh would never have made it into the picture. She used him all along to connect the missing pieces to the puzzle. She had grown to love him but his whole purpose was to buy her some time until she could walk off into the sunset with the man she truly loved, Karim.

Marrissa laid the book down and took a hold of Heaven's hand. She began to rub the scars where the wounds had healed. Every day she applied cocoa butter and witch hazel to Heaven's scars, trying her best to bring her daughter's color back where her scars were very dark. Her aid helped but she had to face the reality that Heaven's wounds would never disappear. Those scars will remind her every day of the tragedy that she suffered.

Marrissa felt pressure being applied to her hand, but her mind was so far gone that she didn't acknowledge it right away. It wasn't until she heard a small groan that she realized what was taking place. Marrissa quickly looked at Heaven and when she saw her with her mouth wide open Marrissa grabbed her chest. It felt like all the oxygen had left her body in an instant. Heaven groaned again, this time much louder. "Mom," she tried calling out for her mother.

Marrissa snapped out of the trance she was in and darted for the door to call out to the nurse. When Marrissa returned with the group of nurses, Heaven had her eyes wide open with confusion. The doctors rushed to her side and started checking her vitals. One of the doctors took a small light and shined it into both of Heaven's pupils. Heaven jumped away from the shiny light, indicating that her vision was still there. Marrissa dialed some numbers on her phone before placing it to her ear. Her hands trembled as she struggled to keep the cell phone steady. The doctors ran more tests to make sure Heaven hadn't lost her memory or hearing.

"Her heart rates a little over the top right now because she probably has no idea what she's doing here. But other than that, everything seems to be okay," the doctor assured. "We ran a few more tests to make sure everything goes back to normal. Just make sure she stays hydrated. Her body needs fluid," the doctor finished before opening up the path so Marrissa can finally reunite with her baby girl.

Marrissa pulled both hands over her mouth as she stepped closer to Heaven's bed. Tears appeared in her eyes faster than a magic trick as soon as she seen heaven sitting up in her bed. She rushed to her side and hugged Heaven so tight that she made her daughter groan again. The doctors left the two alone. No words were spoken for the next few minutes. Marrissa just held her daughter tight no matter how much she groaned. "What ... happened to me?" mumbled Heaven.

Her voice was raspy, but Marrissa understood every word. Marrissa released her daughter and looked into her eyes. "You don't remember," replied Marrissa. It was a statement more than a question, but Heaven shook her head anyway.

Marrissa had been waiting on this day to come to find out what Heaven remembered, now all hope was lost. Heaven had no idea why she was lying in a hospital bed.

"What day did this happen to me?" Heaven started to feel down.

Nine months she'd been in a coma, living inside a dream. She became confused because she thought she was awake the whole time. She was enjoying life with her best friends Stacy, and April. Skipping school to hang out with her boyfriend, Blackboy. "The day of your graduation. Some mad person came speeding up the street —"

"Graduation?" repeated Heaven. Marrissa nodded with tears in her eyes. "So, I spent my birthday in this place?" Heaven asked. Shedding tears of her own.

"Yes honey, but me and your father sang Happy Birthday. He even bought you those balloons."

Marrissa pointed to the balloons floating in the corner of the room which she had to re-inflate every time the balloons deflated. At the mention of her father, Heaven smiled. "Where's Dad?"

"He'll be here shortly. He rushed out from work as soon as I told him the news," replied Marrissa.

She was overwhelmed by the sound of her daughter's voice. "Have my friends been to see me?"

Marrissa was taken aback by the word, *friends*. Heaven only had two friends, and one of them had passed away. "April brought you flowers once, after that her and her mom disappeared," Marrissa admitted.

"And what about Stacy?" Heaven's question dropped like a brick on her mother's ears. *She has to remember what happened to Stacy*, Marrissa thought.

"Don't you remember?" asked Marrissa. Heaven shot her a questioning look that answered her mom's question. "Stacy accidentally shot and killed herself two weeks before graduation, you were there, honey. Of course you remember."

Heaven began to cry again. "I remember but I *don't* remember. One moment she's there the next moment she's gone again. I don't know what's real and what was a dream," cried Heaven as Marrissa wiped away her tears which was replaced by new ones each time.

"It's okay. honey. It'll all come back to you in due time but for right now just try to relax." Marrissa held Heaven's hands inside her own. "When you're feeling better maybe you can tell me about everything and I can help you separate the truth from the dream, ok?"

Heaven nodded. There was so much that she wanted to know about. She had dreams of being intimate with Blackboy. Even being pregnant, the thought made her rub her belly. *Thank God*, she thought to herself, feeling that she had no baby bump. "Did I go to Stacy's funeral?" Heaven's twenty-one questions began.

"No, the funeral was a day prior, but you didn't want to face Stacy's mom ..." Marrissa began to explain the incident from the moment Heaven ran out of the auditorium.

"So, what about Timo, Tay B, and Blackboy?"

"What about them?" Marrissa countered. She didn't have the softest heart in the world when it came to the little gangsters. She blamed this whole ordeal on them.

"If the girls hadn't skipped school to hang out with some thugs Stacy would still be alive and no one would be gunning for Heaven," Marrissa told the detectives one day.

Heaven noticed her mother's demeanor change and left the topic alone. "It's like I can almost separate the truth from the dreams, but it all seemed so real. Well, except this one thing." Heaven smiled. Marrissa smiled back. "I had the funniest little dreams about Principal Hobbs being my real father and you and my dad had broken up, but then you got mad at principal Hobbs because ..." Heaven went on and one about the reality which she thought was all a big, interesting dream.

She heard everything, Marrissa thought as she listened to her daughter. When Heaven finally decided to take a break to catch her breath Marrissa decided now might be just as sensible as any other time. "Heaven," Marrissa looked her daughter straight in the eyes. Neither one of them spared a second to blink, "let's say that the dreams you had weren't actually dreams." Heaven looked at her mother like she had grown an extra head. Marrissa continued. "Maybe you were dreaming, but you were more-so putting a visual to the conversations you heard while you were in a coma." Marrissa looked at Heaven to see if she was on the same page.

"I don't follow you," replied Heaven as if she can read her mother's mind.

"What I'm trying to say is–" Marrissa's sentence was cut short by the sound of the room door swinging open. Heaven became more confused at the sight of Josh and Mr. Hobbs both standing in the doorway.

"Dad?" Heaven directed her words to Josh but both men replied.

"Yes!" The men shared a brief stare and came to an agreement with their eyes. Josh wanted Heaven to know that she'll always be a part of him, no matter what. He was just happy to see that she pulled through even though it might not seem that way. He gave Heaven a kiss on the forehead then made his exit. Karim stepped up to Heaven's bed next.

"Mr. Hobbs." Heaven smiled but her face held that same look of confusion.

"Heaven –" Marrissa stepped up and solved the riddle in Heaven's mind.

"Karim– Mr. Hobbs is your real father."

Heaven started seeing double. "Wha ... huh?" The girl couldn't believe her ears.

"As I was telling you before we were interrupted," Marrissa shot Karim an evil look. "Your dreams weren't dreams. You might have seen them a different way, but they were nothing less than the truth. This is your biological father and we're a couple now." After those words Heaven fainted.

Chapter 17

Miracle

Miracle and her teammates took warmup jump shots before their game began. Miracle played starting point guard for Orr High School and today they played Marshall's varsity team. At 5'7" and one hundred and thirty-five pounds Miracle favored the singer Aaliyah. Outside of the gym no one would've ever pictured her to be so athletic. She averaged twenty-five points per game and shot 78% from the 3-point line.

On the court she was very aggressive but she was far from a tomboy when the jersey came off. She had the cutest dimples in her face and matching ones in her back. Her boyfriend sat courtside watching her booty jiggle as she knocked down threes from long range. Boozer groped himself at the thought of seeing her flawless body without clothes. Miracle and Boozer met at Walmart when she was working there for a summer job last summer. Boozer had stolen some wife beaters while Miracle was watching him. Once she clocked out, he was standing there with money in his hand to pay for them. "I just wanted to see if you was solid," he told her and they exchanged numbers at the bus stop.

Since then, they'd been a force. Miracle looked at Boozer and noticed he was holding himself and smiled. She loved how he loved her. Their story was like *Love &Basketball*

only Boozer's only jersey had come from 'D.P' (Division & Pulaski). He had mad game but the park he sold drugs in was as far as he took it. The only rock he cared to pass was that crack.

The time on the game clock hit 0:00 and the buzzer sounded off for the jump ball. Boozer took his seat on the sideline with his homie Bizzy and a few more guys from his hood. They all sported leather Pelle coats with fur hoods, True Religion jeans, and wheat Timberland boots. The referee tossed the ball into the air and the ball stopped in Miracle's hand by Kara, the starting center for their team.

The moment the rock landed in Miracle's hand, Boozer started clapping. "Let's go baby!" He already knew what time it was. Miracle pushed the ball up court and signaled for a screen. Kara ran to set the pick then ran by into the paint while Miracle faked the 'Pick-n-Roll' and shot the ball from the left wing. Nothing but net. The crowd roared. "That's what the fuck I'm talkin' 'bout," shouted Boozer from the sideline.

Bizzy couldn't help himself from smiling at his homie being in love. All Boozer ever loved was the park he grew up in, selling rocks and blows.

By the end of the game Miracle had put up an amazing thirty-four points. Scoring 5 out of 7 from the three-point line. They blew Marshall out 76 to 32 with Miracle scoring more than their entire team. The audience started to make their exit as Miracle and her teammates made their way to the locker room to change out of their uniforms.

Miracle felt a tap on the shoulder and turned around with a smile. She had gotten used to sponsors and colleges coming out to watch her play in hopes of getting her on their team.

"Hey, Miracle," the woman spoke. "You're amazing out there on the floor."

"Thanks," replied Miracle. She searched the woman's clothing for a school or team logo but came up empty-handed.

As if she could read her thoughts, the woman said, "I'm not one of those beggin' reporters, or nothing like that. Actually, I came here because I need your help." Miracle showed a hint of confusion. "I know it sounds crazy but if you give me at least five minutes of your time I will give you a better understanding," the woman assured.

"Okay, umm ... let me go change and I'll meet you at the Burger King across the street," said Miracle.

The woman showed a sign of relief that Miracle had agreed to talk to her. "Okay, thank you so much," the woman said before walking out of the gymnasium.

"Who was that?" asked Kara.

"Hell if I know."

"So why you going to meet a stranger? Don't you know people are creeps?"

"It's only across the street, plus she looks like whatever she gotta tell me is very important," Miracle stated, concerned.

"Yeah, like she needs a kidney, and you have the perfect set." Both girls began to laugh. "Naw, for real I'm goin' witchu," Kara stated seriously.

"Girl, you kill me. Let's go see what this lady wants."

"She looks like she can be yo mama," joked Kara as the two walked to the locker room and changed.

Inside Burger King, Miracle and Kara spotted the woman sitting at a table in the corner sipping from her drink. They approached the table and took their seats. The woman batted her eye at Kara. "Miracle, what I have to tell you is very personal. If you want to share our conversation with your friend that's totally up to you but I don't wanna catch anybody by surprise more than the truth will already shock you," the woman spoke truthfully.

"Give us a second, bestie," Miracle said.

"I'll be right over here," Kara shot the woman a look before leaving them two alone.

Once the woman was sure that Kara was out of earshot, she cut right to the chase. She went into her purse and pulled out a manilla envelope. She reached inside and retrieved some photos and sat them on the table "Do you know who this girl is?" She pointed to the photo with a beautiful baby girl that looked to be about three years old. The child was playing with a Barbie doll. Miracle looked closely at the picture. "This is me," Miracle stated undoubtedly.

She hadn't ever in her life seen a photo of herself this young, which made her wonder, "Where did you get this?" she asked curiously.

"I'll get to that part, sweety. I promise you I'm not here to play witcho' mind." She showed Miracle a second picture of her and a man. Miracle was on his shoulders. The two appeared to be having the time of their lives. Miracle became emotional. It's like she could remember the moment.

"Is this my real father?" she asked. The woman nodded her head.

"Sure is, and he thinks about you every day."

Miracle felt tears building up in her eyes. "So, he's alive?"

"Yes, he's been in prison since you were four years old, but you can reunite with him and start fresh. You're all he thinks about."

"But he raped me." Her response caught the woman off guard.

"No, sweety, he loved you. He would never do anything to harm you."

Miracle's heart became filled with emotions. The rumors of her old man molesting her had made Channel 9, ABC, and Fox 32 News. Big time drug dealer Juan Alverez, faces rape charges. Miracle had googled the article once she grew old enough to understand. Her innocence was taken from her by her own father, the one who was supposed to protect her from the monsters. "The news is not gonna just lie on someone. He had to do it–"

"The news didn't lie on him. I did," the woman admitted. She showed Miracle one last picture. A picture that she had in her dreams for thirteen years. Miracle picked the photo up.

"Mom!" she whispered as a single tear escaped from her eye. In the picture Miracle was sitting on her mother's lap with a Tweety bird stuffed animal in her hands. The same bear that Ciara had seen at her sister's gravesite.

Miracle started having dreams of this same woman in this photo when she was ten years old. The woman guided her through life and protected her from harm. Miracle's first foster parents used to molest her as well until one day Miracle came home from school and the house was burned to ashes with her foster parents melted to their sofa.

"Your mom was my baby sister. Your dad was my husband until I found out they were having an affair behind my back while I was in the hospital dying from cancer." Her words had pain to them. Miracle felt remorseful towards her.

"I hated them so much I could've killed them myself, but death would've been too easy. I wanted them to suffer like I had to suffer. My own sister went behind my back and fucked my man and got pregnant with you." Ciara felt tears of her own streaming down her cheeks. She felt fire inside her soul every time she took this trip down memory lane. "I couldn't give Juan a baby, I was high risk, me and the baby would've died for sure or at least that's what the doctor said."

Ciara grabbed a few Burger King napkins and wiped her tears away before continuing. "Since the day you were born, I sat and plotted on a way to make all of y'all suffer, even though you were innocent. I waited until you were old enough to understand who Mommy and Daddy were, then I executed my plan. I called Juan one day to have a talk, knowing that he still loved me. I knew it would've been easy to get him to deceive Cynthia just like he did me. We had sex that night and I drugged him and took his house keys. Then I snuck into your home and raped you and planted your father's semen in your underwear—"

"You what?"

Smack!

Miracle slapped the taste out of her auntie's mouth. Ciara wiped blood from her lip. "I know I deserve worse but please, just let me finish," Ciara begged. She needed closure. It was her dying wish. "I called the police and had your father arrested for a very long time but he's back on an appeal and I'm gonna admit to everything that I've done. Including killing my sister."

Those words made Miracle dizzy. Ciara put her head down and continued. "I paid a friend of mine to sleep with your mother, I knew he had HIV. Back then I thought it was the right price to pay for betrayal. I wasn't thinking about you and your brother and what y'all had to go through."

"Brother?" Miracle repeated.

"Yes." Ciara grabbed a picture from her purse and handed it to her.

It was a photo of Baby J at his basketball game. "He just turned thirteen and plays like a pro already. I want you to meet him. My cancer came back, and I don't have long to live but I know he's gonna need support. He doesn't have anyone. He loves me too much for me to tell him this so can you please wait until I'm gone to tell him the truth?"

Miracle couldn't believe this woman was actually asking her for favors after she had ruined her entire family's life. Miracle snatched the photos from the table and stood from her seat. "Don't you ever in your fucking life come around me again. You're fuckin' sick." Miracle hawked up a glob of saliva and spat in Ciara's face then stormed out of the restaurant with Kara in her tail.

All eyes were on Ciara as she used another napkin to wipe her face. She knew the situation could go sour, but she had to do what she thought was best for her nephew, Baby J.

Since she'd met him, she'd seen the world in a whole new light. He made her feel needed again. For a long time, she had forgotten what it felt like to be loved, to have family. Now she had that in Juan Jr.

Miracle and Kara raced across the street to catch the Chicago Avenue bus. The bus was only one stop away. Kara searched for her school permit and bus card so she can pay both of their fares. Miracle stepped onto the bus and rushed to the rear of the bus. Kara inserted her bus card and flashed her permit before following her friend. "What was that? And what did she say to make you so mad?" Kara asked.

She'd seen Miracle slap the woman senseless. Miracle broke down, crying her heart out like never before. Her friend would never understand the trauma she felt as her auntie admitted all the sick things she had done to her own family. Kara wrapped her arms around Miracle and held her tight the entire ride. Miracle's phone rang off the hook, but she didn't bother to see who was calling.

She just wanted to get home, shower and cry herself to sleep. She was supposed to meet up with Boozer, but he'd just have to understand. Kara pulled the stop rope, alerting the driver that their stop was approaching. The bus pulled to the next stop and both girls exited on Lockwood. Normally, Kara would've stayed on the bus until it reached Central which was about three stops away but today, she would stay and comfort her friend until she was sure she'll be okay.

Miracle dragged herself up the stairs of her apartment building until she reached the third floor. Her hands trembled as she struggled to find her house keys. Kara knew Miracle could've knocked and had the door opened within seconds but she understood that her friend didn't want to be bothered by anyone, so she kept her thoughts silent. Miracle finally managed to find her keys and opened the door. Her mouth dropped at the sight of the person sitting on the living room couch talking to her parents.

Chapter 18

Blackboy

Blackboy, Milo, and Ceasar all sat at the table counting dead presidents while Chapo was out handling the big business. Chapo made Blackboy believe that he was the master key to the operation with his adequate whip game on the stove, but the others knew better. Blackboy's brain wasn't big enough to imagine the amount of drugs Chapo was pushing. With Chindo gone the plug laid full responsibility on Chapo. Chapo's plan was to get the three boys sharp enough to run his brother's half of the operation so that he could go back to his regular schedule.

While Chindo was the fully committed drug dealer, Chapo had his focus on going legit. He already owned twelve properties across Texas including two funeral homes and a casino. Chapo always tried to convince his little brother to go legit since his right-hand man put a hole in their operation by turning into a rat in a federal courtroom but Chindo had his mind made up. "I'll leave the game alone when I have enough money to buy the entire country of Mexico," were his exact words each time Chapo pressed the issue.

Since coming to Texas a little under a year ago, Blackboy had already counted a little under a quarter million dollars. He bought two whips and a condo just to show himself some appreciation for his hard work. Him and Chapo's boys had to step on a few niggas necks for trying to stick their nose where it didn't belong. Blowing that iron was one thing Blackboy knew how to do. He grew up to gunshots and police sirens, but the heat Chapo had given him for war time was something he only saw in movies. One tap on the trigger and there go five hollows headed your way.

It took a while for Milo and Ceasar to loosen up to Blackboy but even when they didn't like him, they had to admire his heart.

"What time is it?" Milo asked.

Blackboy checked his iced out watch which presented the wrong time before pulling out his iPhone. "5:48. Why, you got somewhere to be?"

"Shit, I was supposed to handle something for pops at 5:30, gimme a second," Milo said as he got up from the table. He walked to the door with the three deadbolts and slid them to the left.

"Whatchu gotta do down there? You know Chapo don't want nobody to go into the basement." Blackboy warned.

"He just don't want you two down here. I don't know why, it's not like it's a whole lot to see anyway," Milo said as he stepped into the basement and closed the door.

"What the fucks so special about that basement anyhow? It's not like we'd steal something." said Ceasar half-jokingly.

"I don't know, but whatever it is yo' pops act like he'll smoke us over it," Blackboy replied.

"He probably will. That motherfucker doesn't have a soft spot for nobody," Ceasar said as he continued to count.

Blackboy spotted a little hint of light coming from the basement through the crack in the door. His mind couldn't care less about what went on in that basement but his heart was pulling in. *Maybe it's just curiosity,* he thought as he continued to count.

Suddenly Ceasar's phone rang on the table and *Ariel* flashed across the screen. Ceasar smiled as he reached for his phone. "Hold up, I gotta take this real quick," he said as he grabbed his phone and walked out of the kitchen.

Blackboy kept counting the stacks, wrapping rubber bands around every twenty thousand counted. He heard a little noise coming from the basement. He looked towards the door for a moment to see if the noise would return. After a few seconds passed by he went back to counting aloud. "6, 7, 8, 9, seven thousand, 1, 2 –" a louder noise came from the basement. More like a scream. "Shit!" Blackboy cursed himself for losing count and having to start over. "1, 2, 3, –"

BOOM!

A loud unmistakable sound of a gunshot caused Blackboy to jump out his seat and grab a hold of his banger. Ceasar came rushing back into the house with his Glock in one hand and cell phone in the other. "What the fuck was that, yo?" asked Ceasar, directing his attention towards the basement door.

"Nigga, I'm right here with you how the fuck I'm 'posed to know?" Blackboy replied as he closed the distance between him and Ceasar before walking towards the basement door.

It seemed like it had taken them forever to reach the door. The boys shared a look before Blackboy reached for the door. Chapo's instructions not to enter the basement, and the fact that they just heard a gunshot was pulling the boy's consciousness in two different directions.

"Fuck it," Blackboy said, snatching the door open.

"Boo!" Milo yelled and scared the shit out of both boys, nearly getting himself shot by both of them as well. "HAHAHA!" he bust into laughter. "Man, you should've seen you bitches faces."

"Naw, you should've seen this bullet 'bout one second from changin' yo' ass. Why the fuck you play so much, folks?" snapped Blackboy as he concealed his pipe.

"Don't be such a pussy, yo." Milo gave Blackboy chest a friendly punch. "I was just foolin' around."

Blackboy noticed that Milo's body was covered in sweat and his pants were unzipped. "What the fuck was you doin' down here? You all sweaty and shit," Blackboy purposely left out the fact that his fly was open.

"Nothing pussy, just handling a little something for pa'/ Let's get this bread counted so we can go about our way I got shit to do."

Blackboy gave him a funny look as Milo locked the basement door *Nigga's weird as fuck*, Blackboy thought to himself as he hit the table and continued to count.

After they finished counting, Milo bagged the drug money up in a black duffle bag and they all left the house, locking the spot up behind them but leaving the basement door unlocked.

Tiffany laid in her own pool of blood, in the same fetal position Milo left her in with a bullet in her stomach. Despite the pain, she tried to stay as quiet as possible until she was sure that the boys had left the house, and she was alone. Chapo had given his oldest boy specific instructions to rape Tiffany then shoot her in the stomach, killing her unborn child while she die slow in her own blood. He was told to do so while she was sober so she could suffer and die a slow, painful death.

He did exactly as he was told. His only mistake was leaving the basement door unlocked giving Tiffany a chance to seek help. Tiffany pulled herself up from the ground. She felt an unbearable pain in the pit of her stomach from both the gunshot wound and the deceased fetus trapped inside of her. Her naked body was covered in blood. She began to make a trail as she slid along the wall to keep from falling over. Her eyes scanned the room in hopes of spotting a house phone but was unfortunate. She used her will to live to get up the basement stairs, she knew Chapo or one of his goons could be arriving any minute.

She needed to be as far as possible by the time they arrived. Her fear gave her the energy to pick up the pace as she searched for the doorknob in the dark. She twisted it to the left and her heart skipped a beat as Tiffany gave the door a push. The light from the kitchen nearly blinded her as it shined through the house like heaven gates. Tiffany squinted her eyes for protection as she limped through the place in search of a t-shirt at the very least. She didn't want to wander along the road naked but she would if she had to.

She found one of Chapo's dress shirts in the closet and threw it over her shoulders without unbuttoning it. While trying to fit her head in, she stumbled and knocked over a picture frame, breaking the glass. She picked the picture frame from the floor and sat it up right. Her heart stopped when she saw Blackboy along with two Hispanics holding up catfish they had caught while fishing on Chapo's boat. It seemed like forever since she saw her baby boy. His whole personality seemed to have changed over the past.

"Shit, how long have I been in that damn basement?" Tiffany asked herself as she stared at the photo. She kissed the picture and put it in her shirt pocket before heading out of the room and back into the kitchen. She walked over to the stove and turned on all four eyes without igniting the fire, causing gas to fume from the stove. Then she turned on the oven before rushing out of the house. Tiffany walked as far as she possibly could before she passed out from losing too much blood.

When she finally opened her eyes, Tiffany was connected to a breathing machine with IV needles injected into her arm. The medication she was given had her seeing double, but she felt little to no pain. The hospital lights were blinding Tiffany as she tried to pay attention to her surroundings. Her vision was blurry, but she could see the doctor's faces covered by masks. She could hear them talking but their words echoed through her eardrums. It sounded like they were speaking through bull horns as she tried to make out their words.

"Ma'am, can you hear my voice?"

Tiffany nodded.

"She's still heavily sedated, give her a minute to come down," a doctor with short red hair demanded. She didn't care that there were detectives waiting around to question Tiffany about the gunshot wound she suffered from. Those detectives would just have to wait until she recovers.

Chapter 19

Heaven

"Does it hurt?" Marrissa asked.

She and Karim had given Heaven permission to get her first tattoo. She'd bugged them about it until they finally agreed to let her get Stacy's name tattooed on her shoulder. "Not really, after the car accident I think I'm numb to pain," Heaven admitted as the needle worked its way around her collar bone.

Heaven sat as still as a statue in her wheelchair while Ryan, the tattoo man from Jade Dragon's tattoo shop perfected his work. Heaven still had some healing to do, her bones in her legs were still recovering but her memory returned in full effect. Sometimes she wished that it hadn't. Something's she'd rather forget forever. "Pretty soon you're gonna look like it never happened," Marrissa lied.

She knew that some scars would be stuck with Heaven for the rest of her life. Both Heaven and Marrissa wanted to believe those words, but it was physically impossible. Heaven had screws in her hip that caused her pain whenever it rained, which meant springtime would never be the same. "Tattoos may be able to cover some of these scars, but they can't hide the pain I feel every time I think of my situation, or the feeling I get when I wake up to use the bathroom and my legs don't move." Heaven became frustrated with being handicapped.

She wanted her normal life back. Her friends April and Stacy. She wanted to see how high school felt but she still wasn't ready to go out into the world yet. Her mom had moved her to the west side of Chicago, away from her friends in hopes of starting a clean slate. Karim bought them a three-bedroom house in the Oak Park area where it was quiet and clean. Once Heaven built up the courage they would let her decide which school she might be fit for.

"I know it's hard for you right now, but I pray for you so much that God has no choice but to hear my prayers. He's gonna shine the light on you and when he does, the world's gonna see the most beautiful star that ever fell from the sky." Marrissa thumbed her daughter's cheekbone where a scar healed to the best of its ability.

Heaven couldn't help herself from smiling. Her mother always had a way to bring the sun out on a gloomy day.

Ryan put ointment on Heaven's tattoo and wrapped it up so that Heaven can pull her shirt sleeve over it without ruining her clothes or infecting her tattoo. Marrissa tipped him before leaving the shop.

"I still can't believe I have to get used waking up, seeing Mr. Hobbs in our home, calling him Dad, is gonna take at least twenty years," joked Heaven. She didn't want to admit it, but she enjoyed Karim's company. The love she felt from him was three times the fatherly love she felt from Josh. she just hoped that it never changed.

"You're not fooling anyone, Sister. I see the way you smile when he's making your favorite breakfast, then try to keep a straight face when he turns around," Marrissa called Heaven on her bluff.

She looked at Heaven for a brief second before returning her eyes to the road. Heaven was slightly blushing from imagining her father cooking breakfast. "I smile because he doesn't know how to flip omelets," Heaven laughed.

"He calls them scrambled omelets," Marrissa chimed in.

A call came through on Marrissa's phone as it sat in the cup holder near the armrest. She came to a stop at a red light before reaching for her iPhone and answering. "Hey babe."

"Hey, my love. Where y'all at?" Karim's voice came through the receiver. He sounded bothered by something and Marrissa noticed it.

"We're gonna stop at Subway then we'll be on our way home. Is something wrong?"

"Um, naw. I'll just talk to you when you get home. Love you."

"Love you too. Muah."

"Muah."

Click!

The call ended. Marrissa became bothered by Karim's energy, so she skipped the fast-food restaurant and went straight home.

When Marrissa walked through the door Karim was sitting on the sofa with a drink in his hand. From the opened Patron bottle sitting on the living room table, Marrissa knew that his cup wasn't filled with water but the way he gulped it down he could've fooled anyone. "Hey honey, did you miss us?" Marrissa pushed Heaven's wheelchair to where Karim was sitting before leaning and kissing him on the cheek.

"You know I did." Karim's normal swagger was far different from his principal facade. His words came out smooth yet demanding. They were full of authority.

"Hey sweetheart, how did your new tattoo feel? I don't have to go back up there, do I?"

Heaven smiled at his joke. It was that same smile her mom caught her with plenty times before. "No, he did a good job, wanna see?" Heaven started wiggling out of her North Face jacket.

"Of course, I do." Karim helps his daughter remove her jacket so that she can show off her tattoo. He gently peeled off the bandaged until the full tattoo was on display. Stacy's name was beautiful, occupied by two doves. "That looks nice; you got more heart than me," Karim said half-jokingly. He hated needles.

"So, what did you want to talk to me about, babe?" Marissa asked.

Karim turned his attention back to her. "Follow me, I need to show you something."

He walked towards their bedrooms with Marrissa right behind him. She was hoping he had candles lit and rose petals across the bed. Marrissa was stuck on Karim's loving. She followed him across the room until he stopped at the dresser and grabbed something from atop. "When did you start wearing this?" Karim held up a perfume bottle from Bath & Body Works named *Love Spell*.

"I don't," Marrissa grabbed the bottle from his hand and sniffed it. "Where did this come from?" Marrissa looked at Karim oddly.

"The whole house smelled like it when I woke up this morning. Then I found this bottle on the kitchen counter when I went to light my blunt. I know I'm not tripping. I could've sworn I smelled this same perfume a couple months ago at the hospital."

"So, what's the big deal?"

"The big deal is I only know one person who wears this shit." Karim replied. Now he had Marrissa's undivided attention.

"And who might that be?" Marrissa asked, turning up her nose.

She'd been through enough with Karim over the years and she would not accept any more drama. Karim leaned to the side, peeking his head out the room to see where Heaven was at, then he whispered something in Marrissa's ear that caused her to drop the bottle. The carpet prevented the glass from breaking, but it made a loud thud. "Her perfume, in our home?" Marrissa asked. Karim hunched his shoulders. "Did you make a mistake and pack it?"

"Hell naw, what would it be doing in my house?" Karim countered.

"Do I really need to answer that question?"

"Marrissa, listen to what you are saying, I haven't been with that woman in years, why would I still be holding on to her belongings? If anything, the shit is starting to creep me out," Karim knew how much he loved the smell but the fact that the owner of the perfume was no longer in his life and this sudden smell seeming to follow him just doesn't sit right.

"What are you saying…" Marrissa exploded with laughter.

"What the fucks funny? I'm dead serious." Karim frowned. He didn't catch the joke.

"I'm sorry honey, look, just throw the perfume away and I'll remove the smell okay?" Marrissa leaned in for a kiss and Karim wrapped her in his arms. What they would call "the eye in the sky" was actually "the eye in the closet" as their intruder watched them make out from their bedroom closet.

Chapter 20

Miracle

"Six-four my way. Check ball," Miracle called out her score versus Baby J's.

She challenged him in a one on one to see where his skills were. For his age his game was official. Miracle couldn't slack on him or she would be taking a 'L'. Baby J passed the ball back and took his lockdown defense stance. Miracle's best game was her shot, he knew she wouldn't challenge him in the paint, so he needed to stop her quick release.

Miracle dribbled the basketball at a steady pace. Baby J extended his arm, blocking her view from the basket while his right hand protected her left-handed crossover. Miracle stepped back and faked a 3-pointer; Baby J kept his feet planted and as soon as she set up to bounce the ball he knocked the ball away and recovered it.

"Defeeense!" Baby J yelled. Now it was Miracle's turn to contest his inside domination. Baby J had the height of his father standing 6' at just thirteen years old.

"Come on, show me what you're made of baby brother," Marrissa taunted.

Baby J wiped the bottom of his Jordans with each hand giving him more grip on the YMCA floor. "I'm about to show you alright," Baby J smacked the ball.

He let the ball fall free from his left hand, Miracle reached. Baby J swiped the ball with his right hand, taking it through his legs then he faked right and shifted hard to the left as Miracle attempted to reach again. She missed the entire ball and ended up stumbling. By the time she recovered Baby J was back shifting to his right.

"Mixtape!" someone called from the sideline as Baby J took two steps and raised above the rim with his left hand behind his head and the other gripping the ball tight as he floated.

Slam!

He dunked the ball and hung onto the rim. "Oooohh!" the crowd roared.

Miracle underestimated her little brother. He had game like the varsity players at her school. She couldn't wait until he graduated. She would be sure to let everyone know whose bloodline came to take over Orr High School. "Damn, baby bro, it's like that?" Miracle joked; she was stunned by his performance.

"Just had to show you a lil' some'n some'n, I still love you though." Baby J flashed his charming smile.

He checked the ball, and it was time for Miracle to show her little brother why she was number 1 in the state. After the game ended Miracle had 11 to Baby J's 9 making her the winner of their bet. Baby J told Miracle that if she beat him in a 1 on 1; he would enroll in Orr High school for his freshmen year. But if he won, she would have to transfer to Clemente High school which was his pick.

Since Ciara brought Baby J to Miracle's home they'd been locked in like Batman and Robin. Ciara's sickness became more severe, to the point where she was being escorted back and forth to Mount Sinai hospital leaving Baby J to look after himself with the help of his sister.

Miracle still hated her aunt for the trauma she took her through as a child, but she made Ciara a promise to look after her baby brother, she was all he had left. Baby J mentioned Mari to Miracle on several occasions and together they made plans to seek professional help with finding the youngest seed of their bloodline.

Their father, Big Juan, had been granted an appeal and was back in Cook County Department of Corrections on a retrial. Ciara had turned over valuable evidence to Juan's attorney, she had plans to take the stand but she recorded a video confession just in case god decided to call her home sooner than later.

Baby J told Miracle about him seeing their mother calling her name when he was younger. He thought that she was an imaginary friend up until a few months ago. They had taken a trip to the cemetery to visit Cynthia's gravesite. The stuffed animals they had placed there were stills standing strong. Miracle and Baby J changed back into their street clothes and left the gymnasium together. "Imma walk you home then go around the corner to my boyfriend's house, okay?" Miracle told Baby J as they made their way across the street.

"I don't have to be home yet. Imma go get up with my homies they live right around the corner," Baby J lied. He didn't want his big sister all in his business. Truth was, he was going to meet his Porshia and chill with her for a little while.

"Well, I'll walk you to meet them," Miracle insisted.

"Sis, I'll be okay, they live right up the street. I'll call you when I make it," Baby J said as he backed away from Miracle, heading towards the opposite direction.

He felt himself bump into something causing him to stumble. "Watch where the fuck you going, shorty," Baby J heard just before he felt a shove in his back.

He turned around to see a group of teenagers pushing past him. Miracle stood in their way. "You didn't have to push him; it's not like he saw you." Miracle placed her hand on her hip as if she were waiting on an apology.

"That's what he got eyes for, tell 'em use 'em next time, sweetheart. You too fine to be dealing with a lil nigga like him anyway, you need a real man." The leader reached for Miracle's hand, but she pulled back.

"Boy please, yo dumb ass can't think pass go," Miracle spat, causing the other boys to laugh.

"Bitch, I can buy you—"

"Who the fuck you calling a bitch?" *Whack!* Miracle slapped the taste out of the boy's mouth.

Before he could react, Baby J hit him from the blind side, busting his lip. He was outnumbered but he was willing to take a loss over his big sister. The other two boys tackled Baby J to the ground and rained kicks and punches on him while Romeo, the leader held Miracle against the brick wall by her throat. "Bitch, I'll kill you. Don't move." He tightened his grip around her neck.

Miracle's eyes were glued to her little brother being pulverized. Baby J balled up into a fetal position while they continued to slam their Timberlands into his rib cage. Miracle wanted to scream but Tyri's grip had her gasping for air. She fell to the ground with tears in her eyes as Romeo went into his waistband and pulled out his Smith & Wesson nine-millimeter. He walked over to Baby J and pointed.

"Nooo!" Miracle found strength out of nowhere and hopped up to her feet. She rushed Romeo and attempted to take him to the ground, but he had too much weight on him. He pushed her away and went across her face with a back hand.

"You know you crazy, right?" Romeo mugged Miracle before pointing the gun at Baby J once again. Miracle had no strength to recover from the blow. Her face was stinging. "Back up," Romeo demanded the other two boys to stop their attack. Baby J wasn't moving. He had blood spilling from his mouth and nose.

"Let's see how tough you be at his funeral."

BOOM!

Miracle's heart shattered to the sound, she fell to her knees and crawled to where Baby J was lying there motionless. She picked his head up and placed it onto her lap.

"Come on Ty, what the fuck?" the shortest of the three looked at Romeo like he was insane.

"Shut up pussy and come on." Romeo led the pack without looking back.

Miracle rushed in her pocket to grab her phone and dialed 911. "911. What's your emergency?"

"Hello, someone just shot my brother."

***

Boozer

Boozer was at the park hustling when Miracle called his cell phone crying. He couldn't make out the words she said but he knew something was seriously wrong. He could hear someone in the background saying, "Stay with me."

That's when he started to lose his composure. "Miracle, where you at man?" he yelled into the receiver.

"On our way to the hospital," she cried.

"What hospital? And who is *our*?" Boozer was becoming anxious by the second.

"My brother got shot, we're going to Mount Sinai—"

"Shot?" Boozer repeated.

"Yes, jumped on *and* shot," Miracle felt tears building up again.

"We'll talk when I get there, I'm on my way."

Boozer hung up the phone and walked across the street to the liquor store where he knew he would find his homie Bizzy. When he walked in the store Bizzy and his right-hand man, Teezo, were purchasing a fifth of Remy Martin and cranberry juice. "Aye Bizzy come run me to the hospital right quick, I got gas money."

"Hospital? Fuck you burning or some'n?" Bizzy joked. Teezo started laughing which caused Boozer to smile a little, lightening the mood.

"Naw bitch, my girl's lil brother just got shot. I'm finna go check on her." Boozer had told his friends about Miracle finding her long lost blood relatives.

Boozer had plans to meet him one day, but he just hadn't found the right time. All Boozer knew was trap and play ball. He heard her little brother had game, but Division & Pulaski Park (DP) wouldn't be the spot to see what his game was about.

Boozer was used to the action, but he kept Miracle far away from the park. Any moment a shoot-out could occur and somebody could end up hurt or worse, dead. There's been a lot of bloodshed over the years between the four corner hustlers and the double I's over territory. The park was a gold mine for pushing any kind of drug. You could've probably got rich off Tylenol who knows? But no one wanted to sit at the table and eat together so it was, "get down or lay down."

"Shot? He cool?" Bizzy asked, sounding more concerned than before.

He knew Miracle's lil' brother couldn't have been no older than thirteen years old being that he was still in middle school. "I don't know, foe, she said somebody jumped 'em then popped 'em–"

"Come on then, nigga, fuck you waiting on." Bizzy snatched the door open and the three of them marched out of the liquor store without paying for the liquor.

Boozer walked into Mount Sinai hospital with Bizzy and Teezo behind him. The place was crowded with police. Boozer's first instinct was to turn around and get the hell out of there. But he had to check on his girl. He spotted her talking to a nurse by the emergency entrance. "Hold on, y'all." Boozer gestured for his boys to stay put while he went to check on Miracle and get a little more details on what took place.

Boozer's blood began to boil as he got closer. He spotted the bruise under her right eye. Miracle was very bright, so her scars appeared in 3D. "What the fuck happened to you?"

Boozer didn't even acknowledge the nurse who was standing there with a chart in his hand. "Can you excuse us for one minute, please?" Miracle asked the nurse.

"Sure, go right ahead, just ask for Dr. Bush if you need me," the doctor replied then walked away with a limp. A smart person could tell right away that Dr. Bush was working with a prosthetic leg.

"Some boy hit me but I'll be okay., I'm more worried about my lil brother. The doctor says he ain't get shot. He just took a beating, but I seen the boy pull the trigg–"

"Seen what boy? Where y'all was at?"

"We were walking up Hamlin. I was gonna come chill with you after I walked him to his friend's house. That's when Baby J accidentally stepped on one of the boy's shoes. Next thing I know I'm getting the life choked out of me while my lil brother is being jumped. I stopped resisting until I seen the boy who was choking me pull out a gun." Boozer took in everything Miracle said but he just wanted to know two things.

"Where you say this happened at?" he asked.

"Hamlin and Augusta."

"How the boy looked who choked you?"

"He was dark-skinned with dreads and about yo' height."

A light bulb lit up inside Boozer's head. "Call me when you ready, imma come get chu'. And tell yo' lil bro I said get well soon." Boozer kissed Miracle's bruise under her eye. His demeanor had her panties soaked and the kiss put the cherry on top.

"Ok, but we might have to stay for a few days. The doctor said he has a broken rib but I'll call you."

"That's cool, just call me." Boozer turned and walked away, leaving Miracle standing there, daydreaming about what she wanted to do to him right here in front of all those people. She smiled at the thought and went to call for Dr. Bush.

***

Boozer, Teezo, and Bizzy were all at Bizzy's OG house with the room door locked. Bizzy threw his boys all black hoodies and the same color jeans. From the description Miracle had given him, Boozer knew exactly who he wanted to bring the smoke to. Romeo and his gang were four corner hustlers that called themselves H&A (Hamlin & Augusta). Boozer and his boys have had conflict in the past but nothing too serious. That would all change tonight. Somebody had to teach the H&A boys a lesson they would never forget.

Even though Boozer been hustling since he was 10 years old, his friend Bizzy had more street smarts. He bought all the guns that came his way just for a time like this. Bizzy put on his gloves and went to the back of his closet where he had an old speaker box. He pulled the box out the closet and laid it across his bed. Then he took a screwdriver and loosened the screws around the speaker until he could pull the speaker right out.

Bizzy reached his hand inside the box and came out with a Glock, then a Ruger, and the last gun he pulled out was a Springfield XD 40 with a lemon squeeze on the back of the handle. "Yea, this me right here," Boozer said as he grabbed the pipe from Bizzy.

"Put one up top," said Bizzy as he cocked back his Glock 9. Teezo grabbed the P89 Ruger and followed suit.

Knock! Knock! Knock!

"Who is it?" asked Bizzy as the boys tucked their pieces.
"It's Danky," Bizzy's little brother called out.
Bizzy opened the door just a little. "Wassup shorty?"

"Where y'all 'bout to go? Let me slide with y'all" asked Danky.

He looked up to his big brother. Everything Bizzy bought Danky wore to school, styling and profiling. "Imma come grab you after we finish handling this business, lil bro," Bizzy promised.

"A'ight I'm finna put on some clothes."

"Don't go in my closet pussy," joked Bizzy.

He knew exactly where his lil brother was going to freshen up. "You know I am." Danky smiled and went back to his room.

Bizzy put the speaker back in the closet and the boys went out on a mission.

***

"Grab this one right here." Bizzy pointed to a black Impala.

Boozer pulled his hoodie over his head and jumped out the back seat with a crowbar and a screwdriver in his hands. Thirty seconds later the black Impala came to life. Boozer was a pro at stealing cars. Bizzy looked in his rearview mirror and waited for Boozer's signal before pulling off.

Boozer followed Bizzy to the park where he parked his gold Buick LeSabre and both him and Teezo jumped into the steamer with Boozer. Teezo and Bizzy tucked their dreads under their hood and tied them tight, leaving only their eyes visible. Boozer wore a ski mask under his hoodie because he was light-complected.

They sat in the stolen car watching Romeo and his homies sell dope in front of Mama Luchi's house. Mama Luchi was the mother of every hustler on the block. They paid her bills and did whatever she asked them. In return she let them use her apartment to tuck their drugs and guns when the blue & whites came. "Terrell, get in this house! It's almost yo' bedtime."

The boys could hear Mama Luchi yelling at a younger kid across the street. It didn't take long for the child to make his way down the street and into the house. On cue, all three boys hopped out of the Impala and started creeping along the parked cars until they were close enough to spring into action.

Boozer acted first, raising his XD, he let off four shots in Romeo's direction. Romeo fell into the gate of Mama Luchi's house. Teezo and Bizzy joined the action.

Boom! Boom! Boom! Fa! Fa! Fa!

It was a fireworks show in the middle of May, as Bizzy and Teezo stood side by side letting their guns bark. One of Romeo's friends tried to run up the stairs of Mama Luchi's apartment and caught two slugs to the back, dropping him right at the front door. Romeo tried to reach for his piece when he felt something hot burning through the flesh of his leg. Another hole appeared in his stomach, staining his white t-shirt. "Aarghh!" Romeo screamed as he felt each bullet cooking his tissues where they landed.

The last friend made an escape through Mama Luchi's gangway the moment he heard the first shot. Romeo and Mook wouldn't be as lucky. Boozer ran onto the sidewalk to get up close on Romeo as he tried to crawl under Mama Luchi's stairs.

Boom! Boom! Boom!

Boozer sent bullets flying into the chest of the nigga that dared to put his hands on his girl. "Bet you think twice before you touch another nigga's bitch."

Boom! Boom!

Boozer let off two more shots rocking Romeo to sleep. "Night night," he said, turning around. As he was about to jog back to the stolen car, he heard Mook groaning from the porch.

He was about to finish him off when Bizzy yelled "Come on foe, twelve 'bout to hit this bitch." Boozer aimed his gun towards the porch and emptied his clip, hoping he hit his target before running to the Impala. Bizzy drove with Teezo in the passenger seat and Boozer hopped into the back seat.

Blue lights appeared in the distance just as they were pulling away from the scene. Boozer's phone rang in his pocket. He pulled it out and read 'Wifey' on the home screen then he answered "Hello."

"Can you bring me food? I'm starving."

"I'll be there in thirty minutes, hold fast okay?"

"Okay, I love you." Miracle's voice was soft and innocent.

How could I not love her, she's perfect in my eye's, Boozer thought to himself before replying "I love you too," in front of his boys. He didn't care if he sounded soft, those were his true feelings.

Chapter 21

Chapo

Chapo had been tight on the boys since the explosion happened at his spot a few weeks ago. "I never met three brains so stupid," he told them when he found out the explosion came from the oven being left on for so long without being ignited. The moment his bodyguard stepped a foot into the place with his cigar in hand the place blew like the world trade center.

However, that wasn't Chapo's biggest concern. He expected the fire department to discover Tiffany's body burned to a crisp with a slug in her stomach. But to his surprise the house was completely empty. He gave his son specific instructions not to take Tiffany from the basement. He wanted his face to be the last thing she seen before she crossed over.

The first thing Chapo did was call every hospital within ten miles of his home to see if they had a patient by the name of Tiffany Coleman. Chapo knew she had to be rushed to a hospital in order to survive but when plan A went dry, he went with plan B and roamed the streets of Dallas looking for either a dead pregnant woman sprawled out across the sidewalk or a very strong dope fiend seeking two different fixes. Either way, Chapo wouldn't be satisfied until he found her.

Meanwhile, Chapo had other business to attend to. Someone hit up one of his stash spots while it was left unattended. Chapo lost four bricks of cocaine, ten kilos of heroin and $250,000 in cash. The loss was chump change, but it was the principle. No one had ever taken from the Molina's and lived to talk about it. Whoever it was had to be playing Chapo very closely. They managed to disarm the alarm system and all the cameras without a hench. Chapo was pissed off behind this mess and someone had to answer for his loss.

Blackboy and Chapo's boys sat in the back of Chapo's black minivan, across the street from Lalo's biggest drug spot in Texas which was only a few miles away from Chapo's headquarters. Lalo was the Molina's biggest competition when it came to the drug game. Coming second to Chapo in position never set well with Lalo but the two agreed to squash the beef and boss up like real men, that way everybody eats and nobody has to die.

That seemed like a good plan until two weeks ago when Milo had words with Lalo's son, Turbo, over a chick they both were sticking their dicks in. Milo said some words that he knew would push the wrong buttons in Turbo's heart and they had a gunfight outside the strip club. Since then, it's been clueless robberies and kidnappings happening on Chapo's territory. Tonight, someone would pay for waking up the sleeping bear.

Chapo sat behind the wheel of the van, scoping out all the traffic coming and going from inside the trap house. A dark blue Dodge Caravan pulled up and two Mexicans about the same age as Milo hopped out with duffle bags in their hands. They scanned their surroundings before walking into the house. Chapo hit the locks on the van and the boys sprang right into action. All three boys crept up on the Caravan with their ski masks on and guns aimed, ready to kill. Just as they were about to snatch open the door and take the driver hostage, a hole appeared in the driver's side window. Blood spread across the window instantly. The boys looked back to see Chapo rolling his passenger window up.

The boys waited for a few moments until they heard the door open. Chapo told them the drop-off would be quick, so they had to move fast. The moment the door swung open Milo hit the first guy in the nose with his AR pistol, breaking it instantly. Ceasar grabbed the same guy by his shirt, forcing him to stand. Blackboy made his way inside the trap and hit the second guy with a silenced 9mm shell right to the middle of his forehead. Ceasar dragged the first guy back into the trap by his collar.

Inside, there were three more guys and two chicks all attending to the new order they had just received. None of them were paying attention and that cost them. No one looked until they heard a thump. Ceasar let the boy he was holding hostage fall to the ground. Before the others could react, Milo was peeling wigs back. The closest two caught .556 slugs to their heads, making them fall in slow motion. Blackboy squeezed the trigger of the shotgun he held in his hand and sent the biggest Mexican in the room flying out the window. Chapo had instructed them to make it merciless and messy.

The chicks were useless, so Ceasar ended their lives with head shots from his Mac 11. After all the motion stopped in the living room Milo stood over each victim and twisted their bodies up even more with his AR pistol. Blackboy and Ceasar took the duffle bags from the table and the backpacks filled with money that the boys were carrying outside. Chapo's boys ransacked the entire place while Blackboy carried the bags to the van.

Blackboy got stuck in his tracks when he saw a police car cruising up the street. He had flashbacks of his episode with the police in Chicago. He wasn't about to lay down this time. He was ready to go out with a bang. He started reaching for his piece as the police car pulled next to Chapo's van. Chapo rolled his passenger window down again and shortly after that the police car was on its way. Blackboy looked to his left and spotted the body he had blown out the window with his guts spilling out over the grass.

When he looked back to the right the police car was out of sight. Blackboy ran to Chapo's van and opened the back door before throwing the bags filled with money and drugs into the backseat and hopping in. Chapo was sitting there with a smile on his face. "I see you were ready to send buck shots flying at my workers," Chapo said, referring to the cop.

"Hell yeah, I ain't going back to jail."

"Way to go, those bastards are filthy but as long as you feed them right you don't have to worry about them. I'm guessing that's your work." Chapo nodded towards the body lying on the ground.

Blackboy smiled. "You said make it messy, right?"

"Damn right I did."

Chapo gave Blackboy a fist pound just as the two boys came running out of the house as flames chased them out. The house was going up in flames quickly. Ceasar and Milo hopped into the van with two more duffle bags they found full of drugs. "Good job, boys, now let's go eat." Chapo pulled away from the curb like nothing happened.

Chapter 22

Karim

Karim was in his office sorting out papers when he heard a firm knock on his door. "Come –" The twisting of the doorknob stopped Karim from completing his invitation.

"Mr. Hobbs?" the man asked.

"We'll let yourself right on in." Karim smiled but under that smile was noticeable irritation.

"Oh, I'm sorry about that. How rude of me," the man returned the phony smile. "But anyway, I'm Detective Mason and this here is my partner Detective Diaz."

Diaz reached out his hand but was left hanging. "Well, how can I help you, Detectives?"

"We're working on a case, and our sources tell us that you may know of a Tiffany Coleman. We hear that she's been a teacher here for several years."

"Well, did your *sources* tell you that Ms. Coleman hasn't stepped foot in this school since last year?" Karim remarked with an attitude.

"Actually, they didn't, which is why we came to you. We've come to believe that Ms. Coleman is missing. Would you be able to tell us the last day you saw her here at work?"

Karim sat up straight in his office chair at the mention of his best teacher being missing, raised his antennas. *I knew she wouldn't just up and leave us like that. Something had to be wrong,* Karim thought to himself as he began to feel bad about despising her for leaving without notice. "The last day I saw her was sometime in June. She was supposed to teach summer school here for the third graders that flunked last year but she never showed up. I thought maybe she quit but inside I knew she wouldn't just up and leave," Karim admitted.

Detective Mason reached inside a folder and withdrew a photo. "Have you seen this young man before?" He held up a picture of Blackboy. It was his mugshot from his most recent arrest.

"Can't say that I have," replied Karim after taking a closer look.

"This here is Ms. Coleman's son, he's missing as well. He's a key witness as well as these two girls who attended school here." Detective Mason presented two more photos of April and Heaven.

"Key witnesses?" Karim repeated.

"Yes, we've been working on the case with your former student Stacy Lomax. We're trying to determine rather this case is a suicide or homicide."

Karim had his eyes glued to Heaven's picture. "Homicide? I thought the poor girl shot herself. At least that's what I was told."

"That's the story we were told too but we have reasons to believe otherwise, and the possible suspect has recently came out of a coma. He's not speaking at all, at least not to us. So, if you happen to see any one of these people can you do us a favor, and give us a call?" Detective Mason held out his card.

Karim hesitated for a moment before accepting the card. The entire time the detective was talking Karim had been trying to remember\ where he had seen them before. Then it came to him. These were the same detectives who showed up at the hospital when Heaven had gotten hit by the car. *Do they remember me?* Karim thought to himself. "Uh, sure I'll give you a call if by some odd chance one of my former students happens to stop by for old times sake," Mr. Hobbs lied. One of his former students was at his home probably eating cereal after she had just finished her therapy.

Detective Mason shot him a funny look. "Alright, you take care, principal." Detective Mason extended his hand, and this time Karim accepted it with a slight smile to warm the mood.

"Will do."

The detectives walked away, and Karim's fake smile was replaced by a look of disgust.

After he was sure the officers were long gone, he called Marrissa on his cell phone. The phone rang three times before Marrissa answered. "Hey babe," she greeted him through the receiver.

"Hey, my love, what you got going on right now?"

"Nothing just finished helping Heaven with her therapy now she's eating cereal while I ran some bath water," Karim smiled at how well he knew his family. "How's work going?" she asked.

"It's okay, I was just finishing up when those two detectives from the hospital came bothering me."

"Did you tell them we don't know who hit Heaven? We just want to go on with our lives."

"They didn't ask about that. They're looking for Heaven and her friend to question them about Stacy's accident, they say it can be a possible murder, and they have a suspect in their reach." Marissa sat on the other end of the receiver in silence for a moment. "Hello," Karim spoke into the receiver.

"Yes, honey I'm here it's just … I don't know why they're bugging Heaven. She told them everything she knows already plus she's got her own issues going on right now." Marrissa sighed.

"I know honey. You're right baby. I just don't want these dick heads snooping around every day. I don't feel too good about the police so should we just let her talk to them one more time?"

"Hell no, tell them fuck off . We can't help them. The story she told them was the truth, what more do they want from her?" Marrissa snapped. Heaven had been through enough for one lifetime she just wanted her baby girl to live.

"You know what, you're absolutely right. The next time they stop by that's exactly what I'll tell them. Heaven don't need no more problems on her plate, and it seems like them assholes are just fishing for a bonus anyway. Do you know them motherfuckers didn't even knock—" Karim's sentence was cut short by the face of another uninvited guest making her way into his office.

"Oh no, they didn't come into your office without knocking?" Marrissa giggled.

"Baby, I'll see you when I get home. I have some work to do," Karim tried to rush Marrissa off the phone as quickly as possible.

"Ok honey. I love you. See you when you get home."

"Love you too. Muah."

Click!

Karim ended the call and stood up from his seat. "What are you doing here, Simone?"

"Is that how you talk to your wife, Karim?"

"Ex-wife," Karim corrected her.

"Last time I checked it wasn't final." Simone reached for Karim's dick, but he grabbed her wrist.

"What are you doing?"

"Karim, cut the bullshit, I know you're not happy with that white bitch and that bastard child. Come home, I miss you." Simone gave him the puppy eyes.

"Watch your mouth talking about my daughter; you made your decision. You could've accepted my child when I came clean about her, but you wanted to leave." Karim turned off his desktop computer and walked towards the door. "I got somewhere to be, Simone," he said as he prepared to leave.

Simone threw herself against the door. "You can handle your business after I get what I came for." Simone locked the office door and closed the window blinds.

Karim didn't want to deal with Simone's toxic ways, but he couldn't resist her sex appeal. Simone looked similar to Lisa Ray when she acted in the movie "Player's Club". She had an hourglass shape with no stretch marks. Her lips stayed glossed up and she always wore open toed heels to display her perfect toes. Karim knew he had to escape her presence before his new relationship was at stake. "And what did you come for?" He furrowed his brows at Simone.

"I like when you play dumb. It makes my pussy so wet." Simone bit her bottom lip and stuck her hand under her miniskirt. That was Karim's weakness. She noticed his ten-inch bulge through his dress pants. "Well, if you don't know what I came for, he sure does." Simone grabbed Karim's manhood and pulled him closer.

Before he could utter a single word, her tongue was down his throat while her hand massaged his cock. Karim begin to tongue her back, matching her motion like she knew he would. Simone backed him away from the door until they were back at his desk. She turned around and swiped all the papers off the desk before taking a seat on top of it. Her juice box was running down her thighs with no panties to stop the flow. She helped Karim unfasten his pants and freed his magic stick. Simone threw her legs over her head and cuffed the back of her thighs with her arms, giving Karim a close up on her pussy which was pretty and pink on the inside, and shining like a glazed donut on the outside.

Karim wasted no time filling her up to capacity. He entered her slow and deep, savoring the moment. After a few breathtaking thrusts her vagina began to adapt to his length. Karim let out small groans from Simone being so tight and slippery. He grabbed her by the hips and started pumping faster and more aggressively with each stroke. Simone was taking it like a champ as Karim rotated his hips, knocking her walls down from different angles.

"Ooh, beat this pussy up daddy! Beat this, aahh!" she cried out in ecstasy as he hit her g-spot again and again. Her moans drove Karim crazy. He flipped her over and bent her over his desk. He knew she loved her some backshots so he wanted to hear her cheeks clap. Her juices ran down the length of his dick as he waited for her to take her position. Karim shoved his thick fully erect ten-inch dick inside Simone's walls. His left hand gripped the back of her neck to keep her in place while his right hand smacked her ass cheeks, leaving his large handprint just how she like it.

Smack! Smack! Smack!

"Shit, I can't take it," Simone moaned. Charging Karim up.

He pumped harder like he was trying to bust a new hole in her pussy. "Take this dick, you miss it?"

"Yesss!"

"Say you miss it!" *Smack!*

"Eeww, I miss this dick daddy," Simone screamed. Karim spit on her ass cheeks and rubbed it around her hole before working his thumb all the way into Simone's backdoor love button.

That sent her over the top. She started throwing it back on Karim with force. Karim felt his head swell up as he tried to hold back. "Fuckkk!" he groaned as he felt himself exploding.

"I'm cumming, arghh!" Simone met him at the top of the mountain as they both released seeds. Karim's body limped over hers as she laid across his desk. She reminded him why he married her to begin with. Karim knew once she laid the pussy on him it would make it hard for him to leave. No woman alive could put it down like her. There was only one other woman that rocked his world like Simone did and she took their secrets to her grave.

Chapter 23

Marrissa

Marrissa had just finish helping Heaven climb into her bubble bath when her cell phone started ringing. She quickly dried her hands on her black yoga pants and grabbed her phone from inside her bra. She read Karim's name across the screen and pressed the green phone icon as she was leaving the bathroom. She didn't want Heaven to overhear their conversation just in case Karim was calling to discuss the detectives again. "Hey babe," Marrissa said through the speaker as soon as she placed the phone to her ear.

"Eeww, beat this pussy up daddy! Beat this, aahh!" Marrissa thought her mind was playing tricks on her as she heard the moans of another woman on the other end of the phone. She took the phone away from her ear and read the screen again to make sure it was Karim's name that she was staring at before placing it back to her ear.

"Hello?" This time she said it much louder.

All she heard was the sounds of a woman moaning along with a clapping sound. *Smack! Smack! Smack!* Marrissa couldn't believe her ears. She sat on the phone in silence, but her heart was screaming on the inside. *After all I've done for this bastard he still has the nerve to mistreat me— like I'm some piece of trash. We were doing perfectly fine without him*. She thought about Heaven and how this might affect her in the end.

Heaven had gotten comfortable with waking up to her real father, feeling that unconditional fatherly love and Marrissa didn't want to take that away from her. Marrissa sat there daydreaming with the phone placed to her ear. It wasn't until she heard Karim's voice loud and clear say "You know I love you, Simone."

When she finally snapped out of her trance. Marrissa couldn't believe her ears. *'How could this son of a bitch go creeping with his ex-wife after all I've done for him'* she thought as she continued to listen to their conversation.

"Then why can't you forget about them and start a family with me, your wife?" Marrissa heard Simone say.

"It's not that easy; my daughter needs me in her life. She's been through too much for me to just give up on her."

"No, *I've* been through too much, Karim. You gave me H.I.V and think you can just move on with your life, that's not how life works, nigga."

Those words made Marrissa drop her cell phone causing her screen to shatter. It felt like she had taken a karate chop to the throat as she tried to swallow.

Marrissa held her chest as she searched for a place to sit. *H.I.V.?* Her mind kept replaying the moment. She couldn't believe her ears. She found herself leaning on the kitchen counter for support. The room started to spin in slow motion. "Mooom!" she heard Heaven's voice yell, but her legs wouldn't move. "Mom, I'm finished," Heaven yelled again from the bathroom.

Marrissa slid to the floor and picked her phone up. The phone call had ended and the screen was black. Marrissa rushed to her feet and prepped herself before attending to Heaven's needs she walked into the bathroom with a smile on her face. "Sorry, honey, I was cleaning the kitchen," Marrissa lied as she strolled Heaven's wheelchair closer to the tub.

"I was starting to think you ran away and left me," Heaven joked but it hit Marrissa in a different way because she was thinking just that.

"I would never leave you." Marrissa grabbed Heaven's dry towel and sat it in her wheelchair before helping Heaven out of the tub. Marrissa's heart was heavy after listening to her man cheat with his ex-wife on the other end of the phone. But to hear he was infected with H.I.V. made Marrissa's world come crashing down. She wanted to pick up and run away, leaving everything behind.

"You better not," Heaven smiled.

Marrissa helped Heaven get dressed as quickly as possible so she can tell Heaven all about the secrets she's been desperately trying to figure out. Marrissa slipped Heaven's pink bunny house shoes on her feet for her. "We're 'bout to take a little trip, honey. There's a lot of things I've been wanting to tell you at some point in life and I know you've been dying for answers." Marrissa left Heaven sitting in the living room in her thoughts while she stepped into her bedroom. Marrissa returned with a yellow envelope in her hand. "Okay you're ready?"

"Um, I guess," Heaven replied. She was kind of confused by her mother's sudden change of energy.

"Okay, let's go," Marrissa strolled Heaven out the door.

They pulled into the Oakland Cemetery and followed the road all the way to the end of the graveyard. Heaven's brows furrowed. She was clueless. She'd only seen a cemetery in movies and even then, there was either a funeral or something strange taking place. "What are we doing here?" Heaven asked.

"I brought you here to meet someone. There's a long story behind who you are, honey." Marrissa climbed out of the passenger seat and helped Heaven into her wheelchair. Heaven was anxious and it showed through the goose bumps that appeared on her arm. "It's okay, honey. I'm just as nervous as you are. I haven't been to this place in years. There's just a lot that you need to know and I'm hoping now is just as good as any other time." Marrissa sighed.

After Heaven was settled in her wheelchair, Marrissa strolled her through the field. Heaven's wheelchair rolled over the tombs that were buried into the ground. She tried to read the names as she stumbled across them. Eugene & Scarlet Mayfield 1979 - 1981. By the photo engraved in the tombstone Heaven could tell the tomb belonged to two small twins. Her heart cried for them.

'Cynthia Johnson 1975 – 2004'. Heaven continued to read the names until her wheelchair stopped rolling. She was sitting next to a tombstone that was quite different from the ones she was reading. This tombstone stood up 20 inches from the ground and was in the shape of a heart. Marrissa stared at the tombstone in awe. Surprisingly, the tombstone had been recently cleaned and even had flowers next to it. If she had to take a guess, she'd bet her life on knowing who placed them there. Marrissa took a deep breath and exhaled. "Huughh. Heaven, this is my best friend Gabriela Guzman born September 9th, 1976, died December 15th, 1996." Marrissa noticed a quizzical look appear on Heaven's face. "Yes, on the same day you were born." Marrissa answered the question Heaven was thinking. Heaven was still clueless. "She's beautiful, isn't she?"

"Yes, she looks like someone I've seen before," Heaven replied.

"I bet she does." Marrissa smiled. She went into the envelope she had been carrying and retrieved a few photos. "This here is a few photos of us before she died," Marrissa handed Heaven the pictures.

Heaven flicked through the photos, saving each picture to her memory. She came across a picture of her mother and the woman standing outside of McDonald's. The woman was undoubtedly pregnant. "She had a baby?" Heaven asked.

"Yep, a beautiful baby girl."

"What happened to the baby?"

"Don't you wanna know what happened to Gabby first?" Marrissa asked.

Not really, Heaven thought to herself as she stared at the picture for a moment longer. "How did she die?"

"Why don't we start from the beginning…"

Marrissa picked up her house phone and dialed Karim's number. After a few rings his voicemail came on. "This is Karim. I'm sorry I'm not available to take your call –"

Click!

Marrissa ended the call before pressing the redial button. This time she got an answer "Yo," Karim said with a raspy voice.

"Karim, Gabby's going into labor you need to get over here fast," *Marrissa's voice cracked from the pressure Gabriela was putting on her right hand from squeezing it to death. The other line went silent for a few moments then finally Karim spoke again.*

"Hello?"

"Did you hear what I said?" *Marrissa's voice grew louder.*

"Yes, I heard what you said. But you know better than to call my phone at this time in the morning what's wrong with you?" *Karim snapped in a low tone.*

Marrissa and Gabriela both knew that calling Karim's phone at 5 a.m. was unacceptable but Gabby forced Marrissa to make the call. Karim had a wife at home, but he was in a three way relationship on the side. Karim made a promise to be with them and leave his wife when Gabriela dropped a positive pregnancy test in his mailbox. She was becoming fed up with him leading her on. So, she threatened to tell his wife about their relationship if he didn't decide what he wanted to do.

Marrissa didn't care much for Karim, she was in it for the orgasms. However, she did have deep feelings for Gabriela.

Her best friend. Gabby and Marrissa been friends since the fourth grade. Marrissa never had a thing for girls but she was drawn to her best friend. Gabby on the other hand had been bi-curious her whole life. Karim convinced Gabby that a threesome would prove her love for him and Gabby put that same spell on Marrissa. The Cindy Lyn hotel became a second home to the three of them.

The more time Karim spent with them, the more time Gabby demanded. They had sex in his office at school, in the back seat of his Mercedes Benz, even in the public restroom at McDonald's if Gabby wanted the dick. When Karim finally tried to push the brakes, Gabby poked a hole in his condom, setting the trap that she thought would bond them together for life.

"Gabby's going into labor, that's what's wrong with me," Marrissa snapped back. "You need to come take her to a hospital."

"Why you ain't just call an ambulance?"

"Because I didn't fuck an ambulance, you bastard!" Gabby yelled from the background.

Click! Karim ended the call. Marrissa pressed redial to find out his cellphone had been powered off.

"Fuck him, we have to get you to a hospital," *Marrissa searched for her car keys before helping Gabriela out the door of her apartment and to her car.*

Marrissa made it to John Stroger's emergency room in record breaking time. She played the father role while Gabby went through six long hours of labor.

Gabby pushed out a beautiful seven pound baby girl. She had Gabby's green eyes and long hair but her nose and cheek bones came straight from Karim's face. Once the doctors cleaned the baby and dressed her, they handed her over to her mother who waited anxiously. Gabby's heart melted the moment she laid eyes on her bundle of joy. Tears formed in the corners of both eyes as the thought of once aborting her biggest blessing came to mind. Then Karim came to mind. "Where the hell is he?" Gabby cursed.

"He never showed up. I called him several times since we arrived, no answer," Marrissa shared the news that she knew would hurt Gabby's heart but she needed to hear it.

"Hand me your phone," Gabby demanded. Marrissa gave up her cell phone without resistance. Gabby dialed Karim's number off the top of her head. She expected the phone to at least ring but she was caught by surprise when the operator came on "The number you've reached has been disconnected."

Click! Gabby slammed Marrissa's phone close and threw it across the room, grabbing the doctor's attention.

Marrissa didn't bother to chase after her phone. She knew how hurt Gabby had to be to have to go through labor alone. After all those promises Karim sold her and she bought every one of them. "It's okay Gabby, that son of a bitch is gonna wake up one day and realize what he's lost and it'll be too late come back. Look, I think she's hungry." Marrissa turned her attention to the baby who was starting to whimper. "She's so beautiful, Gabby. What are you gonna name her?" Marrissa asked as she reached for the baby.

"I'm still undecided. I'm sure I'll come up with something. Risa, can you do me a favor and go home and gather me some change of clothes? I wanna be able to walk out this place the moment they discharge me."

"Sure, thing sweety, you feed her and I'll be right back," Marrissa collected her phone and the battery that had fallen out and walked out of the room.

Marrissa had made it three lights away from the hospital when it dawned on her. "Shit! I forgot the keys." She stopped at the red light and busted a U-turn going back to the hospital. When she arrived, she double parked and turned her hazards on. She knew she wouldn't take long going to grab Gabby's house keys, so she didn't worry about being towed.

Marrissa caught the elevator to the third floor and stepped out. She still had the visitor tag on her shirt, so she was able to get back to Gabby's room without a hassle.

Once she made it to room 311, she knocked twice before twisting the knob and opening the door. Marrissa's eyes roamed around the room. If it weren't for the chart sitting by Gabby's bed with her name on it, Marrissa would've sworn she was in the wrong room. Marrissa stepped back out the room to grab the nurse's attention. "Excuse me?"

A chubby female doctor with finger waves looked up from her chart she was reading. "How may I help you?" she asked in a polite voice.

"My friend was in this room right here, can you tell me where they've transferred her to?"

"What's her name?"

"Gabriela, Gabriela Guzman."

"Aw, the pretty Latina girl. Give me one second let me find out." The doctor walked towards a nurse who was looking at something on a computer screen. Marrissa couldn't quite hear the words that the two women were exchanging but she saw the nurse that was seated at the computer point in her direction.

The chubby nurse nodded her head then walked back over to where Marrissa was standing. "She hasn't been moved anywhere ma'am. Are you sure you were in the correct room?"

Marrissa thought that had to be the dumbest question in the world being that she was standing right in front of the room. "See for yourself," Marrissa stepped aside and let the nurse twist the knob and let herself in. Marrissa stepped in behind her to see the bed that Gabby once occupied was totally empty. No Gabby. No baby ...

Gabby jumped into the back seat of a yellow Taxi with her baby in her arms. She had on nothing except her hospital gown. The baby began to cry and Gabby did the only thing she could do to keep her quiet. She pulled her breast out and popped her nipple into the baby mouth. The taxi driver adjusted his rearview mirror so that he could get a glimpse of what was going on. Gabby paid him no mind until she heard a loud honk from another car.

The taxi driver was so busy nipple watching, he had run the red light. "Watch the road, you fucking idiot," Gabby cursed.

"Sorry, sorry," the Jamaican guy apologized and proceeded to drive straight.

Gabby scanned the block for Marrissa's car when she was satisfied with its absence she hopped out of the Taxi without paying. After nearly causing an accident and getting caught being a peeping tom, the Taxi driver knew he had nothing coming. He just kept on pushing.

Gabby wasted no time running to her apartment to collect clothes along with the baby's car seat. She thought about packing the baby a diaper bag but she decided against it. "This will be the last time he makes a fool out of me," Gabby said to herself as she strapped her daughter into her car seat.

Gabby went into her kitchen and grabbed a fresh bottle of Hennessy from the countertop. She peeled the gold seal and drank from the bottle until the brown liquid was only visible through the bottom of the bottle. As the liquor started to settle in, Gabby grabbed a marker and a napkin from the kitchen counter and wrote something before folding the napkin and stuffing it into the baby's car seat. The Hennessy was taking effect quickly as Gabby stumbled across the room. She picked up the car seat and left her apartment without locking the door.

Gabby found herself parked three houses down from Karim's house in Chicago Heights. She finished the last of her Hennessy and opened the door of the grey Nissan she had stolen. She knew her cover would be blown instantly had she driven her own vehicle. She climbed out of the car with the empty bottle still in hand and grabbed the car seat with the baby in it before slamming both doors. She stumbled all *the way to Karim's door step and sat the car seat directly in front of his door.*

"Pussyyy biiitch," Gabby's words came out in a slur "You think you can play a bitch like me, Karim? This is your child and you're gonna accept her rather you like it or not," Gabby was talking to the door as if it was Karim standing there face to face. "Fuck you! And fuck you're ugly ass wife!" Gabby yelled as she launched the empty bottle of Hennessy with all of the strength she could build up.

The bottle flew through the front window and made a loud crash. Gabby made her way back to the Nissan and peeled off before anyone could answer the door. The car nearly slid into a parked car from the slushy snow from last night's storm.

Karim snatched his front door open with a baseball bat in his hand. He didn't notice the car seat right away; his eyes were on the Nissan that passed by with the tires screeching. It wasn't until he heard a small whimper come from beneath him, did Karim look down and notice the baby bundled up nice and warm inside the pink and gray car seat. "Karim, what was it?" his wife yelled from the threshold of their bedroom door.

"Nothing, I took care of it. It was some bad ass kids throwing snowballs," Karim lied to keep his nosey wife from checking out the scene for herself. He quickly grabbed the car seat and walked it to his Chevy Trailblazer. He placed the car seat in the back and turned on the heat so the baby could stay warm.

Karim pulled his cell phone out of his pocket and dialed Gabby's number. The phone went straight to her voicemail without ringing. "This bitch is crazy," he whispered to himself before attempting to reach her again. Her voicemail came on again.

Next, Karim decided to give Marrissa a call. He knew she would have some type of answers for him. She picked her

phone up on the very first ring. "Hello!" Her voice boomed through the receiver.
"Marrissa, this Karim, is Gabby with you?"
"No! She's not fucking with me, you asshole. She snuck out of the hospital to do lord knows what. She's gonna get that baby so sick and it's gonna be all your fault," Marrissa spat through the receiver. She never sounded so pissed in her life. ""If she's not with you, where else could she be?"
"Do I look like some sort of human tracking device? All I know is you better find her and do it quickly because if something happens to my friend or her baby I'm gonna give you hell." Marrissa continued to chew Karim's head off.
"Calm down and listen to me. She left this baby at my doorstep this girl is fuckin' insane."
"She what?" Marrissa asked in disbelief.
"You heard me! She left this baby at my doorstep crying in the cold. I need you to come get this baby while I figure something out."
"No, you're gonna take that baby in the house and I'm gonna find my friend."
Click! Marrissa ended the call.
The baby's crying drew Karim's attention. He peeled back the baby's blanket that hung over her head and the baby was staring at him with tears in her eyes. She had these beautiful eyes just like her mother. Karim caught butterflies from the newborn. He took his thumb and rubbed it across her cheek. Karim searched the car seat for a baby bottle or even a pacifier, but he found neither one. All he found was a folded-up piece of napkin sitting between the baby legs. He took the napkin and unfolded it. He read see you in hell written in marker. Karim quickly dialed Marrissa's number back.
She answered after a few short rings. "You better have some damn good news." Marrissa barked into the phone. Karim could tell she was beyond pissed.
They both knew the damage Gabby is capable of when she's mad or drunk. And it's ten times worse when she's both.

"Marrissa, I need you to meet me at Gabby's apartment. I have a feeling she about to try some'n real fuckin' stupid."

"And how long did it take you to come up with that brilliant idea?"

"Marrissa, just cut the bullshit and listened. She left this note in the baby's car seat and it say 'see you in hell.' Now we both know that this is not some type of sick joke. This ain't the first time Gabby tried to pull some suicidal shit."

"Oh my god!" Karim could hear the panic in Marrissa's voice.

"Calm down, okay. Let's just get to her crib asap."

"I'm on my way."

Click! Marrissa hung up again.

Karim looked at the baby again and smiled before safely strapping in her car seat before heading to Gabby's apartment.

Karim smelled smoke from a mile away. But as he turned the corner his heart pounded at the sight of Gabby's building going up in flames. He parked his truck and watched as the fire department, ambulance, and police tried to rescue the tenants. Then he called Gabby's cell phone again. With no luck reaching her, Karim dialed Marrissa's number. Her phone rung endlessly until her voice mail came on. Karim noticed the paramedics strolling someone out on a stretcher with a sheet over their body. His heart dropped to the pit of his stomach, nearly making him vomit as he tried to swallow.

He jumped out of the car and tried to run towards the paramedics but was stopped in his tracks by two officers. "Sir, you can't go any closer." One officer placed his hand on Karim's chest. Preventing him from stepping any closer.

"I just want to know which apartment the body was found in!" Karim heard a familiar voice trying to reason with the paramedics.

"Ma'am, you're gonna have to let us do our job first. Once we're finished I'm sure one of the officers will be more than happy to answer all of your questions." Karim looked past the two officers and spotted Marrissa standing in the middle of the street trying to wrestle her way into Gabby's building. Her face was beet red from the cold air hitting her pale skin.

The two officers that held up Karim turned their attention to Marrissa who was putting up a fight to get some sort of information. Gabby's car was parked right in front of her building so she had to be somewhere in the building. So far, the fire fighters had rescued eight people including three children. Only one had died in the fire but Marrissa didn't notice Gabby's face amongst the individuals that had survived so her chill button was broken.

The two officers walked over to handle the situation, leaving Karim standing there. "What seems to be the problem?" the short stocky white officer asked both Marrissa and the paramedics.

"She says her friend lives here in the building, maybe you can answer her questions. We have to get these victims to the hospital." The paramedic strolled the body away and shoved it into the back of an ambulance.

"Ma'am, what is your friend's name?"

"Gabby ... Gabriela Guzman."

"Gabriela Guzman," the officer repeated the name. He sat there trying to figure out where he heard the name from. He walked to a blue squad car with two investigators sitting in it running names through their computer. He said a few words then waited a moment until one of the investigators handed him a clear plastic evidence bag containing a burned state of Illinois driver's license.

He held the bag closer so that he could read clearly before making his way back over to where Marrissa was standing, anxiously waiting for some answers. He held up the bag so that Marrissa can see. "We found this in one of the victims' pockets." Marrissa couldn't read the ID clearly but she could see her friend's name melted across the plastic.

"The victim was found in apartment 2E burned to a crisp," the officer finished.

"2E?" Marrissa repeated.

Hearing her friend's apartment made her sick to her stomach. *"Yes, 2E. That's where the fire was initially started, that's why we were unable to save the victim. By the time we discovered her she was stuck to the floor of her own kitchen,"* the officer informed.

Marrissa covered her mouth with both hands as tears appeared in her eyes in an instant. She didn't want to believe what the officers had said. There was no way her friend could just die and leave her in this world alone. Life isn't that unfair, *she thought to herself just as she noticed Karim sneak past the yellow tape that was tied around a tree and a light pole. She rushed towards him with steam coming from her head.*

Smack!

"This is all your fault. I don't know what she saw in you, you lying, cheating son of a bitch." Karim held the left side of his face as shame set in his heart. He didn't move or ask what he did to deserve the slap to the face. Gabby didn't give him enough time to make a decision. She wanted him to act like his wife never existed and that was something his heart couldn't fake.

"I know, Marrissa, I tried to fix it but I was too late. I'm sorry." He wrapped his arms around her as she broke down.

She felt something in the pit of her stomach that she never felt before when dealing with Karim. *Why does it feel so good when he holds me? I don't love him, do I?* she asked herself as she melted under his embrace. Then she thought about the baby. *"Where's the baby?"*

"She's in the car, let's go check on her."

Karim grabbed Marrissa's hand and led her to his Trailblazer. He opened the door to hear the baby crying loudly. Karim had no experience with infants so he had no clue what to do to stop her cries. Marrissa picked the baby up from her car seat and felt her diaper. It wasn't soaked. Next she searched for a bottle, guessing the poor baby had to be hungry. "Where's her diaper bag?" she asked Karim as he climbed into the driver seat and closed the door to keep the cold wind from blowing in on the baby.

"I don't know. This is how I found her." Karim shrugged his shoulders.

"We have to go get her some milk."

"Okay. then what?" Karim asked.

"What do you mean, then what? We feed her, that's what, silly."

"I know that but where do we go from here? This baby lost her mother. She's my child, I'm fully aware of that but I still have a wife at home."

"Are you really saying this right now?" Marrissa snapped. "You had a wife the entire time you were sticking your dick in both of us and not once did I hear you mention your shitty little relationship." Marrissa spat with a hint of jealousy.

"Look, I'm not saying I don't want anything to do with her but you and I both know this baby can't come stay with me. I don't want her growing up in foster care, I'll handle my part financially and you can adopt her legally. I know it's what Gabby would've wanted."

"Don't you dare say her name. You don't deserve to. All you've ever done is mind fuck both of us while you go play house with your whore at home." Marrissa made it clear that Karim wasn't only pulling the strings to Gabby's heart but to hers too.

"I'll take this baby and you'll never hear from us again. I hate that I ever met you." She began to cry as she placed the baby back in her car seat.

She was preparing herself to move on with her life. She wanted to be done with Karim and leave everything he stood for in the past but as she reached for the door of the car Karim grabbed her arm. "I don't want you out of my life

Marrissa. I don't want this baby out of my life. All I ask for is a little more time." Karim stared Marrissa directly in her eyes. She felt like he was staring into her soul with those charming hazel women seekers. *"All you talk about is time. How much time will it take for you to be the father this baby needs? She didn't ask to be here."* Karim went into his pants pocket and pulled out his wallet.

He shuffled through his credit cards until he found the right one. *"This is the account I opened when I found out Gabby was pregnant. I had no intention of leaving her hanging with a fatherless child. This card will stay loaded and if you ever need more I'm only one call away."*

"Until you change your number again." Marrissa snatched the card and opened the door to let herself out.

"Wait," Karim grabbed her arm. *"You not gone tell me her name?* He asked. Marrissa realized that Gabby and her never came up with a name for this beautiful baby.

"What do you see when you look at her?" Marrissa asked. Karim stared deep into the baby's eyes.

It's like he got hypnotized as he searched for the answer to Marrissa's question. After a long pause he answered, *"Heaven."*

Heaven didn't realize that she had tears running down her face. For all these years, she had been looking for answers to who she really was. Now, it was like a ton of bricks had been lifted from her shoulders then dropped right back down on her head. She had heard the old saying, *the truth hurts,* but she didn't know how much until the stones hit home. Marrissa wiped away Heaven's tears until she found herself drowning in her own.

Heaven leaned forward and hugged her with all the strength she could muster up. After they held each other for what seemed like hours, just crying, Heaven sat up straight in her wheelchair. She had reason to feel the pain she felt, but she had no reason to be crying. She was raised under a good roof with a silver spoon in her mouth and the best children's fashion money could buy. So, what if she was adopted. The mother she grew to love treated her better than most kids who were raised by both of their biological parents. However, she did feel a lot of hatred in her heart for this woman in the pictures.

The woman who brought her into this cold world just to abandon her, leave her out to freeze. *I didn't ask to be here*, she thought to herself as the fire built up inside. "How could you walk out on your own child?" Her lips spoke her thoughts.

She found herself talking to the tombstone in front of her. "I'm sure those were never her intentions sweety. I'm just sad that you had to live this long life of lies and only she can make sense of her actions. I saw the way she stared at you after the doctors handed you over. Those eyes showed unconditional love." Marrissa attempted to take some of the pressure off Gabriela, but the more she tried to lighten the situation, the more livid Heaven became.

She didn't want to yell at her mother, but she just wanted her to stop talking. "I just want to get away from here. I don't wanna ever hear that story again. You're the only mom I know, and Josh has been my father since the beginning and I'm okay with that."

"What about Karim?" Marrissa asked.

"What about him?" Those were the perfect words for Marrissa's ears.

"You're right, let's get out of here." Marrissa stood up straight and strolled Heaven to their vehicle.

Chapter 24

Baby J

Baby J opened his eyes to see Miracle standing in front of the TV channel surfing. He had been laid up in a hospital bed for three days and his sister never left his side. The TV stopped on channel 9 News and Heaven turned the volume up a few notches. The headlines read *2 dead, 1 injured in Humboldt Park shooting.* Miracle listened closely as the news reporter went into details about the incident. "Two people were found dead including a forty-seven year old woman who was shot in the chest after a stray bullet flew through the window of her home. Another victim was identified as 18-year-old Romeo Washington. A known gang member with multiple juvenile convictions. The other victim was a lifetime resident of the Humboldt Park neighborhood. At forty-seven years old Ms. Loretta Loomis AKA Mam Luchi has been the neighborhood hero for many years ..." The news reporter went on about the tragedy and the life that the victims lived.

    Miracles' mind was stuck on the photo the reporter presented of Romeo. Her gut told her that she knew the suspect behind the shooting, but her heart didn't want to believe it. Her hands began to tremble as she tried to refocus on the TV, the reporter had switched the camera to a young boy who was the son of Mama Luchi. He just stood there crying. "No one is in custody."

Click!

Miracle hit the power button and turned around to see Baby J looking like he'd seen a ghost. "Turn it back on!" he yelled a little above his average calm voice. Miracle hit the power button on the remote, turning the TV back on. The news went into commercials.

"It's gone on commercial." Miracle held the remote towards the TV getting ready to change the channel.

"Leave it here. I just wanna see somethin'," Baby J demanded.

Miracle wondered if her baby brother was thinking the same thing, she was thinking but she couldn't have been more wrong. Baby J couldn't care less about the death of Romeo or who did it. He knew that he'd gotten what he deserved. Baby J's attention was on something totally different. He didn't know what he felt but he felt something when the little boy cried on camera. He could feel a connection to the child for some reason.

Maybe because he knows how it feels to lose a mother. "Are you ready to get up out of this place? The doctor said you can go home today," Miracle snapped Baby J out of his trance.

"For real?" Baby J asked excitedly. He was tired of being laid up in the hospital. He thought all hospitals smelled like dead people.

"Yep, they're gonna write you a prescription for pain medication and we'll be on our way. I'll just have to bring you to your follow up Friday," Miracle said as her phone started vibrating in her pocket. She pulled it out and answered. "Hey baby ... okay we'll be down in a second." Miracle hung her phone up just as the nurse came in with the discharge papers.

She allowed Miracle to sign them. "Look who's awake." She smiled at Baby J. He returned the smile, feeling a little shy. He kind of had a crush on the nurse. She looked a bit young for her occupation, yet she was gorgeous which made him think of his girlfriend Porshia. He couldn't wait to get home to call her over.

Miracle handed Baby J a bag of fresh clothes and pulled the curtains closed while he put on his underwear. Then she helped him put the remainder of his clothes on trying her best not to add salt to his injuries. Once Baby J got dressed Miracle helped him make his way to the elevator, holding her arm around his waist for support.

Baby J had slept off his medication so the pain in his ribs began to return quickly as he managed to make his way to the car that was awaiting them. Baby J got stuck in his tracks when the door opened, and Boozer jumped out of the passenger seat to help him climb into the car. Miracle felt resistance as she tried to guide him into the backseat. "I'm good," Baby J told her.

"Okay Superman, help yourself" Miracle taunted him as she freed him from her grip. She stood back to let Baby J help himself into the car but was taken aback when he began to limp away from the car. "Baby J, where are you going?" she called after him.

"Don't worry about me, I'll find my way home."

"Boy, you must be out of your mind." She followed behind him until she closed the distance between them. "What's your problem?" She reached out and grabbed his hand gently, making sure not to pull or squeeze too tight.

"Is that yo' boyfriend? Tell me it's not, Miracle." Baby J shook his head in defeat.

"Yes, that's my boyfriend, why? What's wrong?" Miracle became confused.

"Everything's wrong." Baby J found a bench at the bus stop and took a seat. He knew that the bus stop he was sitting at would lead him in the opposite direction of home. At the moment, he didn't care where the bus would take him. He just wanted to get away.

"Miracle, what's going on?" Boozer yelled from the car. Miracle held up one finger, instructing him to wait.

"Baby J talk to me, what is it?" She took a seat next to her little brother.

"Remember when I told you how I found Mama dead with a needle in her arm?"

"Uh-huh," Miracle replied. She didn't like how the conversation started so she was sure that she wasn't going to like how it ends.

"I watched *that* nigga sell mama those drugs. Miracle, he's the face I see in my dreams every night. If it wasn't for him our mama would still be alive." Baby J felt a tear trying to escape his left eye and quickly swiped it away with the back of his hand.

Ciara told me that our mama was sick. She took those drugs as an easy way out." Miracle's attempt to lighten the pressure backfired.

"It doesn't matter. He's not God. He don't get to decide whether our mama lives or dies on his watch– you know what... never mind, fuck it," Baby J cursed. He only used that language when he was very angry but never towards his big sister. "If you wanna go with him, go. I'll find a way home." Baby J struggled to his feet and limped to the opposite side of the street.

Miracle followed him. "Baby J, I'm sorry!" she called after him. Since she met her little brother her life started to make so much sense. She finally understood who she was. She wasn't about to let that go down the drain for some street thug she was loving on.

Hoonk! Hoonk!

Miracle turned around to see Boozer holding his hands in the air. She turned back around and continued to follow Baby J.

Baby J took a seat on the bench and Miracle sat beside him. "Brother. I'm sorry. You're right, he doesn't decide who lives or dies. I wasn't there so I don't know how it felt to see your own mother die with a needle stuck in her arm. And to know who sold her the drugs must be hard on you." Miracle gave Baby J a hug. "You're my little brother and no boy in this world is gonna come between us. We're gonna take the bus home and I'm never gonna talk to him again," Miracle promised as her phone rang in her pocket.

She knew exactly who was calling. She just let it ring. She was falling in love with Boozer, he was so sweet and protective of her. She didn't see this train coming until she was already hit by it. *Blood is thicker than water,* she reminded herself. As the bus approached, her phone began to ring again. This time she retrieved it and seen Boozer's name flash across the screen. She declined the call and blocked the contact. Her heart hurt more than ever as she tried to fight back tears. She knew who killed Romeo and she knew why. Boozer promised her he'd put his life on the line for her love and that's what he did.

Baby J noticed the hurt on his sister's face. He felt bad about coming between his sister and her boyfriend. He was still young, but he understood that Miracle would never have the same love as he had for their mother. If only if he could show her how many times he caught their mother crying over Miracle's old toys, begging God for forgiveness. "Sister, I'm sorry. Maybe I've been taking this thing the wrong way. In my heart I knew that my – I mean *our* mother's death was her own decision. Whatever the doctor told her that day made her feel like life was over. I saw it in her eyes, but I was too young to understand." Miracle listened as Baby continued to vent. Ciara told her about their mother's H.I.V. but that part of her life was still a secret to Baby J.

One day he would understand the full history of his twisted family but for now. Miracle's job was to keep him safe and out of the hands of DCFS.

By the time they looked up, the bus was coming to its next stop on Pulaski Rd. Miracle pulled the stopper and helped Baby J to his feet. She could tell that he had a lot on his mind, but she just wanted him to get some rest.

The Pulaski bus dropped them off at Ciara's doorstep. Baby J held the railing of the stairs as he made his way up each step. He was about to use the house keys his aunt had given him when the front door came open. Baby J was surprised to see Ciara standing in the doorway with a smile on her face. He noticed that she had company. This wasn't the normal white guy she snuck in and out of the crib. This appeared to be some sort of businessman, Baby J thought as he took a mental note of the white guy's folder along with his sharp grey suit and tie.

"Hey auntie, what chu doing here?" Baby J asked, surprised.

"Um, this is my house too, big head," she replied jokingly. Her smile was replaced when she noticed that Baby J was holding his side and Miracle seemed to be holding him up. "What's the matter witchu?" Her brow furrowed as she stepped aside and let them inside.

"Nothing, I'm okay. How long have you been home?"

"Since this morning. I tried to call you and let you know I was home, but you didn't answer."

Baby J reached in his pocket and grabbed his iPhone. He clicked the power button and nothing happened. "Phone dead," he replied.

Before turning his attention back to the white man. "Nephew this is Tom Hardnick—"

"Hi, nice to meet you. I've heard so much about you," Tom eagerly cut Ciara's sentence short, extending his hand for a friendly shake.

Baby J was hesitant. "Tom is a private investigator." Those words lit Baby J's face up like a Christmas tree as he quickly took the guy's hand and embraced him with a whole new demeanor. He'd forgotten all about his injury.

"Nice to meet you, Tom." Baby J greeted him with a smile.

"And you must be Miracle, the fantastic big sister." Tom's words made Miracle smile as well. The day was beginning to make life more pleasant because it began with hell.

"Hi, how are you?" Miracle took the investigator's hand.

"Tom is gonna work very hard to help us find your little brother. I found Tom online and he's the best in the city," Ciara assured. Baby J was so overwhelmed with excitement it felt like his lungs had collapsed. Miracle helped him over to the couch where he took a seat.

"What happened to you?" Ciara asked again as she finally noticed the bumps and bruises Baby J had on his face. She had been so excited to tell him the good news that she hadn't noticed the bandages over his left eye.

"He got jumped a few days ago. He got a broken rib but the doctor said he'll recover just fine. It's gonna take some time but he'll be back in shape to be a big brother." Miracle added.

Baby J couldn't believe his aunt had actually hired help to find his baby brother. He wished he could jump into her arms.

"Who the hell jumped you?" Ciara had the look of a gangster in her eyes as she searched Baby J's face for answers.

"Nobody auntie, I'm good, trust me." Baby J brushed her off.

He was growing up so fast, Ciara couldn't keep up. Ciara's phone rang in her pocket, she retrieved it and answered. "Hello … Hold on. I have to take this call; the investigator is going to ask you a few questions. Just answer them the best way you can, nephew," Ciara said as she disappeared into the privacy of her own room.

The last thing Baby J heard was, "Girl, where have you been?" He only knew of one 'her' his aunt could be referring to but none of that mattered. His only concern at that moment was to help find his little brother. "Let's start off with a name," he heard the investigator say.

Chapter 25

Karim

Karim parked his car in the driveway before deading the engine. He blew up Marrissa's line on his way home, but he had no luck reaching her. He became confused when he noticed that her car was missing from the driveway. Last time he checked, she didn't have any plans.

Karim walked up the steps to his home with his mind racing, Marrissa would've at least returned his calls. This whole missing in action thing was new to him. Karim twisted the doorknob, surprisingly it came right open. He scratched his head as his mind wondered. Stepping into his house he didn't notice anything out of place.

He took a detour through the house, checking all the closets and bedrooms. He didn't realize anything was missing until he reached the master bedroom. All the drawers were wide open. Right away he noticed that all of his clothes were left untouched but there were no signs of Marrissa's belongings. The closet had been emptied of Marrissa's property. Karim wanted to know what the hell was going on.

He spotted a napkin on his bedroom dresser. He grabbed the napkin and read the note. *'See you in hell'*. That made his blood boil. It was one thing for Marrissa to pack her things and leave with his child but the note on the napkin was crossing the line.

Last time he received a note like that, a woman he loved had killed herself on his behalf. He couldn't think of what he could've possibly done to make Marrissa so angry. He pulled out his phone and texted her. '*What type of sick ass game are u playing?*'

His message didn't deliver, in fact it appeared green instead of the normal blue apple message. *Red flag!* he thought as he dialed the number private, figuring that she must've blocked his number.

'*The number you've reached has been disconnected -*'

Karim ended the call. He was becoming furious by the second. He paced back and forth for minutes, thinking of a solution. Finally, he unlocked his phone again and dialed Heaven's number with hopes of getting through. He held his breath as the phone rang.

"Hello," Heaven answered.

"Hey, baby girl, where's yo' mama?"

"Um, she's in the room with the doctor."

"The doctor? What doctor? What's going on?" Karim asked curiously. Marrissa didn't tell him anything about a doctor's appointment.

"Um, she says we're moving back into our own home, but I can still talk to you if I chose to." Heaven sounded sad yet satisfied. She appreciated her mother being considerate of her feelings. Karim might have abandoned her in the past but over the past few months he'd been a great father to her. With Josh, she felt loved but finding out the truth made everything make sense.

"Can I talk to her?" Karim asked. The phone line went silent for a moment before Heaven spoke again.

"She said she doesn't want to talk, I gotta go." Click!" Heaven ended the call, leaving Karim more lost than before.

He grabbed his car keys and headed out the door. Heaven said they were at the doctor. Marrissa only went to one hospital that he knew of.

Karim jumped in his Mercedes Benz and went looking for his missing lady.

Chapter 26

Tay B

Tay B walked into Timo's room feeling anxious. A year ago, his best friend attempted suicide. Blackboy had fallen off the face of the earth since the day the tragedy happened so the chances of him knowing Timo had survived was slim to none.

Tay B had been laying low. He now knew that Timo had woken up, the jakes would be snooping around, looking for answers. With Blackboy missing, Tay B guessed that he snitched for a 'get out of jail free' card. He had been planning his get back for this day.

Tay B slid back the curtains and smiled, "Look who's alive and kicking." He grabbed Timo's hand. Timo hadn't fully recovered but he was fully awake at least. Tay B pulled up a chair and sat beside Timo's bed.

"Man, I was sick when I heard what you did, skud. On BD I was lost without you. And I ain't seen that nigga Blackboy since he got bumped off. He damn sho' ain't in the system. That nigga gotta be feeding them people lies because they been snooping around all at Granny's crib. Push come to shove imma put that shit right back on him. I told you that nigga been moving funny since he came back from Texas." Tay B talked while Timo could do nothing but listen. Here and there his brows would furrow, indicating that he understood the foul shit he was hearing.

For the last few days Timo couldn't understand what he was doing alive. *I know I died for sho. I even saw the light people be talking about.*
The flashbacks of Stacy ending her own life had him catching sweat chills. Sleep wouldn't come easy for him.
"I ain't believe it when they posted on Facebook that you woke up. I had to come see for myself. You better not ever let another bitch make you feel like that." Tay B noticed Timo face frowned up. "My bad skud, no disrespect," he apologized, "but just know them people gone come looking for answers as soon as you're able to talk. You can either tell them the truth— which they might or might not believe depending on what Blackboy and them bitches told them— or you can point the finger at Blackboy and save yourself from a long trip to the joint."
Tay B gave his friend something to really think about. Deep down Timo didn't want to believe that Blackboy was trying to set him up but he asked himself, *Where the fuck is he then?*
Timo wasn't cut from the same cloth as the rats and neither was Tay B, but sometimes you had to think like a rat to trap them. "I love you, bro. I'll be waiting for you to come home. Let me bounce before they try to catch a mufucka slipping." Tay B pounded Timo's hand and threw his hoodie over his head before leaving Timo's room.
He walked to the nearest elevator and pressed the silver button on the wall, calling his ride back to the lobby. He watched the numbers over his head light up as the elevator got closer. 8...7...6. The elevator was a stop away when Tay B heard, "Octavius Bennett." The voice was so close Tay B felt the heat from the person breathing on the back of his neck, making the hair on hwer neck stand up. *Fuck,* he cursed himself in the back of his mind as he felt a strong hand grab his wrist roughly and spin him around until he was facing two detectives. He heard the elevator door open but there was no point in running. He had nowhere to run.

"Relax kid, we just wanna ask you a few questions," Detective Diaz assured. "You're not under arrest; we just have to detain you." Detective Diaz placed Tay B's hands behind his back and cuffed him.

Down at the precinct Tay B sat handcuffed to a bench for what seemed like hours before the same two detectives came into the room. They uncuffed him and pulled up a chair for him to have a seat.

"Where you been, Mr. Bennett? Or should we just call you Tay B? Which one do you prefer?" Detective Mason ruffled Tay B's feathers a little bit.

"Call me what you want, just don't call me collect." Tay B played the tough guy role but on the inside his stomach was doing flips.

"Oh, we got us a wise guy here," Detective Mason chuckled. His presence made Tay B sick. His aura screamed *dirty cop* And if Tay B wasn't careful he could get himself in a lot of trouble. The detective laid out those same photos he presented to Mr. Hobbs. Tay B gave the photos a quizzical stare. "We know that you know exactly why you're here, so we gone cut the bullshit, alright?" Tay B just stared at the detective like he was dumb. Detective Mason continued his approach. "These girls here," he pointed to a picture of Heaven, Stacy, and April. "They told us that you were present the day Stacy Lomax was killed, so tell me, what exactly went down."

Killed? Tay B repeated in his head. "She wasn't killed; she shot herself."

"Bullshit! Is that the story you and your little friend rehearsed? Is that why he went into hiding the moment he posted bail?" Detective Mason thought he was turning the pressure on. What he didn't know was that Tay B hadn't seen

Blackboy since he was shoved into the backseat of a squad car.

Now that Tay B knew that his friend wasn't snitching, and the officers were just fishing for information he began to feel more comfortable. As a matter of fact, now was his chance to prove he had balls like those gangstas he'd seen on television. "I don't got shit else to say to you dick heads. Call my lawyer," Tay B said with is chest poked out.

"You're not the one who needs a lawyer. We found her body at your friend's house with the murder weapon with his prints on it. He probably was pissed that she was pregnant, tried to talk her into getting an abortion, then when she refused he shot her. Ain't that right, Octavius?" Detective Mason pressed.

Tay B was laughing on the inside. *This dumb ass nigga couldn't be more wrong in his life.* "Then he turned into a pussy and tried to end himself, huh?" Detective Mason continued.

"Look, you heard what I said: Call my lawyer." Tay B was worried about Timo. The picture Detective Mason was painting would stick in court, especially if these two detectives lucked up and got one of the girls to agree with the story. But for right now they had nothing or else someone would've been gone through processing at Cook County jail by now.

Detective Mason became frustrated and left the room. The other detective stood up and followed but before he left Tay B alone, he turned around and winked. Tay B thought it was weird, but he had a good feeling about it.

***

Detective Mason planned to let Tay B starve for seventy-two hours for his poor cooperation but Detective Diaz snuck him McDonald's every morning. All Tay B could think of was the trouble his friend could be in and the whereabouts of Blackboy. No one knew where he was.

Tay B felt bad for doubting his loyalty. He had to make a trip back to the hospital and clear Blackboy's name. He silently prayed that Timo stayed asleep for a little while longer while he found Blackboy and got something figured out. What he didn't know was Timo had been pretending to be unresponsive for the last couple of days. He didn't want the police coming in to question him. Timo had no plans of ever answering any questions. If he had it his way, one day those detectives would show up and he'd be gone.

"Bennett, let's go." The morning shift officer woke Tay B up from a deep sleep. It was three days later, and Tay B felt like he'd been in the station for weeks.

"Where I'm going?"

"Home unless you wanna stay another night."

Tay B jumped to his feet like he had ants in his pants and threw his arms into the sleeves of his shirt. It was time to go and he wouldn't spend another minute in jail.

Chapter 27

Tiffany

Blood was shedding all through Texas between Chapo's men and Lalo's army and it was all because of Tiffany. She had framed Lalo when she broke into one of Chapo's trap houses and picked him for his drugs and money. She had been watching Chapo's every move like a hawk. That made her mission a piece of cake. Tiffany knew when Chapo was having sex, when he was showering; she even knew when he was taking a shit.

Much like Chindo, Chapo was a sucker for a fine woman with a phat ass. Tiffany took the money she stole from Chapo and hired some help. She thought about taking her son and getting the hell out of Texas, but Chapo had done some cruel shit to her and she was seeking revenge. Chapo cursed her with a drug habit that she couldn't shake. Tiffany found herself nodding off in a local crack house whenever she wasn't out plotting.

One night at a bar, Tiffany met a woman named Netta. Netta was light yellow with brown eyes and deep dimples. Her hair was styled into a mohawk. She had a tattoo of a butterfly on the left side of her face. Not only was she drop dead gorgeous, but she was also unique. In fact, that was the name she gave Chapo when they first met. She thinks the name gives her a little more flavor.

Tiffany gave Netta twenty thousand dollars to get close to Chapo, closer than she have ever been to anyone in her life. She wanted Netta to learn about his whole operation so she could rob him blind, then kill him. She promised to break Netta off with a half of million once the job was done. Tiffany started to get a bad feeling about Netta; either she was playing her part better than Jada Pickett in the movie *Set It Off* or she was falling for Chapo, and if that's the case, Tiffany was a dead woman walking.

Tiffany has been calling Netta for two days, trying to pull off her next caper. Each time Netta would decline her call and reply with a text. This was a big problem for Tiffany. She had to think of a plan B. Killing Netta would serve no purpose. She needed to make Netta feel spiteful towards Chapo in order to put her mission back on the right track.

Tiffany called the only person she could trust, a person who was just as sexy as Netta. She called Ciara and after hours of begging she convinced her friend to fly out to Texas. Once Ciara laid her sex game down on Chapo he'll forget that Unique ever existed.

Tiffany stood outside the airport with a blonde wig on and sunglasses that covered her entire face. She waited for Ciara's plane to arrive. She had to will herself away from the drugs for the moment. Although it was nearly impossible, she managed to stand her ground.

Tiffany couldn't control her excitement as she spotted Ciara walking through the glass doors. She stood up and ran over to her best friend and hugged her tight.

She noticed that Ciara had lost some weight but with the mini skirt and halter top she sported, Tiffany would've thought she'd been in the gym if she didn't know any better. But she knew her friend all too well. However, she wasn't in no position to ask questions but of course the questions began the moment Ciara laid eyes on her friend. "Oh my gosh, what happened to you?" Ciara asked in disbelief. She wanted to cry for her friend.

Tiffany had given her a brief summary of the last year of her life, but Ciara couldn't imagine what life had done to her until she finally laid eyes on her. "This is what he did to me. He locked me inside a basement and turned me out to heroin and crack while all his workers ran in me raw whenever their dicks got hard. On top of that he tried to kill me while my son was out here cooking up weight and taking over the city for him." Tiffany let a tear slip under her sunglasses. Ciara wiped her tears away.

"Girl, you know we stronger than that, real bitches don't cry over spilled milk, we milk the fuckin cow for more."

Tiffany smiled; her friend was right. *'This would be the sweetest revenge ever,'* she thought as she led Ciara to a Taxi. In the back seat, Tiffany reached in her purse and handed Ciara a brown paper bag filled with money. Ciara was told to buy a fancy car and purchase a condo on the rich side of town. Of course, Chapo didn't care about her money, but he would prefer a woman with class to match her ass.

"When I'm done with him, he ain't gone wanna see another pussy," Ciara boasted and they shared a laugh for old times' sake.

***

Boozer

It had been months since Boozer heard from Miracle. He couldn't understand what went wrong. He didn't want to ask but he had a feeling it was because of the elderly woman who was killed when Boozer found out Mama Luchi was shot and killed, he became devastated. The night he was shooting recklessly without aiming he never imagined an innocent lady being caught in the crossfire.

Boozer couldn't eat, couldn't sleep. He needed Miracle next to him. She was the only person that could reduce his pain.

Boozer was shooting jump shots at the park when he heard a single gunshot ring out from the alley behind him. He thought his conscience was playing tricks on him until he heard another shot followed by the sound of tires screeching. After killing Romeo, no one caught wind of Boozer's participation, so he went back to his normal routine. At least that's what he thought.

A black Tahoe came speeding out the alley. Boozer ran for cover as shots started to ring out, ricocheting off the fence, park bench, and even the swings on the playground as Boozer fought to escape. His heart was pounding as he laid flat on his stomach in a puddle of water as the sprinklers drenched his back side. He stayed in that position until the shots went silent and the truck sped off into traffic. He heard screaming come from the alley and jumped to his feet, racing towards the commotion. His thoughts went to Mama Luchi. He prayed that another innocent woman or child hadn't been hit by a stray bullet.

Boozer jumped the fence and ran into a small crowd of people surrounding a motionless body. Boozer's heart dropped into the pit of his stomach when he noticed who the screaming was coming from. He stepped closer to see his auntie Ella holding her son Derrick's head close to her chest like he was a small child, rocking him back and forth as he slowly crossed over to the other side.

Boozer wanted to comfort her, but he knew their relationship was more loss than love. His aunt Ella disagreed with his lifestyle, so she felt uncomfortable with letting Derrick hang out with his cousin. Besides playing the video game, Derrick spent most of his time attending to the backyard he used as a shelter for stray Pitbull's he found roaming the streets.

Every now and then he would sneak and shoot hoops at the park with his cousin or smoke a blunt or two but that's as far as Derrick's life goes. Boozer knew that the moment she laid eyes on him, he would be the blame. What reason would anybody have to kill her sweet baby boy? He didn't claim a street gang or carry a pistol for protection.

Ella always told her son that Boozer would get him killed one day. Now she was holding on to him as his life slipped away. What Ella should've told him was that these streets don't love nobody. Protect your peace with your mind, protect your life with your nine.

Boozer slipped out of the crowd with his head down. God doesn't make you pay for your sins with your life. He makes you pay in tears. A million salty tears, that's what Boozer shed that night as he and his homies got wasted.

Bizzy decided to go to the studio that night and record a song for Derrick. He wanted to let his soul bleed through the mic for his childhood friend. Somewhere between laying down a hook and rehearsing the song ended up dragging the three stooges back to the closet to suit up. They drove around looking for answers but so far, the streets had none.

Boozer logged out of his Facebook. He couldn't handle seeing his cousins face down his entire news feed. The news labeled it a robbery gone wrong, but Boozer knew all too well to believe that sweet little lie.

The only way to ease the pain is to give it to somebody else, Boozer thought as his phone chirped, indicating that he had a text message. He retrieved his phone to power it off when he saw Miracle's name flash across the screen. He opened the message and read:

I'm sorry for your loss. My heart goes out to u and the family. I know I'm the last person u expected to hear from, but I love u <3 <3.

Boozer powered his phone off and pulled his ski mask over his face, now wasn't the time to make up, it was time to avenge his little cousin. *Until we meet again*, Boozer drew an invisible cross from his head to his chest and kissed his Glock 40 before he hopped out blasting.

Chapter 28

Heaven

Marrissa took Heaven to church to give a special thanks to the Lord. Heaven's ability to walk had improved and she was now moving with the help of a walker instead of a wheelchair. Heaven now felt comfortable enough to attend school. Since she'd missed her entire freshman year she would have to repeat the ninth grade.

The next morning the two of them were at Orr High School getting Heaven enrolled. Heaven caught butterflies as she stepped inside the huge school. She was nervous but she was ready to interact with the world again.

Marrissa and Heaven made their way to the dean's office. They were greeted by Mr. Pool, the school's principal for ten years and counting.

"Hello, how may I help you?"

"I'm here to enroll my daughter in school, do you guys have space for one more," Marrissa asked with a smile on her face.

"Certainly do. Do you have her physical? And a copy of her transcript from the last school she attended?"

Marrissa handed over a copy of Heaven's eighth grade transcript from elementary school and the principal passed them over to an assistant.

"And finally, I'll need a copy of your driver's license."

"Sure." Marrissa handed over her identification and Mr. Pool started the enrollment.

After he was done, he walked back over to where Marrissa and Heaven had taken a seat and handed them some papers and two black and gold uniform shirts.

"Welcome to Orr High school. When should I be expecting you?"

School had started two weeks ago. Heaven had all the clothes and supplies she needed so there was no point of waiting any longer.

"Tomorrow," Heaven answered.

"Well in that case, let's get your ID picture taken."

Heaven took her photo for her school ID. She was anxious to start her first year of high school. She was no longer in contact with April, and she needed new friends. She tried reaching out to her old friend, but April's number had been changed. *Maybe her mom didn't want the cops contacting them like they did me,* she thought. *Or maybe her mom thinks I'm a bad friend for taking Stacy's picture instead of talking some sense into her.*

Heaven still had dreams of Stacy being alive, only she had that same bullet hole in the right side of her head. Heaven tried to embrace her nightmares and talk to Stacy but it's like Stacy believed that she was still alive. At least that's what Heaven read on Google.

Heaven showed up to school the next day with her long hair styled into kinky twists. Her beige uniform pants were fitted to show off her curves and she sported black and yellow Jordan 14s to match her uniform shirt.

Even with her scars and bruises from top to bottom, Heaven knew she was beautiful, flaws and all.

Heaven followed the rest of the kids through the metal detector when it was her turn to step through, she became confused. She didn't know how she was gonna step through the metal detector with her walker which was all metal.

"Just step around sweetheart," Ms. Theresa the school security guard instructed.

Heaven pushed her backpack in the scanner and stepped around the metal detector. "I'll just have to wand you then you can be on your way. Are you new here?" The security guard made small talk as she scanned Heaven.

"Yes, today is my first day," Heaven said proudly. She had no reason to be ashamed.

Judging by the students she saw walking into school she didn't even need legs to run with the best of them. That's until her eyes landed on this one girl who seemed to be staring right at her. This girl was beautiful, and she knew it but she didn't seem to take advantage of it. Her attitude was friendly and she kept a smile plastered on her face. She sported the same Js as Heaven. *Good taste gir*l, Heaven thought. The girl placed her backpack into the scanner and stepped through the metal detector. "Hey Ma!" she spoke to Ms. Theresa.

"Hey daughter, that perfume smells hot, what is it?"

"Love Spell. Here…" the girl grabbed her backpack and retrieved a bottle of fragrance. She popped the top and sprayed Ms. Theresa twice. "Now these lil boys gone be all over you."

"I know, right."

Heaven closed her eyes and inhaled the scent. *Love Spell. I've got to tell my mom about this.*

"Aww you like the way it smells too?" Heaven opened her eyes to see the girl talking to her.

"Uh, yeah it's fire." Heaven smiled shyly.

The girl pointed the bottle at Heaven's shirt. "Want some?"

"Uh, sure," Heaven accepted. The girl sprayed Heaven twice and Heaven closed her eyes again and inhaled deeply before holding it in. "Thank you," she smiled.

"No problem, girl, nice shoes."

Heaven blushed at the compliment.

"Is this your first year?"

"First day actually," Heaven replied as she made her way towards the stairs.

"What class are you going to?"

Good question, Heaven thought as she pulled her schedule from her back pocket. "Um, I have social studies, room 204."

"I can escort you to class if you like," the girl offered.

Heaven never thought about how she would make it to and from each class with no elevator. "That would be perfect, I don't know my way around yet," Heaven admitted.

"No biggie. I'm Miracle by the way. What's your name?"

Miracle, that's a beautiful name, Heaven, thought before replying. "My name is Heaven."

"That name fits you," Miracle complimented

"So does yours."

"Thanks."

Miracle walked Heaven to her class and when first period ended, she was waiting outside her classroom to walk her to her next class. Heaven later found out that Miracle was the superstar of the school's basketball team.

Miracle became the big sister she never had. Their taste in shoes were identical. They sported every pair of Jordans on the same day at the same time. Heaven even matched shoes with Miracle at her basketball games. Other girls whispered about Heaven behind her back, but it was all jealous talk. Heaven had overcome her fears and became comfortable with the hand she was dealt.

Miracle managed to buy a car so she drove Heaven home every day after school. At first Marrissa was hesitant about letting her daughter hang out with the senior but realized that Miracle was a good role model. Heaven never missed a day of school, and her grades were on point. Marissa seen joy written on her daughter's face when she came in from hanging out with Miracle. She hadn't seen that facial expression since Heaven lost her friend Stacy, and April had gone ghost on her.

Heaven made plans to visit Stacy's gravesite, she was just waiting for the right time to face her demons. Miracle promised her she would take her when she was good and ready. In Heaven's heart she knew the time was approaching but for now she'll continue to heal physically so that she can walk without her walker.

Chapter 29

Ciara

"Don't be shy, grab whatever you like. This money here goes a long way," Chapo told Ciara as they toured Lenox Mall in Atlanta where Ciara said she was from.

Chapo had been begging to fly down to ATL and visit Ciara since the day she put it down on him. That night Ciara got high off coke and imagined that Chapo was her former lover, Juan, and she fucked his brains out. She put it down so good that Chapo had almost forgotten Unique's name completely.

One day he slipped up and called Unique Ci-Ci while they were having sex. Unique's world came crashing down. She went crying to Tiffany who pretended to feel remorseful. Little did Unique know it was all part of the game plan.

Ciara fought hard to keep up with the lie she sold to Chapo. She had rented a condo with the help of Tiffany and decorated it nicely. Chapo seemed to know the city more than her: he took her to the finest restaurants and shopping plazas.

Ciara didn't expect him to be so sharp when it came to Atlanta. Thank God for Google maps or else Ciara would be in big trouble. She would've never been able to find her way back home.

"I told you I can buy myself nice things, you don't have to buy my love. I'm already falling for you," Ciara lied.

Chapo had seen the gold digger in Unique from a mile away. After a long night of bed rocking sex, Chapo would fill her purse up and send her on her way. He was stuck to her like glue in the beginning because he never had anyone that looked deep into his soul while swallowing his entire dick. Unique amazed him with her tricks until Ciara came and snatched his soul completely, taking his dick to the back of her throat while her tongue massaged his balls. Ciara made Chapo take freaky to another level. She sucked his toes while riding his dick reverse cowboy-style.

"With the things you do to me, you should never have to spend a dime," Chapo spoke truthfully.

Ciara smiled on the inside at how brainwashed she had Chapo. He wanted to spend more and more time with her which made it difficult to keep up with her lies. She was beginning to leave Baby J at home by himself more than usual. Miracle promised to look after him, but she was no more than a big sister, letting Baby J have company in his bedroom and friends spend nights on school days. Baby J basically had the house to himself.

Ciara did a lot of traveling between states over the past few months. One time she even got frisked when the airport security suspected her of smuggling drugs. She told Tiffany that she would have to cut ties with Chapo and take care of her business back home.

Ciara had to refill her prescription every two weeks and attend her doctor's appointments twice a month along with making sure her nephew was doing okay. She needed a break from Chapo's fast lifestyle even though she needed the getaway. Chapo spoiled her rotten with nothing but the best, from her clothes to the Benz 4 Matic he had her pushing. He never bought Unique a car even though he did flourish her with enough money to purchase her own.

Chapo's bank account was $20,000 lighter when they left the mall. Each time he swiped his card Ciara whispered sweet nothings in his ear that made his dick stand up.

Chapo pressed a button on his car remote and the trunk of his Aston Martin opened. He threw all of Ciara's bags into the trunk before opening the passenger door for her. Ciara climbed in with the aura of a proud wife instead of a mistress. Chapo climbed into the driver's seat and zoomed out of the parking lot, rushing to get to Ciara's place.

The entire ride to Ciara's condo, Chapo's phone rang silently in his pocket. He knew it was Unique blowing up his line, so he didn't bother answering. The way Ciara made him feel, he didn't care if he never saw Unique again.

Ciara opened the door to her condo and kicked off her high heels before striding across the living room to grab a bottle of Hennessy from her bar. She told Chapo she loved Hennessy because it goes straight to her pussy. Chapo shipped her enough Hennessy to open a liquor store.

Ciara grabbed two glass cups from her bar and filled them to the top. She turned around to see Chapo staring with lust in his eyes. In his hand he had a small sandwich bag filled with pure cocaine. Ciara saw the hunger in his eyes as she strutted back across the room, pulling her sundress over her head. Her nipples were rock hard as she pictured Juan standing there with his dick in his hand. She handed Chapo a cup of Hennessy before gulping her entire cup. Chapo followed the leader, letting the brown magic burn through his chest as it settled in. Ciara took the bag of coke from him and pushed him onto the loveseat. "We ain't making it to the bedroom tonight," she cooed as she dropped to her knees.

She dug her hand into the bag and pinched a few fingers full of coke. She spread it up the length of Chapo's rod before snorting back and forth until it disappeared. The coke went straight to her brain, giving her a rush instantly. Her nose tingled as she took Chapo's manhood into her mouth. The leftover coke residue made her tongue numb as she deepthroated his full nine inches. She tightened the muscles in the back of her throat as Chapo's dick rested in the middle of her neck.

Chapo tried to grab her head so she could show mercy on him but she removed his hand. Chapo felt his nut building up from his toes, rushing to the tip of his dick, until he couldn't hold it in any longer. His cum shot straight down Ciara's throat. His pole was so deep in her throat that she couldn't taste it until she pulled him out of her mouth and licked the tip clean as Chapo's rod became tender. He wanted to cry out for help. It was now his turn to feast.

Ciara laid down on her back and sprinkled coke on both of her nipples, down the middle of her stomach, and right above her soaking wet juice box. Chapo took his nose and traced the lines. After he snorted the last drop, he went back up to play cleanup with his tongue, sucking her titties one by one then working his way down to her belly button, then her clit. Chapo moved his tongue like a snake. He pulled the hood of Ciara's clit back with his thumb and made love to her clitoris. He stuck two fingers into her pussy, stroking them in and out until two turned into three. Ciara started shaking until her pussy started to squirt all over Chapo's face. She had given Chapo a wristband to her water park.

Chapo felt his manhood stand at full attention again. He flipped Ciara over until she was positioned in the doggy-style position. She expected to feel Chapo's dick filling her up but instead she felt him sprinkling coke around her asshole followed by his tongue swiping up and down. Ciara tried to crawl away; it was her turn to beg for mercy. Chapo grabbed her by the hips and pulled her back roughly, making her cheeks clap in his face as he devoured her booty hole. He had Ciara's ass spread wide open; his face was buried between her voluptuous ass cheeks. Ciara moaned a sweet harmony that made Chapo's mind run wild. She made the type of noises he'd only heard on porn videos where the ladies did it more for the cameras then the actual sex.

Chapo came up for air after ten minutes of Ciara's all-you-can-eat buffet. He grabbed his dick and guided it into Ciara's center slowly, savoring the moment. Her pussy was warm, wet, and slippery. She used her vaginal muscles to grip Chapo's dick as he deep stroked. Ciara didn't want to make love; she wanted it rough. "Don't play with it. Tear this pussy up!" she squealed.

Chapo took the belt from his pants and tied it around Ciara's neck. He wrapped the other end around his left hand to get a better grip. He pulled back on the belt causing it to tighten up around her neck as he drilled her from behind, smacking her ass with his other hand. He made Ciara's knees buckle as he hit her g-spot. She hadn't had sex this good in a long time. "Mmhm, just like that. Eeww, fuck this pussyyy! Dadddyyy!" Ciara orgasm was reaching its peak as she became lightheaded from shortage of breath which made her climax more intense. When she came, she felt it through her whole fuckin' body.

Smack! Smack! Smack!

Chapo smacked her ass while he fucked like a jack rabbit. He came shortly after her and they both collapsed right there on the floor, exhausted but in bliss.

Chapter 30

Tiffany

Tiffany woke up in the middle of the evening to the sound of her phone ringing. She had slipped off into a drug induced coma. She tried her best to fight the urge to get high, but her attempts were useless. Each time she found herself nodding in the safety of her own home.

Tiffany reached for her cell phone and answered the call. "Hello?" Her voice was raspy as she spoke through the receiver.

Unique's voice came through the speaker. She was talking so fast that Tiffany could barely understand her. Unique was two notches passed pissed as she spilled every dirty word in the book.

"Wait! First of all, slow down for a second girl." Tiffany waited for silence before she continued. "Now start from the beginning... what happened?"

"This motherfucker Chapo is somewhere doing something he ain't got no business doing. I been blowing up this nigga phone all day and he hasn't returned not one call..." Unique went on and on with her problems as Tiffany pretended to listen. Meanwhile, she was texting Ciara trying to figure out why she hadn't returned her calls. One of Tiffany's plans seemed to be working while the other one might be falling apart. Ciara seemed to be forgetting the game plan just like Unique had done. Tiffany was becoming frustrated. She expected Unique to jump ship sooner or later but now her best friend was falling for the enemy. "Did you hear me, girl?" Unique asked after noticing Tiffany's long moment of silence.

"Yeah, um ... Where you think he at?" Tiffany asked. She had a plan that would take the top off the war she started for sure.

"That nigga been chasing all up behind some out of town jump off, and the bitch ain't even all that. But he ain't finna treat me like no motherfuckin groupie. I got something for both of they ass." Unique was becoming angrier by the second as she thought about the man she thought was hers ditching her for something new.

Meanwhile Tiffany just wanted to know whether Chapo was in Atlanta or in Texas, that would make a big difference. "So, you think he went out of town with the bitch?"

"I know he's out of town with the bitch. I seen his plane ticket and I went to his house; every car the nigga own is in the driveway collecting dust. Imma kill both of they asses if I ever catch 'em! Mark my word," Unique vowed.

Tiffany had heard enough small talk; it was time to pull a big trick out the hat. "Girl, let me put on some clothes, I'm gone call you right back, stay by the phone," Tiffany lied before ending the call.

A while later, Tiffany pulled into the driveway of Chapo's mansion in Houston, Texas. She had gotten Chapo's address from Unique before she abandoned the mission. She deaded the engine of her Jaguar that she leased under a false identity that she purchased. The Jaguar blended right in with Chapo's collection of cars spread throughout his driveway. Tiffany never told Unique her true reason for keeping tabs on Chapo. Unique thought Tiffany was planning a robbery, but Tiffany was interested in taking something far more valuable than money. Something irreplaceable. She wanted his life. Not only *his* life but she wanted every individual that took part in Chapo's sick act of revenge. Tiffany suffered many months of abuse and rape along with forcefully becoming an addict to a drug she'd never imagined experiencing. That alone gave her the will power to hunt down her enemies like a trained assassin.

Tiffany pulled a ski mask over her head and climbed out of her vehicle, creeping around Chapo's mansion like a thief in the night. It was becoming pitch black outside as the moon became the only source of light. Tiffany reached into the duffle bag she was carrying and grabbed a wire cutter before disassembling Chapo's ADT system. She placed the wire cutter back into her bag and grabbed a crowbar to break into the mansion through the kitchen. Her plan was to take anything of value and set the place on fire. She crept through the kitchen in silence, checking for any signs of a safe. She made her way into the massive living room and searched the wall for a light. Her hand landed on the light switch when she heard clapping.

Suddenly the lights came on. Tiffany's heart dropped when she realized she wasn't alone. "You're pretty clever for a crackhead," a voice boomed over her head, causing her to turn her attention towards the direction in which the voice was coming from. Her eyes landed on Milo, Chapo's oldest son. He was walking down the stairs at a slow pace. Tiffany noticed that both of his hands were empty. Her hand instantly went for the gun she had inside her duffle bag. Her hand gripped the handle of the Glock just as she felt the pressure of a hard object being pressed firmly against her head.

"Drop it bitch," another voice demanded. Tiffany released her grip on the gun and let the duffle bag fall to the floor. Her mask was snatched off and she was shoved in the back. She slowly turned around until she was standing face to face with Unique. The feeling of fear was replaced by anger as Tiffany stared into the eyes of the snake. Tiffany sucked her jaws in to building up as much saliva as she could.

"You should've left when you had the chan–"
Twuuh! Tiffany spat right in her mouth.

Unique backhanded Tiffany with her pistol, instantly drawing blood from her mouth. Tiffany went to tackle Unique when she felt herself being yanked by her hair and slammed to the floor. Milo had a long line of rope in his right hand. He began to tie Tiffany's ankles together before attempting to tie her hands behind her back. Tiffany knew that if she let him tie her up she was as good as dead. She screamed loudly as she wrestled herself free from Milo's grip.

"Bitch, come help me! Why are you just staring?" Milo yelled at Unique as he was being overpowered by the strong black woman.

Unique landed a field goal kick to Tiffany's jaw, causing a cracking sound. Tiffany went into a temporary coma as Milo proceeded to hogtie her. "Let's see you fight back now crack whore,"

Unique snickered at Milo's cockiness.

He got the nerve to be talking shit after he just got done struggling with a female, she thought. "Give me the hammer," Milo demanded as he held out his hand for Unique to surrender her weapon.

"Of course." *Boom!* Unique put a bullet right in the middle of Milo's forehead. "That's for calling me a bitch." Unique stepped right over Milo's dead body as blood spilled from his forehead and soaked into Chapo's Persian rug.

Tiffany tried to wiggle herself free as her mind went to her son. She couldn't die at the hands of Unique; she came too far to give up so easily. If anyone deserved to stop her heart from beating it would be Chapo himself, not some lowlife delusional whore from the strip club. "I wonder how Chapo's gonna feel when he finds out it was *you* who's been setting him up, igniting the war between him and Lalo. I know you're the reason why my man is somewhere in Atlanta getting laid with that out of town trash, I've been following you. At first, I thought it was you who was fuckin' my man but I knew Chapo wouldn't stoop that low," Unique snarled.

This bitch got some nerve. Tiffany stared Unique up and down with rage in her eyes.

"I wonder what he's gonna do to your lil' friend when I tell him she's helping you trap him, hitting all his spots. She'll never make it out alive once I tell him you put a bullet in his piece of shit son's head. This should be fun." Unique grinned as she pulled out her cell phone.

Tiffany felt the rope sawing through her flesh as she tried to wiggle herself free. She couldn't believe how far Unique was willing to go for Chapo's love. In Unique's mind she figured a move like this would earn her a spot in his heart for sure.

Unique dialed Chapo's number and placed the phone to her ear. Instantly, she was forwarded to his voicemail. She became frustrated as she ended the call and stuffed her phone back in her pocket. The ringing of Milo's phone in his pocket gave Unique an idea as she flipped him over onto his back before digging into his pocket to retrieve his phone.

The name across the screen read *Lil brother.* Unique knew it had to be Ceasar so she declined the call before dialing Chapo's number from Milo's phone and pressing the call icon. She guessed that she'd have a better chance at reaching him if she called from his son's phone.

Chapter 31

Chapo

Chapo laid stretched out across Ciara's bed while she slept peacefully on his chest. He could no longer sleep since he woke up from his nightmare. In his heart, he knew something was wrong, he just couldn't put his finger on it. The cocaine added to his paranoia as he tried to calm himself down. The vibration of his phone made Chapo remove himself from bed to take the call. He didn't want to disturb Ciara while she was sleeping so peacefully. Chapo read Milo's name on the screen and answered, "Hola."

A voice that didn't belong to his son but was very familiar yelled through the receiver causing Chapo to pull the phone away from his ear and step out of the room.

Once he was sure that he was out of earshot from Ciara he spoke again, this time in English. "Hello … What are you talking about? Where's my son?" Chapo became disturbed as he tried to figure out why Unique had his son's cell phone and why she sounded so distressed.

"Chapo, just listen to me, you're sleeping with the enemy. The bitch you're laying up with is helping Tiffany set you up."

At the mention of Tiffany's name Chapo's skin turned red with fire. He went deaf momentarily as Unique embedded her story in his brain.

"Tiffany? What are you talking about?"

"You know what I'm talking about. The same Tiffany that survived a gunshot that was supposed to put her out of her misery. She's been out for blood and your son was first to pay his debt."

"What did she do to my boy?" Chapo was now covered in sweat as he tried to remain quiet in hopes of keeping Ciara asleep. If what Unique was saying was true, Ciara was in for a rude awakening.

"She killed him, Chapo. Have you been listening to anything I said?"

"How do you know all this?" Chapo ignored her question.

"I was riding past your house, and I saw another car parked in your driveway so I decided to see what bitch had you declining my calls," Unique lied, "but once I got close up I noticed that your backdoor was open. As soon as I entered the kitchen I heard a gunshot."

Chapo was painting a picture in his head as Unique fed him lie after lie.

"So, where is she?" Chapo finally asked the million dollar question.

"She's right here, tied up. I'm just waiting on your word before I smoke this bitch."

"No, I want her to listen to her friend scream."

Chapo went to the kitchen and grabbed a butcher knife from Ciara's knife set. He walked back to Ciara's room quietly with the butcher knife behind his back. Ciara was still sound asleep the same way he'd left her. Chapo's eyes scanned the room in search of something useful. He noticed a long white extension cord trailing from the back of Ciara's flat screen to the wall. Chapo disconnected the extension cord from the socket in the wall before pulling the cord from the TV out of its receiver. He took the long cord and wrapped it around Ciara's ankles. He tied the cord in a tight knot causing Ciara to move but not wake up.

It wasn't until he tied the second knot when she jumped from her sleep. Before Ciara got a chance to yell, Chapo was sitting on top of her with his free hand around Ciara's neck while the other hand gripped the butcher knife.

"Whea ..." Ciara tried to squeeze out a word but Chapo's grip was too tight. He released the butcher knife and grabbed the cell phone from the foot of the bed.

"You filthy bitches tried to set me up! Did you really think you would get away with it?" Those words made Ciara's eyes shoot open with surprise. *How did he find out?* Ciara asked herself. "Wanna know how I found out, huh?" Chapo asked as if he could read her mind. He turned his cell phone on loudspeaker. "Where's that crackhead whore?" Chapo spoke into the receiver.

"Ruunn!" Tiffany yelled before her words were muffled. Tears formed in Ciara's eyes at the sound of her best friend's voice.

Ciara's days were already numbered, which was the reason she agreed to take the task. But she didn't expect to drop the ball so soon. She was enjoying the lifestyle Chapo introduced her to.

Chapo grabbed a sheet and tied Ciara's hands to her headboard.

"Baby, what are you doing? I have no idea what you're talking about." Ciara tried to finesse her way out of the situation but the more she pleaded the more Chapo became furious.

"I noticed that you weren't very familiar with this city. I never bought your lies, not for one second, but I thought you were lying for a different reason." Chapo glided the butcher knife up and down Ciara's leg, making her skin crawl as she tried to wiggle free. "I hope it was worth it because that will be the last lie your lips will ever tell." Chapo plunged the butcher knife into Ciara's thigh with all of his strength.

"Aaarghh!" she screamed out in agony as Chapo tugged at the knife until it finally broke free from her flesh. Chapo took the butcher knife and hacked away at Ciara's leg again and again until it was no longer connected to her body.

Tiffany sat on the other end of the phone screaming and shouting as her best friend suffered the unbearable pain. Eventually Ciara passed out from losing too much blood but that didn't stop Chapo from completing his mission. He wanted her body in one hundred pieces when he was done chopping. Ninety-nine pieces later, Ciara was dead a long time ago but Chapo was far removed from his being. The butcher knife made clean cuts as Chapo pulled Ciara's hair while he severed her head. The entire room was a bloodbath. Each piece Chapo cut he threw it in a different direction. Once he was satisfied with his work, he gave Unique the green light to put Tiffany out of her misery.

"Put a bullet right in that bitch forehead."

"As you wish."

Boom!

Chapo heard the loud gunshot ring out through the phone.

"Thata girl," he said before ending the call. Chapo realized that he was still holding Ciara's head in his hand. He didn't want to admit it, but Ciara had broken the lock to Chapo's heart. She made love to him in a different way. Her betraying him the way she did sent him over the edge. Chapo gave Ciara a kiss and threw her head across the room. "See you in hell," he said before fetching his pants for another hit of coke.

Chapter 32

Blackboy

She say my leather so soft my top so soft, I probably have it all, these niggas so soft but I go so hard.

Blackboy and Ceasar cruised the streets listening to Lil Wayne's *Leather So Soft* while rotating two blunts at a time. Blackboy got used to the fast life pretty quickly even though he had it all, he never splurged too much. He did just enough to show the watchers that he was on the winning team.

Blackboy was pushing a 2010 Cadillac Escalade with 26" Asanti rims. He wanted to feel like the President when he was behind the tint of the huge black truck. Since he and Chapo's sons applied pressure to Lalo's team, forcing them to go into hiding, Chapo's operation had skyrocketed on the numbers.

Blackboy retrieved his cell phone from inside his cup holder and dialed Milo's number before placing the phone to his ear. The phone rang twice then went silent. "Hello … Hello," Blackboy spoke but received no reply. Out of nowhere, the call ended. Blackboy tried calling back but this time the phone went to voicemail. "The fuck this nigga got going on?" Blackboy said aloud.

Milo was supposed to meet them at Chapo's mansion to stash all the cash from the week's work. Chapo always put Milo in charge when he was out of town. Blackboy got an awkward feeling in the pit of his stomach as he headed towards Chapo's place. Ceasar just laid back in the passenger seat and smoked his brain cells away without a care in the world.

Pulling into Chapo's driveway, the boys noticed an unfamiliar car parked behind Chapo's Bentley. "This nigga got some bop in here, yo pops gone kick his ass," Blackboy stated, assuming the Jaguar belonged to one of Milo's jump off's.

Blackboy deaded his engine and he and Ceasar hopped out the truck and walked straight to the front door. Ceasar rang the doorbell while Blackboy peeked through the glass doors. When they didn't receive an answer, Blackboy pulled out his iPhone and tried calling Milo's phone once more.

"I know this nigga hear his phone," Blackboy huffed as he walked around the back where he knew to find the spare key. To his surprise the back door was slightly ajar, and the alarm system had been disconnected. Alarms instantly went off inside the boys' heads as they drew their weapons and went into killer mode. They crept inside the mansion with their guns aimed, ready to blast at anything moving. Blackboy placed a finger to his lips, signaling Ceasar to keep quiet as they tiptoed through the kitchen. Instantly, they spotted the two bodies sprawled out across the floor.

Ceasar rushed across the living room and dropped to his knees beside his older brother. He placed Milo's head in his lap as blood oozed from his forehead. "Noooo!" he screamed at the top of his lungs. "Milo, wake up brother, wake up!" Ceasar cried.

Blackboy was speechless as he tried to identify the woman lying face down with blood oozing from her head as well. *What the hell happened?. Maybe it was a robbery gone wrong,* he guessed as he raced up the stairs to search Chapo's stash. Surprisingly nothing was missing. Everything appeared to be just the way Chapo left it.

Blackboy raced back downstairs to see Ceasar being held at gunpoint with his own Glock by a woman in all black. The woman didn't bother to take her eyes off Ceasar as Blackboy closed the distance with his gun drawn. A look of surprise spread across his face as he lowered his gun. Ceasar never stood to his feet, instead he stayed by his brother's side. His role model was dead, he had nothing to live for.

"Mama?" Blackboy began to feel like he was dreaming, staring into his mother's eyes.

Tiffany had tears in her eyes as she stared back at her son. Ceasar looked back and forth between the two with absolutely no idea of what was unfolding in front of him. Blackboy raised his gun again, aiming it straight at his mom's head. "Drop the gun," Blackboy demanded.

"What are you doing, son?" Tiffany asked as a look of confusion spread across her face.

"What'chu think I'm doing? You left me hanging like I was a piece of shit. Now that I'm getting rich you wanna come to my rescue. Where were you when I was in that basement, starving?"

"Baby, I didn't leave you, that man done brainwashed you. I was in that same basement, getting raped and hooked on heroin while the enemy had you under a spell," Tiffany cried. She was hurt by her son's assumptions. Blackboy felt ashamed of himself as he looked into his mother's eyes. Her eyes had pain in them and a story to tell that Blackboy couldn't imagine. "Look what they've done to me." Tiffany raised her black hood so that Blackboy could see her bullet wound.

"She's lying, I never seen this lady in my fucking life," Ceasar barked.

"You never stepped into the basement of your pops trap house, but your brother did. Him and every other foot soldier your pops had done ran up in me raw while I was too high to function. I know you don't think the place just blew up on its own," Tiffany revealed.

Ceasar's expression changed from pissed to dumbfounded. He's never known his dad to be so gruesome when it comes to women, but Ceasar felt some truth in Tiffany's words. He felt pity for the woman, no woman deserved to be gang raped and tortured, they were all innocent in his eyes.

Blackboy's eyes turned cold as he fixed his aim on Ceasar.

"Yo, Blackboy I swear on my mom's ashes I knew nothing about this. You know pops kept me away from that basement just as much as you."

Blackboy knew that Ceasar was telling the truth but if his mom was being honest about Chapo's involvement in his mother's horrific journey then Ceasar would be just as guilty as the rest. Blackboy would have to hold his friend accountable for his father's actions. Blackboy caressed the trigger of his Glock... just seconds away from blowing Ceasar's brains out.

"Dennis, this is not who you are. You're not a killer. That man has you brainwashed. I raised you better than this." Tiffany stepped in front of Ceasar and lowered her weapon. She didn't want to witness her son catch another body. Watching him murder his own father in cold blood was enough trauma to last a lifetime.

"Ma, do you have any idea who you're dealing with? This man will come back and kill us and everyone we're associated with," Blackboy warned his O.G. about Chapo's ruthlessness. He'd seen Chapo slaughter families for much less.

"I wasn't scared the first time he tried and I damn sure ain't scared now, but I'll tell you one thing." Tiffany pulled out a box of garbage bags, "he'll have to start at zero." Tiffany tied Ceasar up before robbing Chapo blind of all his money and drugs— every dollar, every brick was bagged. Tiffany even took Chapo's car keys that were hanging on the kitchen wall. "Your father let my son live, so we're even but if we ever cross paths again, I'll kill you myself," Tiffany warned Ceasar before turning her back and walking out the same way she came in.

While she was loading the bags into the trunk of her car she heard a loud gunshot before Blackboy came running out of the mansion with two bags of his own. Tiffany just shook her head as Blackboy hopped into the driver seat of his truck and backed out of the driveway.

Blackboy rushed home and cleared his stash and he and his mother drove back to the only place they knew.

Chicago.

Chapter 33

Baby J

It's your birthday so I know you want to riiide out/even if we only go to myyy house/sip mo-eezy as we sit up on myyy couch/feels good, but I know you want to riiide out...
    Baby J took his time as he entered Porshia's sanctuary. She instructed him to go nice and slow. Porshia promised Baby J that she would give him the panties for his birthday and Baby J couldn't wait to claim his prize. What started out as pain, turned to pleasure as the two caught a rhythm to Jeremih's *Birthday Sex* track playing in the background.
    Despite his auntie Ciara coming up missing Baby J stayed in school and out of trouble. Although he was worried about his aunt's whereabouts, he was afraid to get the law involved. He knew the first thing that would come to their minds would be to take him back into foster care, which wasn't an option for him. Baby J prayed for her to safe return, but in his heart he knew his auntie was gone forever. She hadn't called in months and her phone had been going straight to voicemail. Thank God for Miracle, she did all she could to make sure he was up to part.
    The track changed as the kids worked up a sweat making love. Baby J hadn't imagined it would feel so euphoric, losing his virginity. Porshia fell deeper in love with every stroke. "You love me?" he whispered in her ear as he pleasured her .

"Yessss, I love you" Porshia answered as she stared Baby J right in his eyes.

"I love you too," he responded right before spilling his seed into her. His body went limp on top of hers as she held onto him tightly. She had given him the key to her treasure, and she silently hoped that he would never break her heart.

They showered together before leaving Baby J's home. Miracle had given him a few hundred for his birthday, so he decided to take Porshia and a few friends to Old Country Buffet. If he was lucky enough, he would end his night making love to Porshia again.

Baby J and Porshia stood at the bus stop in their matching Stall & Dean jackets. A familiar car came to a complete stop in front of them. Baby J's body tensed up as the doors of the gold LeSabre eased open and Boozer climbed out of the passenger seat. He opened the back door and gestured for them to climb in.

"We good," Baby J opposed.

"If you wanna make it to where you're going, I suggest you hop in," Boozer said in a serious tone but Baby J wasn't moved by it. "Look shorty, I know you hate me, but you got bigger shit to worry about right now. Rumors been floating around and I know you don't want me to get into all that while your lil lady here, so just let me give you a ride so we can chop it up, bet?"

Baby J looked between Boozer and Porshia as he weighed his options. Porshia never knew the truth about Baby J's injuries. He told everyone at school that he was hit by a car. Baby J went back to living a normal teenage life going to school and playing basketball. He knew the rumors that Boozer was referring to. He also knew that if there are, in fact, rumors floating around, he had a lot more to worry about than some childhood grudge.

Baby J hopped in the back seat and Porshia joined him. Bizzy turned the music up and he and Boozer bopped their heads to a Lil Wayne's mixtape while Baby J and his girlfriend sat in silence.

Once they arrived at the all-you-can-eat buffet Boozer tapped Baby J and they both stepped out of the car. Boozer wasted no time exposing his hand. "First of all, I wanna say I apologize about your ole girl, I was a young nigga tryna survive in the trenches. But you can't go holding grudges about something that only your O.G. could've prevented. If I didn't serve her the next hustler in line would've made the sale, but I do understand your angle shorty and for that I'm sorry. But the real reason I'm here is because I'm sure you know that the night you got jumped by them niggas off Hamlin, one of 'em got nailed and the other one got hit up." Baby J looked Boozer straight in his eyes as he continued. "They don't know who did it, but word onna street is you had something to do with it. Rather you did or not, nigga's gone be tryna get their lick back so I advise you to keep yo' head up." Boozer looked over his shoulders before drawing a .38 special from his hoodie pocket and handing it to Baby J. "Here, take this."

"What's this for?" Baby J asked. He wasn't a gangster and damn sure wasn't a killer. He had dreams of going to the league, not prison.

"It's for safety measures. If nobody tries you then you don't have to worry about using it, but Romeo wasn't just anybody. That's Ray Ray's nephew but them niggas had to get taught a lesson for coming at you and your sister like that. I had to show 'em they bleed just like the rest of us."

Baby J tucked the .38 into his Stall & Dean pocket. "Have you talked to my sister?" Baby J asked.

"Naw, she hasn't been accepting my calls, but I'll be here when she's ready. Love don't just walk away that easy," Boozer said hopefully.

Baby J felt Boozer's love for his sister. He put his life on the line for her and that alone was enough to sweep their beef under the rug. Baby J was becoming a man the older he got the more he understood the game. Heroin was his mother's drug of choice and selling it was Boozer's hustle. "I'll talk to her for you. I'm sure she's been missing you just as much as you miss her," he said.

"So, no more hard feelings?" Boozer asked.

Baby J gave him a fist bump. "Naw, we good."

Boozer smiled as he reached inside his pants pocket and pulled off a few hundreds before handing them to Baby J. "Happy birthday, lil bro. Gon' head and enjoy yo' day with yo' lil lady and remember what I told you," Boozer said as he opened the back door for Porshia.

Baby J patted his Stall & Dean pocket and said, "Fasho," before taking Porshia's hand and walking inside the buffet.

Chapter 34

Heaven

Heaven sat on the edge of her bed, typing a long message to April on Facebook. She had found her best friend's social media page two days ago but she was hesitant to reach out. April seemed to be living a good life without her. *Maybe she blames me for Stacy's death*, Heaven thought as she searched for April's reason for cutting her off.

From looking at April's pictures, Heaven discovered that she was a cheerleader for Proviso East, a high school in a suburban area called Maywood.

Hey bestie, it's been a long two years since we've talked, and I've been missing you dearly. Only you would understand my feelings and there's so much I wanna tell you but I kinda wanna vent in person. You wouldn't believe the info I found out about my family but anyway here's my number in case you've forgotten 773-567-0194. It won't change so hit me up sometime, don't be a stranger <3

Heaven reread her own message before pressing send. Heaven heard her phone ringing just as she was placing it in her pocket. She pulled it back out eagerly but her smile slightly faded when she read Miracle's name across her screen. She thought it was April calling, but she was still thankful for a friend.

"Hello," Heaven answered.

"I'm outside, lil sis."

"Okay, I'm on my way," Heaven ended the call and grabbed her crutch. Since her walking had improved, Heaven preferred to use a crutch to assist her instead of a cane.

Heaven climbed into the passenger seat and threw her crutch into the back. Miracle had invited her to ride along with her to try on her prom dress. She had received a call from her fashion designer, letting her know that her dress was ready. Miracle had been excited to finish her last year of high school and even more anxious to go to prom. Even though she was going alone, she would make it a memory worth waiting for.

Miracle dialed her dress designer's number as she parked in front of her apartment building on the corner of Avers & Ohio street. The woman answered the phone and spoke. "Hello beautiful, are you outside?" Her voice was soft and polite.

"Yes ma'am, I'm walking up to your door right now."

"Perfect, I'll buzz you in. Don't let those lil gang bangers sneak in the hallway, you hear?"

Miracle made sure that the hustlers loitering outside Ms. Becky's apartment heard the woman loud and clear. "I'm sure they know better by now, Ms. Becky," Miracle said as she pushed the door open.

"I don't think we do. Y'all mind teaching us?" one of the boys said as he stepped out of the crowd so that he could be seen clearly.

Miracle looked back and made sure he wasn't stepping too close before rolling her eyes and slamming the door in the boy's face. She stepped aside and let Heaven make her way up the stairs first, then she followed.

Ms. Becky could be heard unlocking her doors on the second floor as the girls made their way to the top.

"Hey beautiful. Oh, there's two of you. God outdid himself with you two." Ms. Becky smiled as she leaned in to hug Miracle. "You and that amazing perfume." Ms. Becky inhaled Miracle's favorite fragrance.

"Hey Ms. Becky. This is my little sister Heaven."

"Hello." Heaven extended her hand to greet Ms. Becky.

"Heaven and Miracle, what a combination. Come on in." Ms. Becky stepped aside and let the two girls enter her home. They followed her into a bedroom, which she used for working.

There were a variety of threads, material, and appliances scattered throughout the room. Ms. Becky had a clothes rack in her room, which she used to hang her completed dresses and suits. She shuffled through the tags until she found the one with Miracle's name written on it. "Here we go." She pulled out an aqua blue dress with silver rhinestones around the breast and crotch area.

Miracle undressed and tried on the dress. Ms. Becky and Heaven both covered their mouths with their hands as Miracle did a 360° spin in slow motion.

"You look like you fell straight from heaven," Ms. Becky complimented.

"She's right, Miracle, you're beautiful, girl," Heaven added, causing Miracle to blush.

"Thanks, y'all," Miracle said as she stepped towards the mirror.

Miracle hadn't worn a dress since 8th grade graduation. It was yellow with ruffles around the shoulders; she'd hated it. Now that she stared at herself in the tall mirror, she couldn't have made a better choice. No makeup, no hair extensions, she was naturally beautiful. The dress hugged her curves perfectly like a mermaid tail. Miracle had her real hair styled into a feather wrap. Staring in the mirror, she can see her mother's features in herself. She could also see her father, Juan's features.

Miracle had been to visit her father two weeks ago at the Cook County jail. He was set to have a retrial sometime in May. Miracle had been reaching out to him ever since her aunt Ciara came up missing. She sent him pictures of Baby

J and herself. He told her he couldn't wait to come home and be with his family. Miracle's foster parents had no idea that she was keeping in touch with her biological father. She didn't care much for their opinions anyway.

Miracle became emotional, thinking about her parents. *Why couldn't I live a normal life like everyone else*, she mused. Suddenly a smile spread across her beautiful face. *What am I sad for, I have a full scholarship to Baylor University, one of the best colleges money can buy. I have my own car and money; I'm much more fortunate than others*, she thought as she rubbed down the curves of her shape to ensure that the dress fit perfectly, which it did.

"I love it, Ms. Becky. It's gorgeous."

"And you make it look that much better, girl," Ms. Becky said.

As Miracle undressed, her cell phone began to ring inside her purse.

"Heaven, can you get that?"

Heaven reached inside Miracle's purse and retrieved her iPhone. The screen read *Lil' Bro'* with a heart emoji.

"It's your brother," Heaven said as she accepted the call.

Miracle quickly pulled her sweatshirt over her head and grabbed the phone from Heaven's hand. "Wassup, birthday boy?"

"Hey sis, can you come grab us from Old Country Buffet? I'll love you forever."

Miracle could feel Baby J smiling on the other end of the phone. "You're gonna do that anyway. You gotta come up with a better deal than that," she joked.

"Ok, well how about I sneak you out a piece of cheesecake?"

"Cheesecake?" Miracle repeated.

"Yep, it's a bomb too." Baby J said, boasting about how good the buffet cake was.

"Deal, I'll be there in twenty minutes."

"Okay, love you."

"I love you too," Miracle said before ending the call.

"Thanks Ms. Becky, I love my dress."

"Here, let me bag it for you, sweety." Ms. Becky took the dress and placed it on a hanger before sliding a cleaner's bag over the top and handing it back to Miracle. "See you later. Don't let those thugs into my hallway ya hear?"

"Of course not," Miracle said before her and Heaven made their way back down the stairs.

Once they made it to the bottom, Miracle reached in her purse and took out her car keys before sticking her hand back inside her purse, this time leaving it. She had a bad taste for the boys hanging outside Ms. Becky's apartment. Heaven opened the door and stepped out into the chilly March's weather as light raindrops fell from the sky. Miracle hit a button on her remote and her car doors unlocked.

"Aye girl," a voice called out as Miracle and Heaven rushed to their vehicle. Miracle can feel someone else's body heat looming over her shoulders. "You can't hear me talking to you."

She felt a hand grip her elbow way too aggressively for her liking. She turned around in one swift motion and maced what she expected to be one person. Instead, there were three boys behind her. Each one caught pepper spray in their eyes before Miracle ran around to the driver's side of her car and jumped in. Heaven wasn't as quick, but she managed to get the passenger door opened before she was snatched by the hair.

"Aarrgh!" she screamed before turning around and shoving her crutch straight into the boy's nut sack, then coming down with a hard blow to the head before dropping the crutch and diving into the passenger seat. Miracle quickly peeled off into traffic as the boys attempted to pull Heaven back out of the vehicle. Heaven kicked and screamed until she broke free and slammed the car door.

Miracle hit the lock button on the driver's side door, locking all the doors as she made her escape.

Boc! Boc! Boc!

The girls heard the unmistakable sound of gunshots followed by glass shattering. Both girls duck their heads below the dashboard. Miracle couldn't believe they were being shot at. Once the shots went silent, Miracle looked into her rearview mirror to see the boys running back to the sidewalk. "You okay?" Miracle asked as Heaven rested her head in her own lap.

She raised her head with a frightened look spread across her face. She looked down and noticed that she was holding her stomach. Blood was spilling through the cracks of Heaven's fingers. "I'm hit, Miracle!" Heaven's eyes filled with tears as she began to think about Stacy and the way she died. *Why is life so hard for me?* she asked herself. Heaven's life was beginning to feel like a curse. Since birth, she's been ending up with the short end of the stick.

"Just relax, I'm gonna get you to a hospital. It's gone be okay you hear me?" Miracle looked at Heaven's wound and tried her best not to panic. She didn't want to scare her little sister to her death.

Heaven nodded as she tried to take deep breaths. A mixture of burning flesh and blood filled the air as Miracle stomped the gas pedal. Heaven was losing consciousness from losing so much blood. "Stay with me, sister, we're almost there." Miracle tried to keep Heaven awake as she made an exit on Central Avenue. Just as she was pulling into the hospital's emergency parking lot, Heaven passed out.

***

Marrissa

Marrissa sat on her couch with her legs folded, watching *Scary Movie 2* and eating popcorn. Since Heaven's ability to walk improved, Marrissa spent more time to herself. She was still devastated by the fact that Karim was H.I.V positive and having unprotected sex with her. Although she later discovered that he had been taking the proper medication to prevent from transmitting his disease, Marrissa was still taken aback by the heart-shattering news her ears heard over the phone several months ago. That, on top of him cheating with his ex-wife, was enough to push Marrissa away forever.

Marrissa sat her popcorn aside to fetch a soda from the fridge. She grabbed a can of Orange Crush and popped the top before pouring the soda into a glass cup. Once she finished, Marrissa grabbed her cup and walked back to her living room where she proceeded to watch the movie. A familiar smell invaded Marrissa's nostrils as she sat on the sofa. She smelled herself to see if the scent was coming from her own clothes. *Of course, not,* she confirmed as she pressed play on the DVD remote. Marrissa didn't wear the fragrance she was smelling but she knows who did. The million-dollar question is, *why is this smell lingering throughout my home?* she asked herself. Marrissa took a sip from her drink, the acid from the soda slightly burned her throat as it went down.

A few minutes into the movie, Marrissa heard her phone ringing on the couch next to her. She picked it up and read Miracle's name on the screen. "Hey sweetie," Marrissa spoke after she accepted the call. "Hold on honey, calm down ... Relax, now tell me what's going on."

Marrissa didn't remember how she got back on her feet, but she found herself dashing through the living room in search of her car keys. Marrissa let her housecoat hit the floor, exposing her naked body as she went to her bedroom to slip on some clothes. "Lord, please have mercy on my child," Marrissa prayed as she slipped on a pair of pajamas and threw a t-shirt over her head. Her tears had no brakes as they drag raced down both sides of her face.

After she threw a jacket on, Marrissa slid her feet into some sandals and headed straight out the door. She started her engine then took her trembling hands off the steering wheel. She closed her eyes and said a silent prayer before pulling into traffic. Marrissa looked back at her home and noticed there was someone staring out the window. Marrissa felt a lump in her throat as she tried to swallow. *I'm going crazy*, she thought to herself as she closed her eyes for a moment before reopening them. She looked back to see that the figure had disappeared. She quickly pushed the moment to the back of her mind and raced to Loretta hospital.

Chapter 35

Miracle

Miracle sat in the waiting area of the emergency room shaking in her seat. She had witnessed Heaven pass out and was afraid that she might be dead. The doctors wouldn't give Miracle any information containing her friend without a relative being present. Miracle called Heaven's mom at her earliest convenience, but it seemed like hours before she finally arrived. Marrissa came rushing through the glass doors. Her skin was blue like she had been holding her breath the entire ride to the hospital. Miracle spotted her and rose to her feet with her hands covering her mouth. The look on Marrissa's face was devastating. Miracle felt terrible inside for the woman she called mom. Marrissa made her way to where Miracle was standing and gave her a tight hug.

"It's okay sweetie. Just breathe, she's gonna pull through," Marrissa said hopefully. She wanted to believe her own words so badly, but she knew God had the final say-so.

"You must be the mother." Marrissa heard a baritone voice boom from behind her. She turned around to see a tall handsome doctor standing there with a chart in his hand.

"Y-mmm." Marrissa cleared her throat before attempting to answer the man's question again. "Yes, I'm the mother. Is my child okay? Where is she?"

"Hi, I'm Doctor Shanklin." The doctor extended his hand for a shake before he continued. "Why don't we go somewhere a little more private," he insisted.

Marrissa and Miracle followed him through a set of automatic doors where the sounds of crying babies, aching dope fiend, and injured individuals all came to an end.

"That's better ... Now I can share the good and bad news."

Marrissa went deaf at the sound of 'Bad news' as the words escaped doctor Shanklin's mouth.

"What's the bad news?" Marrissa asked aloud as her heartbeat pounded through her chest.

"Why don't I start with the good news to chill you down a bit. Your daughter will survive, she's undergoing surgery as we speak. We managed to stop the bleeding before she bled out completely."

Marrissa relaxed a little, but she was still on the edge of her seat waiting to hear the bad news.

"The bad news is your daughter needs a blood transfusion, and she happens to have a rare blood type which we're having trouble finding a match. Perhaps you or her father can donate some blood to solve this problem." Dr Shanklin suggested.

Blood? I certainly don't have the same blood as her and her father's blood is infected and can't be much of any help at all, Marrissa thought.

Miracle noticed the look of defeat spread across Marrissa's face and became apologetic. She knew the family's biological secret; however, she didn't know Heaven's father was H.I.V positive. As far as she knew he was just out of the picture.

Marrissa placed her hand on her forehead, her legs wobbled as she became dizzy. Dr. Shanklin quickly grabbed her and guided her to an empty seat. He gave her time to recollect herself before he fetched a cup of water. Marrissa pulled out her cell phone and began texting. Miracle stood next to her in silence, hoping everything would be okay. Her phone started vibrating in her purse. She dug into her Michael Kors purse and grabbed her iPhone, reading Baby J's name across the screen before walking away to answer it.

"Hey," she spoke in a low tone. "Here I come," Miracle said after Baby J informed her about his arrival.

She walked to the entrance to the emergency room to meet her little brother and was taken by surprise at the sight of Boozer standing next to Baby J. Miracle stopped in her tracks and took a deep breath. Boozer wasted no time stepping into her personal space. He wrapped his arms around her. She could hear his heartbeat as she laid her head on his chest. *Gosh, I missed him so much*, she thought to herself. But the other side of her wanted to pull away.

"You okay?" Boozer asked sincerely.

Miracle nodded her head before looking at her little brother who was standing there with his hands in his jacket pockets. She broke free from Boozer's embrace and hugged her little brother, that's when tears began to flow. If life had its way it could've been *her* laying in that hospital bed fighting for her life and that would've left her baby brother hanging on with a strand of hope. That thought alone brought tears to her eyes.

"It's gonna be okay, sis. Whoever did this is gonna pay." Baby J's words made Miracle look up at him. Her eyebrows furrowed as she let the words register in her head.

"Why are you talking like that? Boy, what's wrong with you?"

"Ain't nobody gonna take advantage of my family, sis. Ain't no nigga just gone shoot at you and get away with it. You're most precious to us."

Miracle noticed how Baby J included Boozer in his notion. Miracle pushed her brother a few feet away from Boozer and whispered. "What's going on? What are you doing with him?"

"He dropped me and Porshia off at OCB. We kinda had a talk and he gave me his number. When you told me what happened I called him for a ride, and he came. He's pretty cool, I apologize for being so childish. He cares about you and I'm tired of seeing you moping around like you lost your puppy so go talk to the man and I'll be over here."

Baby J headed to take a seat in the waiting area. Miracle walked back over to Boozer, still confused. "What did you do to my lil brother?"

"What chu mean?" Boozer felt offended.

"Why is he so happy to be here with you? And why is he talking like he's gangsta? He's a kid."

Boozer smiled. "I just told him what's real, baby girl."

Boozer thumbed Miracle cheek, something he did right before he told her how beautiful she was. This time he just smiled. Miracle waited until the handsome man who just came into the hospital was out of ear range before she continued.

"*Whatever.* Take him home. I'm gonna go check on my lil sister."

"Can I get a kiss?" Boozer squinted his eyes and shot Miracle that charming look of his.

"I don't know where yo' lips been," Miracle joked.

Boozer pulled her in and kissed her anyway. "Waiting for yours," he responded before cutting her loose. "Call me when you're finished. I gotta go handle some business."

Boozer's charming look disappeared and a cold-blooded killer stared back at Miracle.

"Don't go hurt nobody, Maurice." She called him by his government name.

"You know me well, don't you?" Boozer winked his left eye.

"I'm serious. Promise me you won't do anything stupid."

"Baby, you know I can't promise you that. Nobody plays with my girl and gets away with it." Boozer tried to walk away to prevent confrontation, but Miracle pulled him back by the hand.

"There's a woman that I love very much staying in that building. I know you're gonna do what you wanna do but please baby, no innocents." Miracle's words were heartfelt as Boozer began to think about the old lady he accidentally killed last time someone played with his girl.

"No innocents. I promise." Boozer kissed Miracle lips again.

"I love you."

"I love you too, now unblock my number before I bust all these hospital windows." Boozer smiled.

"Okay Maurice, bye." Miracle went to grab Baby J and escort him through the glass doors. She turned her head one last time to see Boozer standing there biting his bottom lip. She shook her head and smiled before disappearing behind the doors.

Miracle spotted the handsome man exchanging words with Marrissa. They seemed to be having some sort of argument. *That must be Heaven's dad,* she thought to herself just as the doctor came in between the two parents and began talking. Miracle noticed the handsome man shake his head in defeat as he mouthed a few words to the doctor. She wanted to get a little closer so she could eavesdrop on their conversation, but she decided against it. Instead, her and Baby J took a seat in the chairs in front of them and waited.

Chapter 36

Blackboy

Blackboy had elevated his game in the streets since he returned to Chicago. Tay B and Timo's heads spun when they witnessed the new way Blackboy carried himself. His demeanor and swagger had aged by ten years, leaving his homies in their teenage years. He flooded the southside with guns and drugs, buying muscle and hustling the way Chapo had taught him. Blackboy filled his day 1s in on his journey in Texas, from the kidnapping to the great escape and return home to his own stepping grounds. It felt good to be back in the trenches of Chicago but Blackboy could sense the change in his homies attitude when he's calling shots.

Tay B was down for whatever as long as his pockets stayed swollen. Timo, on the other hand, didn't feel too happy about playing foot soldier to somebody like Blackboy. Being the big dawg in the hood was always his dream. Blackboy learned a lot from Chapo, so much that he knew to play his friends very close. *"Snakes don't hiss anymore, they shake your hand,"* Chapo had told him.

"Timo, I need you to drop this package off in the Ickies and collect that bread from Head." Blackboy handed Timo a Nike duffle bag filled with crack and heroin. "Take Lil Keef and Fredo with you," he ordered. Timo accepted the bag and walked out of the trap house. On 65th and Laflin. The door slammed a little too hard for Blackboy's liking.

"What's wit yo' boy? That nigga been acting weird." Blackboy asked Tay B.

"You know how niggas be. Some niggas got pride issues; they don't like taking orders from no nigga they came from the sandbox with, you feel me?" Tay B replied truthfully.

"Is that how you feel?" Blackboy looked up from the money counter and stared Tay B directly in his eyes.

"Nigga, I never had this much money in my life, and I want it to stay like that. All I'm saying is, if we yo' boys bring us to the table with you. Let us look like bosses too."

Blackboy let Tay B's words marinate for a second. He thought back to his time in Texas when he was following orders himself. Chapo told him, *"As long as there's only one person calling the shots, no one will misunderstand their role."*

"It ain't no hard feelings, Tay B, but I went through a lot to get where I'm at. This shit wasn't passed to me on a silver platter, skud. I cooked crack for my own mama to turn into a P, y'all don't know how it feel to see yo' O.G. strung out on that shit." Blackboy's attitude softened. Tay B witnessed Blackboy hop onto the emotional rollercoaster without a seat belt. He'd never seen his homie break down like this before. Only Blackboy knew his story back in Texas; today Tay B would get a step inside his shoes. "My O.G. is gone forever on the inside. I still catch her nodding off that shit from time to time."

A lonely tear escaped Blackboy's eye.

"Look folks, whatever you went through to get where you at, you deserve it. I'm just glad I got my boy back in one piece. Secondly, you broke that bag with yo' day ones look what I'm driving." Tay B whipped out a set of keys to his new Audi and flashed them in Blackboy's face. "Nigga, this yo' work, without you I'd still be scuffin' up my favorite shoes."

That compliment made Blackboy smile. Tay B was right, Blackboy came back and put his whole hood on. If Timo couldn't see the bigger picture, he's a fool.

"That's love skud, for real for real, one day we'll all be able to call the shots. I'm just now getting my feet wet. I haven't even found a plug yet. This shit ain't gone last forever believe that."

"One step at a time skud, it's gone, come to us."

The boys shook hands and dropped the rakes.

"Aye skud, you ain't been seeing April and Heaven around?" Blackboy asked.

Heaven been on his mind since he crossed state lines. Now that he had the money to fulfill both of their dreams. He was ready to make her his wife.

"Aw you ain't heard? Last time I talked to shorty she told me that a muhfucka tried to end yo' girl career after their graduation. April said she was in a coma and it wasn't looking too good for her."

That news created a funny feeling in the pit of Blackboy's stomach.

"Somebody shot her?" Blackboy asked a question his heart didn't want the answer to.

"Naw folks, they said she got hit by a car; broke a lot of shorty bones and shit. I heard it was Stacy O.G.. Or some'n."

"You still got April's phone number? I'm tryna holla at her." Blackboy asked.

He wasn't gonna give up on finding Heaven, rather she was dead or just a couch potato.

"Hell naw, her shit disconnected. She told me that her O.G. was scared or some shit, I know they was moving out of Chicago that's about it."

"Aight bet. Load this cash up and take it to yo' crib. I'll be by later to scoop it. I'm 'bout to go look at this house I'm supposed to be closing on," Blackboy said as he stood from his seat.

"Growth my nigga," Tay B showed the smile of a proud brother as he embraced his friend. "That's what the fuck I'm talking 'bout— boss moves," Tay B said as he patted Blackboy back.

He felt the difference Blackboy made when he returned from Texas, the whole hood felt the difference. Niggas who grew up robbing and stealing, were feeding the homeless now. Blackboy pulled out his cell phone to check the time. His clock read 2:31 pm. He had to meet his broker at the property at 3:00 sharp.

"Damn, I'm late. Lock up I'll be back as soon as I finish up with this business," Blackboy said before leaving the trap house and hopping into his luxury Cadillac truck. He started his engine and drew his Glock 19, placing it on his lap as he merged into traffic. Wacka Flocka pumped from his speakers as he headed towards Lake Shore drive with thoughts of Heaven on his mind. Hearing the bad news about her gave him a small headache. He guided the steering wheel with his knees as he broke down a swisher sweet and dumped the contents out the window. After licking the brown paper, Blackboy filled the blunt up with some of Chapo's grade-A Kush and twisted it up.

He nodded his head to the music as he blew clouds of smoke in the air. The sensation from the weed calmed his nerves a little as he tried his best to push the thoughts of Heaven to the back of his mind. Blackboy floored the gas pedal down Lake Shore drive, passing up the steady traffic. He felt like he was flying an airplane on autopilot as his speedometer touched 100 mph. It wasn't until he looked in his rearview mirror and noticed the flashing lights from a state trooper car, when he let his foot off the gas and proceeded to slow down. Blackboy touched a button on his radio and a secret compartment opened beneath his feet.

Blackboy stashed his gun along with the weed he had inside a plastic bag inside the compartment and closed it before spraying his special air freshener as the A/C pumped through the ventilation system, eliminating the smell of Kush in a matter of seconds. Blackboy slowed down until eventually he came to a complete stop on the side of the road. "Fuck," he cursed himself for zoning out and not noticing the jakes creeping up behind him. *A minor mistake like this could cost you if you don't tighten up your screws,* he told himself as he dusted off his True Religion shirt while eyeing the sheriff as he walked up and tapped on the window.

Tap! Tap! Tap!

Blackboy rolled his window down slowly and looked the deputy in his eyes. In that instant Blackboy realized that he was not in Texas anymore where the police would look the other way when they saw him in traffic. He was back in Chicago where the law was just as dirty as the dealers and didn't give two fucks about a gang or powerful name— in Chicago the police had their own gang.

"How you doing, officer?" Blackboy spoke politely to lighten the mood.

"License and registration please," the redneck deputy demanded. His tone was less than friendly as he gripped his .357 magnum on his hip.

Blackboy was reaching for his registration when he noticed a second sheriff standing on the passenger side of his vehicle with his gun drawn. That's when Blackboy finally remembered that he had a warrant for missing his court appearance on his gun case. He told himself that he'd get the issue resolved but he was living too fast to stand on his word. Blackboy passed the sheriff his registration and threw his hands in the air.

"Step out of the car." the redneck deputy demanded as he snatched the door open.

Blackboy climbed out of his truck just as six more state police cars arrived, surrounding his vehicle.

"What's all this about? All this for a little warrant? I don't think that's necessary, officer."

The officer proceeded to throw Blackboy in cuffs before responding. "I didn't know murder was a little warrant."

Those words made Blackboy's heart drop to the pit of his stomach.

"Dennis Coleman you're under arrest for the murder of Stacy Lomax; you have the right to remain silent ..."

Blackboy went deaf as the sheriff continued to read him his rights. *Murder? ... Stacy? What the fuck is these people talking about?* Blackboy wondered.

"Do you understand these rights?"

"Man, fuck you! Call my attorney!" Blackboy spat at the sheriff.

He was devastated by the news the police had just laid on him, but Chapo made him sharp enough to know that a false charge like this wouldn't stick. Somebody had to be feeding the Jakes false information to bring him down. Somebody that was present the day Stacy pulled the trigger and committed suicide. Blackboy was thrown in the back of an unmarked police car and driven to the station on Belmont and Western where he was fingerprinted and charged with first degree murder.

The next morning Blackboy was transferred to the Cook County courthouse for a bond hearing. Blackboy's attorney Irvin Miller appeared in court dressed to kill in his custom Tom Ford suit and Gucci slacks. Irving Miller had a reputation for walking down murder cases with his eyes closed. That's the reason why Blackboy had him on payroll. He just couldn't believe that he had to dial the number so soon.

"Can you read me Mr. Coleman's background?" the judge asked the state's attorney.

"The accused has an open charge from 2009 in which he was released on bail. A warrant was issued out on June 16th,

2009, when the defender failed to appear in court. Be advised that the defendant hasn't appeared in court since."

After the state's attorney's attempt to drag Blackboy's name in the mud his attorney still managed to get him a million-dollar cash bond. Blackboy knew that posting bail would've brought him unnecessary drama with the feds. Irv told him to sit tight, he'd have the case thrown out in the matter of months. Blackboy was baffled by his attorney's cockiness but he was devastated by the fact that one of his closest friends was trying to frame him and abdicate his throne.

Blackboy had cold ice running through his veins and war on his mind. If they crossed me they'll kill me Blackboy thought to himself. His mental had outgrown his friends, who were still fascinated by fast cars and nice clothes. Blackboy boy's mind was on lifetime investments, something that molds an advantageous future.

Once Blackboy was processed in his first call went to Tay B. the phone rung four times before it went silent. Tay B answered the free collect call with an onerous tone. "Hello," his disturbed voice pumped through the receiver.

"Aye skud, them mufuckas just put Stacy's body on *me*, what the fuck y'all got going on?"

"Wait! What?" Tay B remarked, offended by what he'd just been told.

"You heard what I said, nigga. I go ghost and pop back up with a murder charge that didn't none of us commit but all of us were there. Neither one of them shorties had a reason to throw me under the bus so between you and Timo, one of you niggas ain't right, skud. But we gone get to the bottom of this." Blackboy's ominous tone sent chills down Tay B's spine like never before.

Tay B was stunned by Blackboy's aggressive demeanor.

"Look, I ain't getting down on you if that's what you thinking but I don't think this discussion is for everybody's ears, ya feel me? But imma come see you–"

"Fuck all that! We ain't got shit to hide. These people got me in here on false charges." Blackboy cut Tay B's sentence short. "It was me, you, and three other people in that room and I damn sholl don't see y'all fighting no murder charges. These two girls don't have no reason to lie on me so that leaves *you* and *Timo*, skud. Ain't no way around it. Who lying on me? Who trying to tarnish my name, skud?"

The other end of the phone went silent as Tay B thought about the day, he told Timo to rat on Blackboy before he himself was taken into investigation where he found out that Blackboy wasn't snitching. Tay B tried to clear up the rumor, but the detectives had gotten ahold of Timo first.

"I ain't gone even lie to you, skud. Them people came and snatched us up for questioning after you got booked. We thought you folded on us," Tay B admitted truthfully. "But after I got interrogated and found out you went ghost on the Jakes after you bonded out, I told them bitches to suck my dick and call my attorney— on Dave. I can't say the same for Timo though."

"Is that right? Matter fact, call that nigga and tell him I just got bumped. But don't let him know I'm on the phone," Blackboy said before covering up the mouthpiece of his jail phone.

"Aight, hold on."

The phone went silent for a moment before Timo answered.

"Yooo," he said through the receiver.

"Where you at with it skud?" Tay B started off the conversation with a little small talk.

"I'm hitting P's right now, what's the word?" Timo responded.

"Man, they snatched up Blackboy and put that B on him. We need to locate them ho's and get this shit cleared up."

"How you know they charged him? He called?" Timo asked suspiciously. His gut instincts told him something was fishy, but Timo was too stupid to listen.

"Yeah, he said he might be down for a while. He wanted to know if me and you can hold the fort down," Tay B lied like a paid attorney.

"Hold the fort down huh?" Timo repeated deviously.

Tay B could sense that Timo had a wicked plan stirring up in his mind.

"Yeah, skud, he needs us to keep shit rolling until he bounces back. You feel me?"

"The throne is for the taking my boy. By the time that nigga touch down there will be a new sheriff in town." Timo's remark made Blackboy's blood boil, but he remained silent on the other end of the phone.

"You gone get down on folks like that? He came back and made all this shit happen for the hood. Them other niggas picked they plates up and left," Tay B defended

"I'm not coming second to no nigga. I'm the king of my own castle, that nigga ain't bout to be barking orders to me like I'm a puppy or something–"

"You talking crazy like you happy our boy got wrapped up." Tay B said, noticeably irritated.

"Yo boy?" Timo corrected him. "That nigga always thought he was better than us to begin with. I'd rather be safe than sorry."

"Suit yourself. Imma hold my nigga down until the end. This our boy since the sandbox, ain't no amount of money gone change that."

"Fuck all that sandbox talk if you ever change yo' mind I'll have a spot for you right next to mines."

"Naw we gone save that spot for yo' mama, snake ass nigga. See you in a bit," Blackboy barked through the receiver before slamming the phone down pacing back and forth in the bullpen with murder on his mind. His day one had backdoored him over some paper.

Blackboy was more hurt than angry. The nigga he thought would have his back forever, had crossed him like an AND1 vol. 2 game. Blackboy raced back to the phone which was now occupied by some type of corner store burglar. He was crying to his girlfriend, trying to convince her to post his bail. Blackboy really needed to make another call, but he didn't want to come at the guy the wrong way and offend him.

"Aye skud, I might be able to help you bounce up out this muhfucka. All I need is a quick three-way." Blackboy offered.

The boy who appeared to be no older than 18 years of age, looked up and stared Blackboy right into his eyes.

"Stop the bullshit," he called Blackboy's bluff.

"I ain't bullshitting you shorty, you got a bond don't chu?" Blackboy asked.

"Yeah, my shit ten to walk though. Ain't nobody got that type of bread to be blowing for a phone call."

"Just make the call and find out," Blackboy challenged.

"Bae, call this number real quick."

Blackboy could tell that the person on the other end of the phone was putting up a fight by the color change in the boy's high yellow skin as he became red with rage.

"Man, make the fuckin' call. You ain't tryna come get a mufucka and you 'bout to fuck up my only chance." the boy argued before asking Blackboy "What's the number?"

Blackboy called out the number and the young boy repeated it to his girlfriend before passing the phone to Blackboy. The line was silent for a moment then a voice spoke.

"Who is this?"

"It's me, ma. I'm jammed up right now; can you clean the house and feed the puppies for me until I get this mess cleared up?"

Tiffany knew exactly what her son meant by *clean the house and feed the puppies* what she didn't understand was...

"Why you ain't call me straight through? Is everything okay?" she asked.

"Everything will be okay," Blackboy assured.

"That bump in the road had a body in it, but don't stress yourself out about it, and that nigga Timo through a wrench in the game. I know his mama is gonna be disappointed when she finds out," Blackboy coded for his mama to pay Timo's O.G. a visit.

"Sure is, you go ahead and get back home I'll keep the dogs fed, baby—"

"Aye Ma!" Blackboy cut her off before she got the chance to end the call

"I'm here."

"The person on the phone gonna text you an address. I need you to peel ten and deliver it for me"

"Those words made the young boy's eyes grow wide as saucers.

"Okay. Love you"

Blackboy knew his mother hated any type of communication if it wasn't direct.

"You can text her your address, she'll be there shortly. Make sure you come and get my lil man," Blackboy said before handing the now excited lil boy back the phone. Now it was time to sit back and relax. Blackboy had just pushed the button to send a message that said, "I am not to be fucked with," and Timo will be the first recipient to receive mail.

Chapter 37

Tiffany

Tiffany sat outside Ciara's house in deep thought. She wanted revenge on Chapo so badly that she underestimated the possible outcomes if something was to go left the way it did, and now, she was suffering the consequences. Even though she hadn't witnessed her friend's murder she knew better than to underestimate Chapo's wrath. If Ciara, by any chance, was lucky enough to survive the storm in Atlanta, Chapo had surely put her out of her misery when he discovered both of his son's corpses sprawled out across the floor of his mansion.

Tiffany had been planning this visit since the day she returned to Chicago. She knew how much Ciara's nephew meant to her so for what it's worth she decided to make sure the boy was well taken care of as long as she's alive.

Tiffany wiped a tear from her left eye as memories of Ciara crowded her mind. She knew that her friend was on the brink of death, but she didn't expect it to be a cruel one like she imagined it to be. Her friend deserved a better ending.

After deading her engine, Tiffany reached and grabbed a dozen of red roses along with a manilla envelope from her passenger seat before climbing out of her Mercedes Benz. She sighed, calming her emotions as she walked around a puddle of water from the evening's rain. Her heart rate increased with each step she took.

She became lightheaded as she stood directly in front of Ciara's doorstep. Tiffany made a fist with her left hand and held it up in the air but she was hesitant to knock. Suddenly, the door swung open and Miracle stood in the doorway with a McDonald's soda in her hand.

"Oh, hi," Miracle greeted Tiffany with a look of surprise spread across her face.

Tiffany had seen Miracle in some photos that Ciara had shown her a few months ago but this would be the first time she came face to face with the young lady.

"Hello, my name is Tiffany. I didn't mean to catch you off guard." Tiffany extended her hand and Miracle shook it politely.

"It's okay, I'm Miracle. How can I help you?" she asked as she caught a glimpse of the envelope Tiffany had tucked beneath her arm.

"Actually, I'm here to see Baby J but I'm glad that you're here. I'm Ciara's best friend. Do you mind if I come in?"

Miracle was hesitant to allow a stranger in her aunt's home, but the woman appeared to be unnerved. *Something is really bothering her*, Miracle thought to herself before she stepped aside.

"Come on in." She allowed Tiffany to step inside.

Tiffany walked straight across the living room and picked up a picture frame from the table. Her mood was saddened at the image before her. She walked back across the room and handed Miracle the photo, it was a picture of Tiffany and Ciara at the casino for Ciara's 21st birthday. The photo made Miracle a little more comfortable with allowing a stranger to enter their home, but a second emotion tugged at her heart.

Something was telling her that this woman didn't come here to stare at old pictures and the fact that she didn't ask for Ciara means she had already known where she was. Secondly it may also mean she came to deliver some bad news. These were the thoughts that ran wild in Miracles' head as she held her breath unintentionally.

"Is he here? I think it's best for me to share this news with both of you."

Miracle couldn't respond right away so she darted to the back to find Baby J. After a moment the two siblings returned with disturbing looks on their faces. They looked like twins standing there in the living room holding hands. Tiffany cleared her throat and re-introduced herself to Baby J who looked unpleased to meet her. He figured she had to be a member of DCFS coming to take him back into custody.

"Hey Baby J," she greeted him by his nickname. "I'm Tiffany, your auntie's best friend."

Baby J's mood lightened at the mention of his aunt Ciara. His eyes roamed around the living room where there were pictures of Tiffany and Ciara all over.

"No wonder you look so familiar." Baby J sighed a breath of relief.

Tiffany smiled for a moment before her mood quickly changed. "I'm here because I know you've been wondering where Ci-Ci been." Tiffany pinched the bridge of her nose to prevent a tear from escaping her eyes.

"Well, Ci-Ci came to Texas to help me find my son who was kidnapped. I fucked up by asking her to help me get back at the man responsible for taking my child and ruining my life." At that moment Tiffany was no long fighting to hold back her tears. They were spilling from her soul. I knew the man was roofless when he chained me up inside a basement and drugged me while his foot soldiers raped me day in and day out. I just wanted him to pay for making my life a living hell." Tiffany sniffled and continued. "Everything went left when a bitch switched sides and told Chapo that we were setting him up. Ci-Ci was supposed to help me take everything he owned and live in paradise until it was her time." Tiffany's last words brought a look of confusion to the boy's face. Miracle on the other hand, knew exactly what

Tiffany was indicating. Tiffany noticed Baby J's muddled expression and decided to rewind the film a little. "Baby J, your auntie's cancer came back. She withheld it from the world, but she admitted it to me down in Texas. The doctor said she didn't have much longer to live."

Baby J became nauseated as he tried to stand up straight. Miracle scooped him into her arms and guided him to a seat. It hurt her to see her baby brother so lost. Miracle didn't care much for their auntie but her brother saw her in a different light. The monster in Miracle's closet was the hero in Baby J's dreams. Even though she hated Ci-Ci, Miracle would give her brother the support he needed to survive the storm.

"Anyway, me and Ci-Ci were gonna make that short time worth living. Then she was gonna leave everything to you and your sister but when Chapo found out he ordered death for me, luckily, I was quick on my feet. I don't think Ci-Ci was as fortunate." Those words left a bad taste in Tiffany's mouth as she revealed Ciara's demise.

Baby J's heart fluttered. His head felt as if he had a helmet tied too tight. Miracle pulled him close. As much as he may have needed room to breathe, she created none.

"I know your situation and I've been doing my best at keeping the government out of your business but one of these days they're gonna want to know where she's been. We can't hide something like this forever. This is a percentage of your aunt's share, that's more than enough to hold you down until we figure out the next step." Tiffany handed the envelope to Baby J. "If you ever need more, I'm only one call away." She pointed to her phone number which was written on the back of the envelope.

"What if DCFS pops up and try to take my lil' brother?" Miracle was more concerned about her brother's well-being than some envelope full of money.

"As long as he stays in school and keeps his grades up, he shouldn't have a problem. He graduates this year, so I'll be around to make everything make sense. Until then, stay close to each other and never open the door for another stranger," Tiffany said as her cell phone began to ring in her purse.

She retrieved it and frowned at the caller ID before answering.

"Who is this?" Tiffany waited for an answer before pulling the phone away from her ear. "I gotta step out and take this call" Tiffany opened the door and stepped outside.

"Are you gonna be okay?" Miracle asked.

Baby J just stared off into space. His eyes had lost their color, all Miracle saw was darkness.

"I knew she was sick, I just didn't want to be reminded," Baby J said flatly. He was more disappointed than sad.

"I can't believe she would do such thing when she promised to help me find our brother." Baby J's head hung low with defeat.

Miracle understood his pain. As a big sister she wanted to be there for her brother at times like this, but she didn't know where to begin searching for Ja'Mari. She knew no physical details about her youngest sibling. As the two sit there with helpless thoughts Tiffany returned to say her goodbyes.

"I have to handle a situation for my son but if y'all ever need anything–I mean *anything*—just give me a call," Tiffany sounded sincere, but all Baby J could think about is the broken promise that his auntie told him right before she disappeared.

"Thank you so much, we'll keep in touch," Miracle said as she escorted Tiffany back out the same door she came in.

Tiffany spotted a black SUV parked directly behind her Benz. the engine wasn't running but she could feel eyes staring at her through the tinted windows. She put her hand in her purse and clutched her Glock 23 tightly as she hit a button on her key fob, unlocking her car doors. Her heart began to pound and her hands became sweaty as she neared her vehicle with her eyes glued to the black truck. *To hell I'll go before I become somebody's lab rat again*, she thought to herself as she hopped behind the wheel and locked her doors before starting her engine and speeding into traffic.

Tiffany's Glock was now in her lap as she focused on her rearview mirror. The black truck didn't budge, in fact it disappeared in the distance as she drove further down the one-way street.

Her heart rate slowed as she began to relax. Then she turned on her radio and listened to Fantasia sing her heart out as she headed towards the 290 expressway. Blackboy had gotten himself in another jam and Tiffany as a mother was willing to do anything to save him. She pulled out her cell phone and called the most recent caller back.

After a few short rings, a young lady answered the phone with a feisty attitude. "Hellooo!" Her tone almost made Tiffany give her the dial tone but she was doing her son a favor so she managed to deal with the young lady's attitude.

"I'll be at the McDonalds on Garfield in fifteen minutes to drop off that package, come by yourself please," Tiffany instructed.

"Oh, I'm sorry ma'am I didn't know who this was," the girl apologized as her attitude faded completely. She became a whole new person within seconds.

Tiffany rolled her eyes

"It's okay, just come alone," She said and ended the call.

With the clear traffic, Tiffany made it to her destination in ten minutes. She picked up her phone and called the same number. This time the young lady answered with much more respect.

"Yes ma'am."

"Instead of going to McDonald's, pull into this Shell gas station across from the BP gas station. I'll be waiting inside." Tiffany instructed.

"Oh, okay cool. I'll be there in two minutes," the girl said and ended the call.

Tiffany waited inside the BP gas station and counted out ten thousand dollars from her emergency stash before placing the other ten thousand back inside her arm rest compartment. She watched as a tan Buick Century pulled inside the Shell gas station across the street. Tiffany made sure the girl didn't have any company before she grabbed her purse and exited her vehicle.

Tiffany headed across the street just as the young lady exited her own vehicle and strutted into the Shell gas station looking clueless.

Tiffany hopped inside the girl's vehicle and placed the money on her seat before jumping out and tracing her steps back to the BP gas station. As she climbed inside her own vehicle, her phone began to ring. She answered.

"Get back into your car and leave," she said before hanging up.

She watched as the girl rushed to her car with her cell phone to her ear. Tiffany's phone started ringing again as the girl climbed into her Buick with an attitude. Suddenly it stopped ringing as Tiffany pulled out of the gas station, heading to pay an old friend a visit.

As she drove up Garfield a text message alert came through. Knowing who it was, Tiffany opened it up and read: *Who are you???* She locked her burner phone and kept driving.

Pulling up to Timo's house, Tiffany felt the urge to get high, as the crack monkey crawled onto her back. *Now is not the time*, she thought as she deaded her engine in front of Timo's mother's house. After grabbing her purse, she climbed out of her Benz and walked directly to the front door of Sabrina's two-story home.

Tiffany tapped on the door lightly, awaiting someone to answer.

Knock! Knock! Knock!

"Who is it?" Sabrina yelled from the other side of the door.

"It's Tiff girl," Tiffany answered with her best impression.

She could hear the locks turning on the other side of the door before Sabrina pulled the door open with a huge smile on her face. Tiffany returned the award-winning smile as she spoke, "Heyyy girl," before giving Sabrina a hug.

"Oh my God, I haven't seen you in a month of Sundays. Come on in," Sabrina invited her old friend inside.

The smell of Hennessy traveled through the house like an open bar.

"To what do I owe the pleasure?" Sabrina asked.

She had no clue why her old friend popped up after all these years.

"I ain't seen you in forever. I came to check on my girl," Tiffany lied. "Is Darryl home?"

"Naw, that nigga somewhere tryna hit a lick, you know him." Sabrina took a seat on her sofa and grabbed her cup of Hennessy off the table in front of her before taking a sip.

"How yo' son been? Last time I heard he was in the hospital recovering," Tiffany lied again.

She had eyes on Blackboy's operation so she'd seen Timo's face almost daily.

"That boy *been* out the hospital. He somewhere running the streets tryna' get himself killed."

"He's always been hardheaded, you just gotta let him learn the hard way. Ain't no sense in stressing 'bout it," Tiffany said as she took a seat on the couch next to Sabrina who was busy putting her problems in the liquor as she refilled her empty glass.

"Girl, I'm not stressing about Timothy's ass. When God is ready for him, he'll call him home. Hell, I got life insurance, and I won't waste a spot in the graveyard burying that evil ass boy."

Sabrina talked about her only son alive like he didn't come from her own vagina. His older brother, Tyshaun, became a victim of hate crime at the age of fourteen. He was gay and he wore his sexuality on his sleeve with pride up until the day he was found dead behind his high school with his own dick in his mouth.

"You want some'n to drink? Girl, you look like you've been doing some stressing yourself," Sabrina said, noticing that Tiffany had lost some weight.

"Girl, you don't know the half," Tiffany admitted as she grabbed an empty shot glass and poured herself a shot before downing it in one gulp.

Tiffany eased her hand inside her purse as Sabrina winded her hips to an old R-Kelly song. *"Sex in the kitchen over by the stove/hands on the table by the butter rolls,"* she sang along as the brown liquor put her in the mood. Sabrina had stretch marks from her two children, but her body was still in shape. She favored Keyshia Cole with a gap between her teeth, but her smile was beautiful. If she hadn't fallen in love with Darryl after her children's father died in Iraq, she could've married a rich white man easily.

Tiffany felt the liquor taking its effect on her as she found herself staring at Sabrina in a seductive way. What she didn't know was that Sabrina kept a pink pussycat pill inside her drink, it was the only way she could get turned on by Darryl after she found out he had been sleeping with men.

Sabrina noticed the look on Tiffany's face and remembered that she had spiked her own drink. *This could be fun*, she thought to herself as she poured Tiffany another shot. Tiffany joined Sabrina on the sofa and took her second shot. Sabrina wasted no time throwing her tongue down Tiffany's throat. Tiffany let her purse hit the floor and rolled on top of Sabrina. Her body was on fire as she started grinding on top of Sabrina. Both of their pussies were throbbing as Sabrina unzipped Tiffany's Chanel pullover hoodie and raised her t-shirt above her breast. Then she freed Tiffany's titties from her bra, watching her brown nipples grow. When Sabrina threw one of Tiffany's titties into her mouth, moans escaped Tiffany's mouth as she felt her juices making a mess inside her thong. With a titty still in her mouth, Sabrina unfastened Tiffany's pants and slid a finger into her juice box. Her hand became drenched with Tiffany's juices instantly, making Sabrina want to taste. She removed her middle finger from inside Tiffany and stuck it into her own mouth, sucking her sweet juices like it was honey. Tiffany stood up and pulled her pants down, revealing her freshly waxed vagina. Her juices were running down her leg. Sabrina noticed a few spots where Tiffany had been stuck with needles in the creases of her thighs.

Despite the dark marks, her vagina looked like it came straight out of a porn magazine. Sabrina grabbed Tiffany's hand and pulled her on top of her as she laid back on the sofa. Tiffany climbed on top of her face and rode it until she experienced a leg shaking orgasm. Now she wanted to see how Sabrina tasted. "Let's go to the room," she insisted. As she rolled over her legs were still wobbly as Sabrina got up and led her to the bedroom.

Sabrina stripped free of her panties and bra before climbing into her bed and holding her own legs behind her head. Tiffany crawled between her legs and planted kisses on Sabrina's pussy like she'd done it before, making Sabrina's juice box ooze from the pleasure. She slid her middle finger in and out of Sabrina as her tongue tickled her clit. Sabrina moaned as she grinded her hips to the rhythm of the beat Tiffany made as she slid a second finger inside her pussy, finger-fucking her while her tongue found its target. In mere minutes, she brought Sabrina to a breathtaking orgasm but she wasn't finished.

Once Tiffany cleaned up her mess, Sabrina went into her dresser and summoned her personal play toy, an eleven-inch dildo. After wiping the long black toy down with a wet wipe, Sabrina crawled back into bed and laid Tiffany on her back before easing the dick inside Tiffany's juice box, giving her deep and slow strokes until Tiffany started to fuck back.

Then Sabrina went faster and deeper, making Tiffany scream out in ecstasy. "Fuuuck!" Sabrina got into the scissors position before filling up her hole with the other end of the two-ended dildo. Both girls tightened their vagina muscles and played a sexual game of tug of war until they both reached their peak and exploded all over the rubber dick. *Killing her is definitely going to have to wait,* Tiffany thought as she laid beside Sabrina who was laying there breathing heavily from the workout they'd just experienced.

"Who would've known a visit from an old friend would end like this?" Sabrina said as she wrapped her arm around Tiffany.

Chapter 38

Marrissa

Marrissa sat in the waiting area of Loretta hospital as Heaven went into her second surgery. *God came right on time,* she thought to herself as she thought about the miracle her daughter had just received. Heaven's blood type match was found amongst a few of her recently donated blood types and organs. Marrissa spotted Doctor Shanklin walking through the double doors with a folder in his hand. This would be her second time seeing him since her daughter's incident occurred three days ago, and just like the first time, he gave her butterflies. Dr. Shanklin approached Marrissa with a warm smile on his face. She returned the smile as she stood to her feet. Dr. Shanklin extended his hand for a shake and Marrissa accepted. His cologne invaded her nostrils and gave her love spells.

"How are you feeling, Mrs. Hamilton?"

"I'm feeling great, just a bit tired," Marrissa replied.

"Losing blood can do that to you but I can assure you'll be just fine. Here, why don't we sit and talk."

Dr. Shanklin guided Marrissa back to her seat. He noticed the disturbed look on her face.

"Is there something bothering you?" he asked.

"I'm sorry, what do you mean by *losing blood*?" Marrissa asked.

"You know, the blood you donated for your daughter's blood transfusion." Dr. Shanklin assumed.

"Oh, I'm not the one who gave her blood. They ended up finding a match in the lab, I guess." Marrissa sounded a bit more comfortable as she figured that Dr. Shanklin was just guessing.

He furrowed his brows and opened his folder, scanning through files with his eyes. "Says mother right here, you are the mother, right?"

"Of course," Marrissa answered as she took a look at the paper.

Her heart dropped as it landed on the signature at the bottom.

"But this is not my signature. Where's my daughter?" Marrissa took off running with Dr. Shanklin right behind her.

She pushed through double doors and checked each room one by one. "Heaven!" she yelled each time she opened another patient's door.

Dr. Shanklin was lost as he tried to catch up with her.

"Mrs. Hamilton, wait a minute!" he called after her as she twisted the knob to open the next door.

She turned around and yelled, "What room is she in?"

"I'll take you to her room but first you have to calm down, and second, tell me what's going on."

Marrissa's face turned blue with fear.

"I never donated any blood. Me and my daughter's blood type doesn't match, she's adopted. Someone's out to get my child. You have to take me to her," Marrissa began to cry.

"Calm down," Dr. Shanklin grabbed Marrissa's hand and squeezed. "Right this way." He pulled her two doors down from the door she had just opened. "Go ahead, open it." He stepped back and let Marrissa twist the knob.

She opened the door and saw a nurse standing beside Heaven's bed. Marrissa rushed over to the nurse and yanked the woman by her shoulder. "Get away from her!" she yelled as the lady spun around, nearly falling.

"Mrs. Hamilton, this is your daughter's assigned nurse," Dr. Shanklin said as he grabbed her, preventing her from continuing.

The small nurse appeared to be frightened as she stood there with a dose of medication in her hand to relieve Heaven of any pain when she awakened.

"Ms. Ortiz, can you give us a moment?" Dr. Shanklin asked the frantic nurse.

She nodded and rushed out of the room, closing the door behind her.

"Mrs. Hamilton, you have to relax. Maybe it's all just a misunderstanding."

Marrissa listened to doctor Shanklin as embarrassment came over her. She felt overwhelmed by all the life changing episodes she endured in the past couple of years. Suddenly, Marrissa broke down and fell into Dr. Shanklin's arms.

He wrapped his arms around her for support, but the feeling became awkward as he felt an emotional attachment. He rubbed Marrissa's back as the temperature began to rise in the room. "Everything's gonna be just fine, I promise," he assured

How can he know that? How would he be able to promise me such a thing? He doesn't know what I've been through, she thought as she continued to cry on his chest.

She never wanted him to let go, she wanted him to hold her forever. She looked up and stared the doctor right in his eyes. His brown eyes marinated inside her soul, hypnotizing her momentarily. She leaned forward and kissed him right on the lips.

He didn't resist the first kiss but when Marrissa leaned in for a second one, he pulled away just as Karim came walking through the door.

"Is everything okay?" Karim asked, causing Dr. Shanklin to break free from Marrissa's embrace and create a little space between them.

"Um, everything's just fine. I was just telling Mrs. Hamilton here that your beautiful daughter had a successful surgery and should be awakening at any moment."

Karim turned his attention to Marrissa who hung her head low in her chest.

"Is that right?" he asked with his eyes glued to Marrissa.

Her look of guilt stuck a dagger into Karim's heart as the fear of losing her forever settled in his mind. Dr. Shanklin was a handsome man who seemed to have his way with the women. Karim saw the sparkle in Marrissa's eyes when she talked to him.

"I'll leave you two to it. If there's anything you need, I'll be in my office," Dr. Shanklin said as he walked past Karim on his way out the door.

Karim walked over to where Marrissa was standing and reached for her hand. She pulled away and turned around, leaving him staring at her back. As she stood there watching Heaven sleep, she felt Karim's presence looming over her 5'5 frame right before she felt his arms wrap around her waist. She imagined Dr. Shanklin holding her tightly, whispering sweet things in her ear. That fantasy was short-lived when Marrissa heard Karim's whisper in her ear

"Is she okay?" Marrissa's body tensed up as she pulled away from him. She turned around to face the man she used to love; the man she put so much on the line for.

"Yes, someone donated blood to her yesterday. They gave her a transfusion this morning." Marrissa sounded worried as the news Dr. Shanklin gave her came back to her head.

"That's good, you should be happy," Karim rubbed a piece of hair that hung lose over Marrissa's left eye and tucked it behind her ear.

"Karim, the donor signed my name. Whoever it was knows who I am, knows who she is," Marrissa pointed to Heaven.

Karim shot her a strange look.

"What chu mean,,, *signed your name?*"

"What I mean is the doctors thought that I was the one who gave our daughter blood. Me and you both know that's impossible, but whoever donated blood to her knows exactly who we are," Marrissa explained as her face turned blue with fear.

Karim stood there in his thoughts as he remembered the day he found a note on his bedroom dresser.

"Remember the day you took all your shit and moved out?" he asked.

"Karim now is not the time for your bullshit" Marissa spat. "Our daughter is being targeted by some insane son of a bitch and you're here trying to fix the unfixable" 'unfixable' Karim repeated in his mind.

"I'm not trying to fix shit; I'm trying to get to the bottom of this bullshit—"

"Well yes, I remember. Next question," she huffed.

"I found a letter on our bedroom dresser that said 'see you in hell' at first, I thought it was you playing some sick, twisted ass game," Karim admitted.

"Why would I do that? You're going to hell by yourself," Karim stared Marrissa in her eyes and noticed that she had become confused.

"So, you don't remember the note Gabby left before she passed away?" Karim asked, refreshing Marrissa's memory.

Her eyes widened with shock as she covered her mouth. "That's what I was trying to explain to you when you wouldn't answer my calls" Karim shot her a mug but Marrissa wasn't feeling the whole victim role, so she cut into him and she cut deep.

"You're really gonna sit here and play this innocent principal bullshit when you know exactly why I left your cheating ass"

Karim brows furrowed with confusion as Marrissa continued her assault.

"You were out there fucking your ex-wife when you could've been at home playing house —"

"Marrissa not now, okay."

Karim put an end to her emotional rollercoaster before it got hectic.

"I'm just saying, don't you think it's weird? How her perfume seems to linger around the house every now and then?"

"Who's perfume?" A grumpy voice asked.

Both parents shot their eyes down to Heaven's bed where she was laying there with her eyes barely open.

"No one's baby, how do you feel?" Marrissa took Heaven's hand in hers and rubbed gently.

"I feel like a crackhead," Heaven smiled.

Both of her parents burst into laughter until they heard a small knock on the door. Karim and Marrissa traded a stare before he decided to walk over and open it. He came face to face with a familiar face. While he was trying to connect the dots inside his mind the person solved his puzzle with a simple

"Hey, Principal Hobbs. Is this Heaven room?"

Karim stood clear of the doorway and gave April a clear view of her best friend. April rushed to Heaven's side and hugged her tightly. Heaven groaned a little as she wrapped one arm around her friend.

"Hi April, where have you been?" Marrissa spoked.

"Ms. Marrissa it's a long story but I'm back and I'm not leaving her side no time soon." Heaven smiled at the sound of her best friend's voice.

"How did you find me?" Heaven asked.

"Girl, you know you couldn't hide from me if you wanted to" April joked.

"Okay I may have needed a little help" she said as she pointed towards the doorway which Karim had left ajar.

Miracle stood there smiling shyly with her hands covering her mouth. Heaven stretched out her free arm, inviting Miracle to the reunion. Miracle sashayed across the room and grabbed Heaven's hand. A tear formed in the corner of her eye and fell freely, landing on top of Heaven's hand. Emotions built up through the entire room as everyone sat there in total silence.

"Don't be such a wuss," Heaven joked as she hit a button on the side of her bed, sitting her up straight. "Miracle this isn't your fault, and I don't want you to guilt trip yourself,"

"I'm fine," Miracle wiped the lonely tear away from her eye. "I'm just happy you're alive. You scared the sh—"

Miracle caught herself from cursing in front of Heaven's parents.

"Karim, why don't me and you talk out in the hallway while these kids catch up" Marrissa headed towards the door with Karim on her tail. Before closing the door, she looked back "We'll be close honey," she said before disappearing.

Out in the hallway, Marrissa picked up the conversation where they had left off.

"So, what's with this note? Do you think someone's playing a trick on us?" she asked.

"Honestly, I don't know. But what I do know is, that was Gabby's handwriting on that napkin"

"And how would you know that?" Marrissa challenged.

"Because I never threw away the old note," Karim said as he went inside his pants pocket and retrieved two balled up napkins.

He unfolded each one before handing them to Marrissa. Her eyes studied both napkins. Not only was the handwriting a match but the napkins were also the same.

"They're identical" Marrissa mumbled with her eyes still glued to the napkins.

"I know, that's why I thought you left the second one," Karim admitted. "Only me and you know about this," he finished.

"I would never play a twisted game like that"

"I know, but that's all I could think of at the moment," Karim shrugged his shoulders.

"Maybe we're being haunted by Gabby's ghost, all of this nonsense didn't start until we decided to be a family." Marrissa's assumption made Karim look at her awkwardly.

Ain't no damn ghost haunting us Marrissa, you're talking crazy now." Karim snatched the napkins and stuffed them back into his pocket.

"I suppose you have a better idea." Marrissa crossed her arms and waited for an answer.

Karim scratched his head, indicating that he was clueless.

"My point exactly," Marrissa said as she grabbed a hold of the doorknob to Heaven's room. Just as she began to twist, a voice called out

"Excuse me ma'am!" Marrissa turned around to see two familiar faces walking in her direction.

An awkward feeling settled in her gut as she released the doorknob and crossed her arms again.

"Yes," she answered with a slight attitude.

The cocky black detective extended his arm to greet her, but she left him hanging.

"I'm Detective–"

"I know who you are," Marrissa cut Detective Mason off. "The question is what do you want?" she asked, staring at the folder under his arm.

Detective Mason let his right arm rest and proceeded talking.

"I know we've been through this already, but we just want to ask your daughter a few more questions about the homicide that occurred on May 25th–"

"Homicide? That was no homicide. That poor child shot herself, I thought my daughter told you that"

"I know what she told me ma'am, but we have reason to believe she may have been concerned about her safety at the time. We have this guy in custody," Detective Mason held up a photo of Blackboy's mugshot. "He's currently charged with the murder of Stacy Lomax, we're just looking for a little help bringing this child to justice" Marrissa shot the cop a disbelieving look. *Something about this cop makes my skin crawl*, she thought to herself before saying

"Seems like you're looking for a paid vacation. My daughter would've told me the truth a long time ago so the fact that you charged someone else's child with murder is sick," Marrissa felt her blood boiling as her face turned beat red.

That could've been anyone's child that the system was trying to make a statistic.

"Ma'am we're just doing our job-"

"Well do your job elsewhere before I file harassment charges," Marrissa snapped before entering Heaven's room and slamming the door in the cop's face.

***

Heaven

Heaven waited until her parents disappeared behind the door then her attention went back to April.

"I can't believe I'm actually seeing you right now. It feels like forever since we last saw each other" Heaven's emotions started to get the best of her.

One side of her wanted to apologize for being a bad friend, the other side wanted to know why her friend went ghost on her while she was fighting for her life. April read the quizzical look on her bestie's face and began to explain herself.

"I know, bestie, I'm sorry. I know I was bogus for leaving your side when you were fighting for your life but the whole situation had me scared. My mama heard the rumors about Tiny gunning for us, and she moved me to the suburbs"

Heaven stared at April as she explained her situation. In her heart she understood April's mother's reason for moving her away. Like herself, April was an only child. No mother should have to experience the heartache Stacy's mother felt.

"Why didn't you text me? I still have the same number" Heaven asked.

"My mom took my cell phone for a whole year, when she finally got me a new phone, I barely remembered my own number. I thought I lost two friends in one lifetime, and I couldn't stomach that for a long time. I even thought you were a fake page when you reached out."

April's eyes were beginning to water causing an emotional rollercoaster to run around the entire room. Miracle even felt for the two girls as she listened to them pour their hearts out.

"No matter what happens, from this point forward I'll stick by your side. My mother couldn't change my mind if she tried," April promised.

The two girls hugged for a moment before April pulled back. "And thank you for bringing us back together," April hugged Miracle.

Heaven smiled at the sight of her two closest friends embracing. She wrapped her arms around them both. After a moment April broke the silence.

"Now, does anybody wanna tell me what Mr. Hobbs is doing here?" she asked, staring between Miracle and Heaven who began to smile.

"He's my dad," Heaven said.

"Dad? Girl, yo' mama fuckin' the principal? Okay, Marrissa girlll!" April cheered.

"April, he's my real dad but we'll save that story for another day"

"Un un, I can't wait to hear this shit—"

Slam!

The slamming of the door followed by the appearance of Marrissa and Karim brought the girls to a silence. Marrissa appeared to be frustrated as she strutted across the room. Heaven figured that her parents might've had an argument right outside the door.

"How are you feeling honey?" Marrissa calmed her temper down a bit to check on her daughter's well-being, although she was extremely overwhelmed.

"I'm fine. Mom, is everything alright?" Heaven could sense that something was bothering her mother and Marrissa couldn't shake the feeling, so she put it all on the table.

"Heaven you wouldn't lie to me about what happened to Stacy, would you?" Marrissa looked her daughter in the eyes as she waited for an answer.

"Of course, not, Mom. What made you ask such a thing?" Marrissa looked at April, then back to her daughter.

"Do you remember those two detectives that questioned the two of you?" Marrissa stared at her daughter, but the question was directed to April as well.

"Yea, the mean, black guy, right?" Heaven answered. She didn't like where this was going. She finally managed to catch up with her best friend and she was afraid that touching the sensitive topic would scare her away forever.

"Yes, exactly. They seem to believe that Stacy was *killed*. In fact, they even claimed to have someone in custody," Marrissa informed.

Her remark caused both Heaven and April to shoot each other clueless stares. Both girls knew that Stacy's death was an act of suicide, but if anyone was to face charges it would be Timo, which was also dead to the girls' knowledge.

"How could they arrest someone? When we already told them the truth?"

"They seem to believe different, that's why I'm asking you girls one last time before I file harassment charges against that crooked cop."

"We told them the truth, Mom. I wouldn't let nobody kill my best friend and get away with it," Heaven assured.

"I know. honey. I'm just making sure." Marrissa held Heaven's hand in hers.

"But I do want to know who they locked up for it," Heaven added.

"When you feel better, if you want to talk to them, I'll give them a call, but for now let's get you home and get cleaned up so I can feed you. You look a little hungry," Marrissa joked, pinching Heaven's arm gently.

"More like starving, let's get out of here," Heaven said before her mother went to fetch the nurse.

***

Timo

The number one spot bitch I'm right here, I'm right here, I'm right here/only the family in my eyes bitch we right here, we right here, we right here.

Timo rode the streets of Chicago like he owned them, listening to the up and coming artist 'Lil Durk' as he floored the gas to the brand new Porsche 911 that he copped with the money he'd stolen from Blackboy. Word had gotten around that he snitched on his homie, so his circle had gotten small as a Cheerio, but Timo didn't care as long as he had Ben Franklin's in his pocket. Symone, the hood's biggest hoodrat, sat in the passenger seat rolling up a blunt of Kush as they headed to the Gucci store downtown. Symone was undoubtedly a gorgeous chick with all the right assets, and she used her beauty to get whatever she wanted, whenever she wanted it. Timo always had dreams of fucking the hood Beyonce, but his bag was never right. She tried to get next to Blackboy once he came back from Texas, but he curved her like a wicked baseball pitch. He knew what she was about, and he wasn't going to spend a dime on her. That was another reason for Timo to be envious towards his day one.

Symone pulled down the sun visor on her side and checked herself out in the mirror. She applied lip gloss and rubbed them together before popping them seductively. Timo watched out the corner of his eyes as his dick bricked up in his pants. He felt like he accomplished something by bagging Symone. His eyes roamed her body from head to toe, causing him to lick his lips. Symone caught him in a trance and smiled.

"You see some'n you like?"

"I see some'n I *love*," Timo replied as he watched Symone spread her legs, revealing her freshly waxed pussy. She was sporting a Chanel skirt with no panties beneath it. Timo could almost taste the juice from her love box as he watched her spread her lips apart, giving him a sneak peek of her pink insides.

"This pussy ain't cheap," she said with no shame.

"And this nigga ain't broke," Timo popped his shit right back to her. He never had game growing up but now he sees the game came with the lifestyle. He had the money to say whatever he wanted and back it up. A broke boy couldn't talk rich nigga shit.

His words made Symone wet. She slipped a finger inside her pussy and stuck it inside Timo's mouth. He sucked her juices off her middle finger like it was a dipstick from the candy store.

"You like how that tastes?" She lowered her gaze to make her chestnut eyes look more seductive.

Symone wore contacts but everyone thought they were her real eyes because she wouldn't be seen without them.

"Hell yeah, you make a nigga wanna pull over right now." Symone noticed the bulge in his pants. *Judging by the size of his erection, he might actually be worth my while,* Symone thought to herself as she rubbed her hand over the length of his penis a shock went through Timo's body causing him to accidentally floor the gas of the sports car. He didn't realize he was approaching a redlight until Symone screamed "STOP!"

Timo looked up and quickly mashed on the brakes, missing the minivan in front of him by an inch as he cut his steering wheel to the left which gave him just enough room to merge into the turning lane. Just when he thought he'd made a clean escape from an accident, he felt a slight bump on his rear end. Not enough to cause any real damage, but enough to piss him off. Timo threw his Porsche in park and jumped out right in the middle of traffic.

He walked up to the old Honda Civic and beat on the window with his fist. He noticed an elderly lady behind the wheel with glasses on. Timo snatched the door open and came face to face with the barrel of a Tech 9. He heard doors being slammed a split second before he was surrounded by three more guns, all with extended clips. That's when Timo realized the old lady wasn't a lady at all. In fact, it was a familiar face he recognized under the wig.

"Throw 'em in the van!"

Timo heard Tay B's voice bark orders right before he was tossed in the back of the same van, he'd nearly hit a moment ago. *'I got caught slipping'* he thought right before he felt a hard object hit him in the back of the head.

Lights out!

The next time Timo opened his eyes, he blinked repeatedly. The room seemed to be spinning as he tried to study his surroundings. *Where the fuck am I?* he asked himself.

He couldn't remember what had transpired a few hours ago. He realized he was hogtied when he attempted to rub his head where he felt pain. The lights came on in the basement causing him to squint. Timo watched three figures walk into view== each of them holding guns in their hand. He felt himself being snatched up from the floor and thrown into a chair. Timo could hear his own heartbeat as sudden fear came over him.

When the fourth figure came into view holding a silver platter, Timo became confused. Tiffany stood over him and removed the top from the platter, making Timo's eyes wide with fear. He squirmed but the duct tape wrapped around his mouth prevented him from yelling. Judging by the tools on top of the platter Timo knew something traumatizing was in the cards for him. A butcher knife, set of needle and thread, pliers, and an injection needle filled with an unknown liquid substance made Timo's imagination run wild. Tears slipped through the cracks of his eyelids as he squeezed his eyes shut and said a silent prayer. *Our father who art in heaven, hallowed be thy name...*

"Don't cry so soon, you're gonna ruin the show," Tiffany said as she watched the goons tie Timo to the chair so he couldn't move.

Timo just knew that he was going to experience a painful death. A sudden pinch to the neck caused him to jump. His eyes shot open just in time to see Tiffany placing the empty needle back onto the platter before snatching the duct tape from his mouth. Timo's neck stiffened as he tried to dodge Tiffany's hand. She squeezed his jaw, forcing him to open his mouth then she used the pliers to grip his tongue. She squeezed so tight that it drew blood instantly.

"Arrrgh!" Timo yelled out.

The liquid that Tiffany injected in his neck had temporarily paralyzed him so that he couldn't put up a fight, but he could feel the pain. Tiffany picked up the butcher knife and waved it past Timo's eyes."

"This is what happens when you go against the grain," she said before giving Timo's tongue a clean chop.

He screamed as he watched her hold up the pliers with the piece of meat dangling inside them. Timo squeezed his eyes shut with disbelief. Sweat ran down his forehead as the pain settled in the back of his throat where the rest of his tongue rested.

"I cut your tongue off, so you'll never live to tell another lie, at least not by mouth" Tiffany placed his tongue inside a clear Ziploc bag and sealed it.

Timo's white Gucci shirt was filled with his own blood. He tried to close his mouth to prevent himself from bleeding out, but it only filled up from the inside until he had no choice but to spit it onto the floor. The extensive amount of blood loss eventually caused him to lose consciousness. Timo knew that this would be the last time he ever closed his eyes.

Chapter 39

Baby J

Baby J and his homies, Lil Danky and Vonnie, sat in the last row at the AMC movie theatre with their dates. Baby J was stuck to Porshia of course, but his friends would leave the movie to hunt for other females every ten minutes. Baby J and Porshia sported matching Hollister jogging suits and Jordan 11's. Since his auntie's friend dropped him off the package he'd been spoiling his girl and taking care of the bills. Porshia fed Baby J popcorn before eating a bit herself.

The movie *2 Fast 2 Furious* played as the kids began to make out. Baby J slid his hand down Porshia's jogging pants while she sat on his lap with her legs spread. His fingers found their way inside her love box, penetrating as deep as they could. Porshia crooned from the feeling. Her box got wetter and wetter the more Baby J caressed her honey pot. The temperature in the room seemed to increase as Porshia began to roll her hips in sync with her boyfriend's fingers.

She felt his manhood rock up instantly, ready for action. The movie theater was crowded but the last row was always empty. The engines roaring through the speakers blocked out any noise the couple might've made while they were making out. Porshia stripped out of her Hollister sweater and used it to cover her waist before pulling her jogging pants below her cheeks. Baby J freed his manhood, and Porshia took her time sliding down the length of his rod until it couldn't go any deeper inside her ocean. The two took their time grinding quietly until Baby J exploded inside his girlfriend's tunnel. After he released the last drip, they both raced to the restroom to clean up their mess.

Baby J took some paper towels and wet them before wiping his joggings where Porshia had left a huge puddle in the crotch area of his pants. He threw the paper towels inside the trash can before standing under the hot air dryer. As the stain began to dry, Baby J's friends came crashing into the restroom.
"My boy got him some ass at the movies," Danky yelled as he and Vonnie shook hands. Baby J turned around and smiled like it was nothing. He knew his friends had been watching along with Porshia's cousins. Neither of them seemed to care. "I was 'bout to get some from DD but her muhfuckin' breath stank," Danky turned up his nose as he joked about Porshia's cousin's oral hygiene. The boys burst out into laughter at Danky's dramatic ways.
"Naw for real, I kept feeding the bitch popcorn, nachos. Popcorn, nachos. That shit just won't go away."
Vonnie started coughing from Danky's joke mostly because he knew his boy was serious as a heart attack.
"Fuck that movie, y'all ready to bounce?" Baby J asked after checking to make sure his pants were dry.
"Yea let's drop them hoes off so I can go brush my teeth," Lil Danky answered.
The boys cracked up laughing again before exiting the bathroom to see Porshia and her cousins standing outside the women's bathroom whispering amongst each other. By the way the girl's attention shot to him, Baby J knew he was the topic of their discussion. He stepped towards the crowd as the girls went silent and grabbed Porshia's hand
"You ready to go?" Baby J asked.

He was a gentleman to his young lady. No one taught him how to treat a woman, he just knew how he would want someone to treat his sister. Or even his mom if she was still living.

The kids exited the movie theater and approached the white Honda Civic that Vonnie had stolen from the Northside. That's the part of the city where the rich white folks like to get drunk and party so hard until they forget where they parked their vehicles, so they catch cabs home. Sometimes they lost their cars. Sometimes Vonnie took them for a test drive for a few days before he ditched it and found a new hot car.

At 5:40 pm on a Saturday evening, the sun was still lingering in the sky. Other crowds came spilling out of the movie theatre and walking to their vehicles. Baby J saw adults and kids making their escape. One crowd in particular caught Baby J's attention. It was a small group of teenage boys and one younger boy who seemed to be about nine years old. The boys looked familiar, Baby J knew for certain that he'd seen them around before, he just couldn't remember when and where. He proceeded to hop in the backseat with Porshia and her cousins while Lil Danky rode shotgun with Vonnie.

Looking out his window, Baby J could see the boys pointing at their vehicle. He tapped Vonnie, who was driving, on the shoulder and whispered something in his ear. Vonnie looked into his rearview mirror to see the boys rushing to their minivan. He started the car up and sped out of the parking lot. He turned left then right at every corner so that the van couldn't follow them.

"Who the fuck was that?" Danky asked, catching wind of the situation.

"That was the niggas who jumped me," Baby J answered, finally putting a face to the person he remembered from the crowd. His Long Live Romeo t-shirt was a dead giveaway. Baby J had the .38 special that Boozer had given him tucked at his side so the girls couldn't see it. Porshia and his homies were the only people that knew he was packing heat. Vonnie made his way to Division and Long street with no signs of the van in sight. He stopped at the red light and waited for it to turn green.

"But I thought them niggas was —" Vonnie tapped Lil Danky's chest to prevent him from saying too much around the girls. He knew how Danky loved to show off. He used to share war stories about his big brother Bizzy to the whole school at lunch time. He even spread the rumor of Baby J having a gun at school. The principal heard the rumor and called the police to search Baby J's backpack. Of course, they found nothing. Baby J was too smart to put his pistol inside his own bag; he instructed Porshia to hold it until school ended each day.

The light turned green, and Vonnie continued to drive to the neighborhood.

Thump! The car was rear ended.

Vonnie looked in his mirror and saw the same Caravan trying to run them off the road. Thump! They hit the car harder this time. Vonnie floored the gas pedal, trying to lose the van but their car was too slow. The van played bumper carts down Division Street.

"Turn right here!" Baby J hollered as the girls started to panic in the backseat.

Vonnie made a hard right turn onto Lavergne street, nearly hitting the curb in the process.

"Aaah!" the girls screamed in unison.

Boop!

Vonnie sped over a speed hump at 40 mph causing the car to float in the air momentarily. Baby J tried to keep calm, but he felt his composure slipping slowly. Porshia squeezed his hand, interlocking her fingers with his. The temperature of his hand told her how heated he was. Before she knew it, the back window was sliding down.

Boc! Boc! Boc!

Baby J fired three shots at the van. *Skiirr!* The van slid, nearly hitting a parked car. Vonnie made a quick left on Augusta Street and stomped the gas like a mad man. The Caravan never appeared behind them, but the police did with their blue lights flicking, indicating for Vonnie to pull over.

"Shitting me!" Vonnie said as he sped right through the red light on Cicero in the middle of traffic.

While the cops were waiting to get past the busy traffic, Vonnie had already made another left turn, then another right. He drove the car at NASCAR speed until he turned in the alley of his home on Avers and Thomas. Vonnie's block had a few vacant lots, which he used to park all of his stolen cars until they were too hot, then he would sell them to the next person for seventy-five dollars.

Vonnie deaded the ignition and all the kids vacated the stolen vehicle before walking up the alley until they reached the back of Vonnie's home. Vonnie jumped the black gate and twisted the lock to let his friends in. "Shhh!" he told the girls to keep quiet. "If my O.G. hear y'all she's gone curse my ass out," he said before using his house key to enter the apartment building through the back door.

"Check it out, Baby J. Aye Lil Danky sit right here with them we'll be right back."

"Aight bet," Lil Danky replied.

His mind was still stuck on the most interesting thing that ever happened in this life. He watched Baby J handle his .38 Special like a pro. Vonnie and Baby J disappeared behind the door while Lil Danky sat on the back porch with Porshia and her cousins.

Vonnie tiptoed to his room with Baby J behind him. His mother wouldn't mind the girls camping out. Vonnie lied because he didn't want the girls to find out his mom was a dope fiend. The only person that knew that secret was Baby J, who admitted to having the same secret up until his mom passed away. Vonnie went through his clothes bag and threw Baby J an outfit out of his wardrobe.

"Put that on right quick and give me yo pipe, imma hide it until we find out what happened," Vonnie suggested.

Baby J stripped out of his clothes and handed his best friend his gun without argument. He knew that Vonnie was a little more seasoned to the streets than him.

Baby J threw the black Nike hoodie over his head and put on the AND1 basketball shorts Vonnie had given him. It wasn't his style, but it'll have to do for the moment. Vonnie grabbed a set of car keys from the back of his closet which belonged to another stolen car he had stashed on the next block. He put the pistol away and threw Baby J's outfit into his dirty clothes bag.

"Come on, let's drop ole' girl 'nem off," Vonnie said.

Baby J dialed Boozer's number as he followed Vonnie out the house.

"Hello," Baby J heard Boozer's voice come through the receiver.

"I need you big bro."

***

Boozer

Boozer threw the dice and snapped his finger "Free Teezo!" he yelled as the dice landed on six, one. He collected his winnings and rolled the dice again. "I said, *free Teezo!*" he yelled the same thing for five straight minutes as he went on a hot streak against his big homies.

He finally crapped out when he heard his iPhone ring inside his pocket. "Fuuuck!" he yelled before retrieving his phone and looking at the caller ID. He read Baby J's name across the screen and answered, "Hello."

Baby J spoke on the other end of the receiver and Boozer could sense that something was wrong. "Wassup? Talk to me," Boozer became concerned.

"Not over the phone. I'll pull down on you."

"You know where I'm at, slide on me," Boozer said before ending the call. He faded his big homie Fresh on the D's "Dice don't hit," he called out as he threw another ten on the ground.

"Bet," Fresh matched his bet and rolled six, five.

"Bet back?" Fresh scooped his winnings and shot the dice again. A black Volvo came to a complete stop right in front of the dice game. Boozer's homie Bizzy gripped his pistol. "That's for me," Boozer said before catching the dice. "Yo' point," he told Fresh, giving him the point. "Let me go holla at my shorty real quick."

Baby J and Vonnie climbed out of the hot car and met Boozer on the curbside.

"That's a steamer right?" Boozer pointed to the car.

"Yeah," Baby J answered.

"Park that muhfucka in the alley it's gone be hot sitting right there," Vonnie hopped in the whip and started it up before pulling the hot car around to the back of the park.

"What chu got going on, lil bro?" Boozer asked, noticing that Baby J had on a hoodie in eighty-degree weather.

"Them niggas that jumped me tried to get up with me today."

"Who? Mook 'nem?" Boozer asked as his temper rises.

"Yeah, they peeped me coming out of the movies on Grand and followed me."

"Where yo' strap was at?" Boozer asked.

"I had it on me, I got them niggas up off me." Boozer cracked a slight smiled and shook hands with Baby J.

"You must need some more food," Boozer said, guessing that Baby J needed a refill on shells.

"That too, but I need you to see if somebody got hit. They had a shorty in the car with them. I ain't tryna hurt no kids, bro," Baby J seemed concerned about the child he saw at the movies.

"You weren't in that car right there, were you?" Boozer asked, pointing his thumb over his shoulder at the stolen vehicle in the alley.

"Naw, my boy swapped it out," Baby J answered.

"Did y'all set the other one on fire?"

"Naw, we just parked it by his ole lady crib"

"That was dumb lil bro. The first thing they gone do is track the vehicle, then they gone swab it for fingerprints. I know y'all didn't wear gloves to the movies."

"We didn't wear gloves at all. We didn't think we would have to get our hands dirty, to be honest," Baby J spoke truthfully.

When Boozer gave him protection he accepted it, but he didn't think the day he had to use it would come so soon. He didn't think it would come at all. Baby J was a hooper and that was all he wished to be. He was a sweetheart like his mother, but he got more than just his last name from his father. His temper went from zero to a hundred in seconds even when playing basketball. His coach told him he'd have to learn to control it, but Baby J blew him off.

"That wasn't smart … that wasn't smart at all lil bro," Boozer said before pulling out his iPhone. If anyone knew what was going on it was Facebook. Social media was a quicker news source than WGN news. If anything went down in Chicago, social media would be the first to broadcast it.

"They saying something happened on Lavergne, was that y'all?"

"What they saying?" Baby J asked, ignoring Boozer's question.

"They saying somebody got shot inside a minivan but they're not saying who," Boozer said as he kept surfing the media for more evidence.

Pull through you got this.
Praying for my boy Slob I know you hard body.

Boozer read a couple of random Facebook posts aloud. Baby J's heart rate increased; he became nervous.

"Look, just have yo' lil man torch the steamer and bring me back the pipe. I want you to lay low for a minute it's gone be straight." Boozer assured him that everything was just fine. Even though he didn't know for sure that everything would be alright, he gave Baby J a sense of hope.

"I'm 'bout to stand on that right now, then imma hit the line."

"Yeah, hit me ASAP," Boozer said before giving Baby J a fist bump and returning to his dice game.

Once Baby J returned to the vehicle, he told Vonnie the game plan that Boozer created.

"Yeah, that sounds like a plan. Imma drop you off by the crib and I'll handle the steamer," Vonnie said

"Naw, I wanna be with you. It's my work"

"It's nobody's work. Imma make this all disappear, just listen to me. If them people get ahold of you and find out that your foster parents are missing you going back in the system and I ain't having that."

Baby J knew his boy was absolutely right, he just didn't feel comfortable leaving his friend's side. Especially when Vonnie was cleaning up *his* mess.

"Just go handle yo' business and slide back to my crib when everything's everything," Baby J instructed.

"You know I got you," Vonnie said as he started up the car and drove off in the direction of Baby J's home.

Chapter 40

Vonnie

After taking Baby J home, Vonnie headed straight to the neighborhood gas station on Pulaski and Grand. He parked the hot car a block away to keep it off camera. After buying a gas can he purchased five dollars' worth of gas and filled the gas can to the top. *Everything's gonna be just fine,'* Vonnie repeated to himself on his way home. He wanted to believe his own words, but reality gave him butterflies. He'd rather take the heat than let the system claim his best friend again. Life has already stuck it to him hard. Baby J had potential with his basketball game and Vonnie just wanted to see him make it.

Vonnie parked the vehicle two blocks over, grabbed the gas can from the backseat and walked up the street to where he had parked the old hot car. He twisted the top off the can and began to pour gasoline all over the stolen vehicle. He reached into his pocket and retrieved a Bic cigarette lighter before popping the trunk to search for a piece of cloth to set on fire. Suddenly, police cars surrounded him, quicker than he could blink, with their lights flickering. All he heard was the sound of tires screeching followed by the slamming of car doors. "Freeze!" the officers yelled with their weapons drawn.

Vonnie threw his hands up in surrender with the light still in his hand. Two officers tackled him to the ground and cuffed his hands behind his back before pulling him back to his feet. After searching him to make sure he wasn't armed with any weapons, the officers threw him in the back of their vehicle while other officers searched his apartment. It didn't take them long to discover the weapon and jogging suit Baby J had left in his room only an hour ago.

After watching the officers walk out of his apartment holding a clear bag with the .38 special, Vonnie hung his head low in defeat. Being slow on his feet had cost him. *It is what it is*, he told himself. There were only two options at this point: r`l at on his best friend or take the blame. He made up his mind the moment the heat hit the fan. Vonnie was a firm believer in God and he knew God has a reason for everything he does so he took the hit like a man.

"You owe me one," he said to himself but the message was for Baby J. The police drove Vonnie to the police station and processed him in, charging him with two counts of attempted murder.

Chapter 41

Blackboy

Blackboy sat at the dayroom table playing spades with a few homies he met in jail. He let his hair grow into a mini afro over the past few months. His mother convinced him to grow his dreadlocks again. "Coleman, you have a visitor," the CO called out. Blackboy knew he had a scheduled visit today, but his mom wasn't supposed to show up until 3:30 pm. It was barely 11:00 am. Blackboy finished his hand and threw on his fresh DOC shirt before running to the bathroom to check himself out in the mirror.

"Come on, Coleman, I have to get you downstairs before I go on break," the correctional officer flirted. Blackboy had pull in division ten. His money stretched a long way especially for his age and Chapo taught him how to use it to get whatever he wanted. Blackboy ate real meals three times a day and even had a cell phone snuck in by Ms. Robinson, the five-day officer for his deck.

"Don't be rushing me, Ms. Robinson, you know it takes time to look this good." Blackboy flashed his perfect smile. Ms. Robinson just shook her head and smiled. They both knew what she wanted to say but she'd have to save her remark until they reach the elevator.

Blackboy went inside his shower bag and grabbed his Gucci cologne and sprayed himself with the fragrance before passing his celly the bag and joining Ms. Robinson in the bubble.

"Just say you miss me, you ain't gotta do all that."

"Boy you so extra, lil black ass. Let's go." Ms. Robinson was hooked on his demeanor. She never saw a young man his age with so much swagger and the pockets to back it up. Not to mention his sex game.

"We gotta take the stairs, the elevator not working," Ms. Robinson said before winking her eye.

"Aw shit, you tryna bust it open for daddy today?"

"I'm tryna bust it open for daddy every day. I can't wait until you come home so I can throw all this ass back on you."

Ms. Robinson put a switch in her walk as they approached the stairwell. Blackboy kept his hands behind his back and just stared. Once they stepped into the stairwell and out of sight of the cameras, Ms. Robinson began to unfasten her uniform pants. Blackboy whipped his dick out and stroked himself into a full erection. Ms. Robinson bent over with both hands on the stairs. Blackboy could see her juices running out of her pussy and down her leg. Ms. Robinson was chocolate complected so the oils that she used made her shine like glaze on a donut.

Her booty hole and vagina were freshly waxed, giving her that magazine-ready sex appeal. Blackboy wasted no time entering her fortress from behind. He went in deep until the tip of his dick touched the back of her walls.

Ms. Robinson bit her lip and squeezed her eyes closed to prevent from screaming. Blackboy was on a time limit, so he banged her back out with no remorse. He spread her cheeks to give him full access to her tunnel. Five straight minutes of pounding and Blackboy was spilling his seed inside the CO. He never gave condoms a thought when having sex with big booty Ms. Robinson. He was just grateful to have the opportunity of having sex while being incarcerated. Ms. Robinson went inside her clear bag and passed Blackboy a wet wipe to wipe himself off before grabbing another one for herself.

After cleaning his tool, Blackboy handed her the wipe and pulled up his pants. Ms. Robinson tucked the wipe away and adjusted her clothes as a voice came through her walkie-talkie.

"Visitation to Ms. Robinson."

"Go for Ms. Robinson," she responded as she rushed down the stairs.

"Did you pull out that one time from 2-girl for visitation?"

"In route," Ms. Robinson responded as she turned the key to the door and pulled it open.

Blackboy stepped in and walked towards the visitation room.

"Enjoy your visit?" Ms. Robinson said with a sweet voice. Blackboy just winked.

"Visitation one time on your door," Ms. Robinson said before disappearing into the stairwell.

The door was buzzed and Blackboy stepped inside the waiting area with the other inmates. A minute later, another door was buzzed and the inmates stepped in to see their visitors. Blackboy scanned the room with his eyes in search of his mother, but he couldn't locate her. He heard a tap on the glass booth where two girls were sitting. They looked like twins from a distance. Their eyes seemed to be looking right at him. He took a step closer, and his heart melted at the sight before him. Heaven was sitting there looking beautiful as the day she was born with a perfect smile on her face. Blackboy couldn't believe his eyes. He took a seat at the booth with a quizzical look spread across his face.

Heaven placed her mouth closer to the speaker and said "Heeyy." Her voice gave him butterflies.

"Wassup beautiful? What chu doin here?" he asked, still surprised to see her face after all these years.

"I thought you'd be happy to see me."

"Oh, believe me, I'm happy as hell. I just can't believe you're here right now," Blackboy said.

He became a little shy in front of his first love.

"Well, I heard you were in some type of trouble, and I couldn't sit around and let you take the fall for something that had nothing to do with you. How the hell did they charge you with this nonsense anyway?"

"That nigga Timo snaked me out, but it's all good. Cat's got his tongue right now." Heaven didn't get the hidden message. What she didn't know is, there was no hidden message. Tiffany literally fed his tongue to an alley cat.

"I thought he killed himself."

"Naw, he survived. But that nigga's a dead man walking."

"I told you that he didn't deserve your friendship, I never liked him," Heaven admitted.

"I know, baby. I'mma need your phone number so my lawyer can reach out to you. I could beat this shit in a motion in a few months if you sign an affidavit letting them know what really went down." Blackboy was excited to see Heaven standing there for multiple reasons. She held his freedom and his future in her hands.

"I can give you that but besides that, how you been holding up?"

"I was good before, but I feel great now. You still my future wife?" Blackboy flashed his charming smile. He looked much better than she remembered. His small afro was neatly trimmed, and he had grown a goatee.

"I don't know about all that. You've probably been cheating on me." Miracle nudged Heaven with her elbow and whispered something in her ear and they both laughed.

"Excuse me for being so rude. Hey, how you doing?" Blackboy greeted Miracle.

"Heyy," Miracle spoke shyly. His presence was overwhelming. He seemed to be much more than what meets the eye.

"I'm the infamous Blackboy that Heaven been bragging about," he joked.

"She told me about you, but I think she told me about the wrong person."

"He's ten times better, right?" Heaven said. She didn't expect Blackboy to change so much in just two years. Blackboy smiled at the compliment.

"So, future wife, how have you been doing since the last time I saw you?"

"Besides being hit by a car, put in a coma for a year, and being shot... I've been okay, I guess."

Blackboy turned his attention to the crutches Heaven held by her side, then to the scars all over her body. His heart broke into pieces. "Shot?" he asked. *I must've heard her wrong,* He studied the rest of her body.

"Yes, *shot*. But none of that matters we're gonna get you home so you can take me on that date we talked about." Heaven smiled to lighten up the situation. She could see the vein that appeared in the center of his forehead. He was a different Blackboy from the teenager she met, although she cared about him the same. Heaven just hoped he didn't outgrow her mentally.

"Who the hell shot you?" Blackboy asked, ignoring Heaven's attempt to shift the conversation.

Miracle knew it was a mistake for Heaven to tell Blackboy she was shot. Miracle saw that same look in his eyes that she saw in Boozers when he found out she had been shot at. That same night, three of the boys were shot. Only two of them were lucky enough to survive.

"Bae, I'm okay. I just want to get you home and live my life," Heaven said.

She would be lying if she said his temper didn't turn her on. She was ready to give herself to him in every way.

"Visit over. Come on gentleman!" the officer yelled through the intercom.

Blackboy pulled out his phone book and a pen "What's yo number?"

Heaven gave him her phone number. Surprisingly, it hadn't changed and Blackboy remembered it. "I'm about to call you in five minutes, pickup," Blackboy said before placing two fingers to his lips and touching the glass. Heaven followed suit and left the visiting cage. Even though Heaven made his day with her surprise visit, Blackboy was disturbed by the news she shared with him. *Coma... Shot...,* he wondered what the hell happened since he was arrested.

Ms. Robinson came back to get him and take him back up the stairwell but this time he refused. "Let's take the elevator. I gotta get back on deck." Blackboy was in no mood for sex. Heaven was on his mind heavy.

"How was your visit?" she asked, trying to make small talk. She could sense that something was wrong. *Maybe he got some bad news,* she thought. To her surprise it was the total opposite.

"That was the best visit I ever had," Blackboy answered. His mind was in the clouds.

"Yo' mama had good news for you?"

"That wasn't my O.G. but she was just as important" Blackboy kept it real. Play time was over.

"Aw, okay," Ms. Robinson felt a hint of jealousy as she pressed the call button on the elevator with much force.

Blackboy sensed her attitude, but he paid her no mind. She was just a chew toy he used to pass time. Now that his time was coming to an end, he wanted nothing to do with her. He knew he would have to play his role for a little longer in order to keep his cell phone and the other perks that came with the game. But as far as sex, Blackboy only wanted Heaven. With all the scars, she was still at a ten on his scale.

Blackboy stepped back on the tier and told Ms. Robinson "Lock me up real quick."

She rolled her eyes and strutted past him, walking straight to his door. She unlocked it and stood aside. Blackboy walked in and closed the door behind himself. Ms. Robinson placed her face to his chuckhole and whispered, "You bet not be calling no bitch," and walked away without waiting for a response.

She knew the whole deck was watching her, but she didn't care. Blackboy had promised her that she wouldn't have to work once he made it out. If it was any truth in his promise, Heaven had broken it.

Blackboy placed a long strip of tissue in his chuckhole as a 'Do not disturb' sign and retrieved his cell phone out of the ceiling light. The first person he called was Heaven. They had a lot of catching up to do.

Chapter 42

Baby J

Baby J stayed at the gym shooting jump shots after a long day of hooping. Since he found out his friend Vonnie was charged with two counts of attempted murder, during which a child had been hit in the chest. This concerned Baby J deeply. Baby J spent all his time chasing his dream. The streets weren't in his future. He wasn't built for the streets or so he thought. Little did he know he had his dad's blood flowing through his veins, which was worse than venom.

Baby J shot up another three and he hit all net. He jogged to catch his own rebound, ran back to the three-point line and shot again. His friend Vonnie could be facing juvenile life and Baby J couldn't live with the thought of his best friend serving all that time for something he didn't do. Baby J told Vonnie that he'd come forward and take the rap but Vonnie told him not to. "This ain't gone hurt me like it'll hurt you, trust me. Just promise me you gone make it to the League so we can become more than statistics," those were his words. Baby J promised him that he'd get them both out of the hood.

Baby J went to the line for another shot. He heard his cell phone ringing inside his backpack which was sitting on the bench. After retrieving it he read the caller ID before answering it. "Hello," Baby J said, waiting for the person to speak.

"May I speak with Juan Alverez?" the person asked, causing Baby J's heart to skip a beat. *Nobody calls you by your government name, but the government,* he thought as he held the phone up to his ear. "Hello," the person on the phone spoke again.

"May I ask who's calling?" Baby J asked. He was two seconds away from pressing the end button on his iPhone.

"My name is Tom Hardnick, I'm an investigator hired by Ciara Jones." Baby J heard nothing past the guy's name which he remembered vividly.

"How can I help you?"

"The question is, how can I help *you*? I have some news for you, but it requires us to meet in person, do you mind if I drop by in maybe an hour?" Tom asked. It sounded like he had the news Baby J has been searching for over six years.

"Sounds good I'll be waiting for you," Baby J said, full of excitement.

"Great, see you in a bit," Tom said before ending the call.

Baby J rushed home and showered before calling Miracle to share the news with her. She arrived thirty minutes later with Heaven and April. Baby J opened the door and spoke to the girls before pulling Miracle into the hallway, out of earshot of her friends.

"What's with the crowd?" he asked.

"You called me in the middle of going somewhere. I had two options, rush here with them," Miracle nodded her head towards the front door where her friends were standing, "or drop them off and risk missing this opportunity." Miracle shrugged her shoulders.

"You know how I feel about this situation, sis"

"Relax, baby boy, you're not the only one with family secrets. Besides, April thinks you're cute."

Baby J didn't care much for Miracle's friends' opinion, he was more concerned about the news he was about to receive concerning his little brother. "Whatever, I just don't want to talk around them. When he comes, we'll talk in the kitchen—"

The bell rang, cutting Baby J's sentence short. He dashed for the door in excitement. The girls stepped aside and let him by. Baby J twisted the knob and pulled the door open,

"Hi, is Ciara home?" the unfamiliar man asked. This was not the man Baby J expected to see. Tom was tall with dark hair, the man standing face to face with Baby J was average height with light brown hair. His street clothes told Baby J that he wasn't there for business.

"Who are you?" Baby J asked.

"I'm just a friend of hers; I stopped by because she hasn't been answering my calls. I was beginning to worry about her."

Now was not the time to discuss his auntie. Baby J wanted the man to leave but he didn't want to come off as being disrespectful. The man noticed the discomfort written on Baby J's face.

"I'm sorry, just tell her –"

"Dad?" Heaven called out to Josh. He looked up and became speechless as he stared Heaven in the eyes. "What are you doing here?" she asked.

"I … uh." Josh's face became red with embarrassment. He hadn't seen Heaven since she was in the coma, now he was here with no words to explain why he was at someone else's doorstep looking for a missing lady. Josh turned around and ran off the porch, back to his car.

Baby J closed the door. "What was that about?" he asked Heaven.

"I'm just as lost as you. All I know is I haven't seen him since I laid in that hospital bed fighting for my life. He ran out on me and my mother." Heaven became emotional.

Baby J began to feel sorry for her. Even though she was beautiful, he could tell she'd been through a lot.

The bell rang again. This time Baby J became fed up. He yanked the door open with force.

"Oh, my bad," Baby J said to Tom who was standing there in his sharp suit with a suitcase in his hand.

"Is everything alright?" Tom asked.

"Everything's fine. Come on in." Baby J cleared the doorway for Tom. Tom followed him into the kitchen.

"Hi, it's been a while" Tom extended his hand for a shake from Baby J, then Miracle. Baby J's expression went from frustration to eagerness. "Mr. Alvarez, I finally have a very useful piece of information I would like to share with you, but first I'll need to discuss a new fee for my troubles. I had to cross a couple of guidelines to discover what I've –"

"How much?" Baby J asked. He was in no mood for small talk.

"Well, the information I gathered cost me two thousand dollars."

Baby J left Tom standing in the kitchen as he walked to his bedroom. He returned a minute later with a knot of bills in his hand. It was the last of what Tiffany had given him a couple of months ago. He handed it to Tom who counted it and stuffed the money inside his jacket pocket before continuing.

"It took me some time, but I figured out *who*, now I just have to figure out *where*," Tom said as he opened the suitcase and presented a picture. "This here is Terrell Loomis AKA Ja'Mari Jones. He was adopted out of foster care by Loretta Loomis, who is now deceased. Since Ms. Loomis was Terrell's legal guardian, he's now wanted by DCFS since she's no longer living ..."

Baby J zoned out on the picture as Tom went on and on about how he discovered who his brother was. Tom figured out who, but Baby J had already known where. His baby brother was lying up in a hospital bed fighting for his life all because of a gunshot wound caused by Juan Alverez Jr. himself. Baby J became dizzy right there on the spot. Miracle pulled out a chair from the kitchen table and caught him before he hit the ground. Baby J sat down in the chair and caught his breath.

"Is everything okay?" Tom asked.

Miracle passed her brother a glass of water, which he downed before responding to Tom.

"Are you sure this information is accurate?" she asked. Baby J wanted to be sure he was given the right information before moving forward.

"I assure you that I'm the best at what I do. The route I took to unfold this information can get some good people fired and thrown behind bars. Everything that I just showed you is 100% percent accurate," Tom assured.

"Thanks for your service, Tom, but we got it from here."

"But don't you need help finding him before the system claims him?" Tom asked, searching for another way to collect extra money.

"No ... I know exactly where he's at."

Chapter 43

Tiffany

Tiffany whistled throughout her huge home in Plainfield, Illinois and her three large pit bulls came charging for their food. Tiffany kept Max, Snow and Phoenix around the house for extra protection. She bought the puppies when they were three months old. At nearly a year, they already looked full grown.

The doorbell rang and Tiffany's eyes shot to her camera system bell. She watched as the FedEx carrier delivered a large box and ran back to their truck.

Once they drove away, Tiffany grabbed her Glock from beneath her kitchen table and walked to the front door with her three monsters behind her. She opened the door and picked the box up. Seeing her real name on the label raised a red flag since she had purchased the house in her alias. She carried the box inside and locked her doors quickly. The dogs jumped at the box with excitement.

"Down!" she ordered. The pups fell to all four legs and stared with their tongues out.

Tiffany walked to the kitchen to fetch a knife. The dogs followed her once again. Whatever was in the box had the pit bull's undivided attention. She cut the tape and opened the box. "Uurgh!" Tiffany puked up her breakfast at the sight before her. Ciara's head was sitting in the box with her eyes wide open and her flesh was decaying.

Tiffany slammed the box closed and broke down into tears. The dogs began to bark uncontrollably. Something was wrong and they could sense it. Fear came over Tiffany as reality set in. The devil had arrived in her town and he came to play. Tiffany knew as long as she kept the battle in her city, she could put up a fight with Chapo, but if he got her back to Texas she could kiss her life goodbye. The law would look the other way at his gruesome crimes.

Tiffany grabbed her cell phone and made a call.

"Hello."

"Bring the whole team to headquarters. We're going to war whoever doesn't comply, cut their water off immediately." Click! Next, she went to her basement and opened a safe. She emptied the safe and loaded guns into three large duffle bags. She had everything from Glocks to Micro Draco's. She's been getting ready for this day. Chapo came bothering the wrong bitch.

Tiffany tucked her Glock on her thigh holster and strapped an AR pistol around her shoulder. She unlocked her front and back doors and let her dogs go take a sniff around like she had taught them. They returned a few minutes later with their tails wagging, indicating that the coast was clear. Tiffany set her house alarm and exited through the garage. She hopped in her black Suburban truck, threw her duffle bags in the back as her Pitbull's hopped into the backseat.

An hour and thirty minutes later, Tiffany pulled into the parking lot of the O'Block community. From her car she could see a huge crowd of killers awaiting her arrival. She dialed Tay B's number so he could help with the bags while she put her Pitbull's on leashes. He was the only person besides Tiffany they were friendly with. Tay B walked to the trunk of the car with two of his goons. Phoenix jumped out of the backseat and charged

"Oh, shit!" one of the boys yelled as he tried to take cover.

"Phoenix, no!" Tiffany called out as she climbed out the truck. Phoenix was the female out of the three dogs, so she was the feistiest. Tiffany grabbed her by the collar and connected her leash. Tiffany held all three leashes in one hand. As strong as the dogs were, they respected her too much to drag her, so they walked at her pace.

When Tiffany got inside the gate the crowd grew much larger. She had just proven to herself how much power and respect she had when she looked at the killers from different sets. The same hoods that shot and killed each other daily were setting their differences aside to aid and assist the First Lady. Tiffany had brought the MOE's from no limit, the BD's & GD's from The Dearborns, The Mickey Cobras from the Ickies, and even the Insanes from Inglewood.

They cleared the path for her as she walked through the O' with her pits. She had a set of keys to an empty apartment. She had the apartment sitting until it was time to shine. Tiffany inserted a key and twisted it to the left, unlocking the door before pushing it open. Inside, there was only one chair and a large table.

Tiffany occupied the seat as she watched the goons fill out the whole apartment. She'd had the walls to every room knocked down to create more space. The apartment was the size of a gym room. Once the door was slammed shut and locked Tay B sat the bags on the table. Tiffany began her speech. "Listen up, I know some of you might not want to be here, sitting amongst your enemy, but right now a bigger problem has arrived at my doorstep and if I have a problem, all of us have a problem." She scanned the room, looking each individual in their eyes for a sign of deception. The goons kept their game faces on. "The drugs these blocks are pushing came from a very powerful man; I'm talking cartel-type of shit. He's in Chicago and he didn't come for drugs, he wants blood. If I die today all those cars y'all buying are done. All those guns y'all buying are done. Back to the basic block hustling. That's why I called this meeting so we can solve this problem and move on with our lives." Tiffany nodded at Tay B who opened each duffle bag and spread the guns out on the table.

The crowd can be heard taunting. "These guns are not here to use on each other. They are not here for music videos," She looked at the few rappers she knew who had a buzz around the city. "Those guns were bought for this man and this man only." Tiffany held up a picture of Chapo. She knew he had come to personally claim her life for the sake of his son Milo, but she also knew he hadn't come alone.

"This man is ruthless. I want y'all to keep your eyes open for anybody with his same skin complexion, they'll buy drugs, snort 'em, and still blow yo' shit off. Anybody who thinks they're bigger than this shit can leave now because once this meeting is over, if I hear about one body being dropped, the shooter and his whole hood will be on SOS."

Tiffany stood up and walked over to the wall where the key rack hung. She emptied the rack and passed out over twenty keys. Each one belonged to a different vehicle. Chapo was powerful but he had come to the wrong place. This side of town belonged to Tiffany. He wasn't about to scare her out of her own city. Just like him, she had killers who would put their lives on the line for her.

Tiffany discussed the shifts for hustling and security and split the guns amongst the hoods before ending the meeting. What she didn't know was that she hadn't given Chapo enough credit. He had more connections than she believed. In fact, he had eyes on her entire speech.

He sat outside in his van, watching her plan for war through a hidden camera he had attached to one of his hired workers in the city. While Tiffany thought she was prepared, Chapo was always two steps ahead of her. She was playing high stakes Checkers against a man who mastered Chess.

But the king of Texas had underestimated his enemy as well.

***

Chapo

Chapo sat in his van eavesdropping on Tiffany's plan to destroy him. He laughed at her ignorance, but he admired her heart. Under different circumstances he would've loved to have her on his team.

Meanwhile, while Chapo was in Chicago stirring up beef, Tiffany had called his #1 rival Lalo and had all his spots hit. Chapo had two vans parked behind him filled with his most trusted killers. Chapo let his guard down by warring with emotions. He wanted Tiffany's head on a platter, and he wanted to severe it himself just like he did her best friend. His son Ceasar sat in the passenger seat with a chip on his shoulder as well. Blackboy had shot him in the stomach and left him bleeding out. Although he knew Blackboy didn't intend to kill him, he wanted his lick back, for himself and for his brother.

Chapo looked at his burner phone after feeling it vibrate in the cup holder. He grabbed it and read a text message: *'Greenlight'*. That was the keyword he'd been waiting for. Chapo sent a text to his goons waiting in the trucks behind him. He had fifteen killers with him, including his son.

Ceasar pulled his ski mask down and cocked back his 300-blackout assault rifle. The security guard that was on duty was in the trunk of his own car. "You know the drill," Chapo said to his son as he saw the crowd spilling out of the project building.

"Make it messy," Ceasar said before hopping out in sync with the other goons.

Ceasar had his target on one person— Tiffany. She had to pay for what she did to his brother. He raised his gun and let it ride.

Blocka! Blocka! Blocka! Tat! Tat! Tat! Tat! Ch-Ch-Boom!

Ceasar and his boys ambushed Tiffany's army like they were playing a game of Call of Duty. A couple of her shooters dropped instantly but many of them spread out and returned fire.

Boc! Boc! Boc! Gla! Gla! Gla!

The Glocks and Dracos made an instrumental together.

Even though Ceasar's killers were seasoned and had an advantage, they were outnumbered 20 to 1. Ceasar couldn't get his target due to so many bullets whistling past his head. The shootouts he had in Texas couldn't come close to the heat he was taking in Chiraq. Chapo didn't tell him that this city lived for killing. He only told him he knew where to find his brother's killer. Ceasar was a gangster, but he wasn't ready to die. Not in Chicago. He retreated and hopped back into the bulletproof van with his pops, breathing hard. "Pops ... it's too many," he huffed.

Chapo knew that Tiffany had stolen enough money and drugs to support a war, but he didn't think she had the brains and balls. "Fuuck!" Chapo banged his fist against the steering wheel as he watched his men get gunned down.

He could hear police sirens in the distance as he pulled away and left his men hanging. He and Ceasar had to get away from the scene.

"You're hit," he told Ceasar. Ceasar followed his dad's eyes to a stain in his left thigh. Ceasar ripped off his bullet proof vest to make sure no bullets had penetrated his armor. He had several holes in his vest, but none went through. Next, he ripped his shirt off and tied it around his thigh tightly.

"Hold tight, I'm gonna get you out of here," Chapo said as he made a hard right turn and headed towards the expressway.

Chapo broke his burner phone into pieces and threw each piece out of the window as he drove to Gary, Indiana. His goons knew to go straight to the meet-up spot behind Harold's restaurant, but he doubted any of them would make it out. He trained them to stand their ground until the end. Since he never signaled them to retreat, they'd take their last breath in Chicago. Even if they were smart enough to break out, returning to Chapo's meet-up spot wouldn't be in their best interest.

Chapo dumped the van and hopped into a Corvette with Ceasar. He took him to another spot where an Indian woman took the bullet out his thigh and sewed his wound up nicely.

Next, Chapo and Ceasar went to board they're private jet and rushed back to Texas. Tiffany had to pay for the damage she caused. She had stolen his drugs, his money, and his family. He had underestimated her by a long shot. He failed to realize that he was dealing with a woman from Chicago with a kid to raise. She looked death in the eyes once, this time she wasn't gonna lay down for no human that can bleed just like her.

Chapo caught a gut feeling as his private jet landed back on his property. He could sense that something was wrong. He finally turned on his cell phone and it began to ring immediately. He read the name on the screen before answering "Hola," Chapo listened to the person talk before ending the call. His face became red with rage from the bad news. "Fuuck!" He slung the phone.

Chapter 44

Big Juan

"Blessings D!" Everybody called out to Big Juan the legendary maniac Latin Disciple. Today is his big day, the day he starts trial. Big Juan knew he was going home; he just didn't know how he would live life with the two women of his life dead and gone. Miracle had told him the story Tiffany had given her and her brother. Big Juan made a mental note to see Tiffany about that situation. She was the only person with the answers to his questions.

"Love," Big Juan said as he stepped off the tier at 5:00 am.

He'd been waiting on this day for thirteen long years. Even though Ciara had crossed him he still loved her. Without the information she had given Miracle to give to his lawyer, Big Juan's appeal would've been nearly impossible to win.

Big Juan went from bullpen to bullpen for five long hours before his trial began.

"All rise," the judge ordered. "Court is now in session."

Miracle showed up to support her father. Baby J thought it was best for him to stay clear from the law for a while.

Miracle watched as the state's attorney attempted to assassinate her father's character, bringing up his prior convictions and alleged mob ties which had nothing to do with the crime he was convicted of, and Juan's lawyer did a great job of making that clear.

"Your honor, I would like to turn over a video to the state's attorney"

"What will this video show?" the judge asked.

"It will show a full video confession of my client's ex-wife admitting that she framed my client. She also admits to raping her own niece at the age of four years old."

Miracle's face became red with embarrassment. She hated to think about what her aunt did to her.

The state's attorney looked surprised. Juan's lawyer held back the key piece of evidence. He knew it would've knocked the state's attorney's socks off when she heard about the video. Miracle knew this would bring a different type of heat to her little brother since her aunt was missing. It didn't sit right with her father's situation either but for now rape was the charge so that's the battle they had to tackle for now.

After a toughly contested trial, a verdict wasc read.

"We the people of Illinois find the defender …"

***

Heaven

Heaven and April spent their Wednesday at the mall shopping for clothes for Miracle's after party. Miracle's prom was the upcoming Friday and the girls couldn't wait. Marrissa dropped the girls off because Miracle was attending her father's trial. Heaven walked inside the top brand clothing store searching around for something cute. She still hasn't become comfortable enough to show off her body with her scars, so she was in search of something flashy but full. She spotted a True Religion jean outfit hanging on the wall.

"Excuse me," she called for help.

The young man at the cashier stepped from behind the counter to assist her. "How can I help you?" he asked respectfully.

Heaven pointed to the white outfit. "Do y'all have that outfit in a size 28?"

"That one just came in, we have all sizes right now."

Heaven was happy to hear that. True Religion jeans made her booty look bigger.

"Well, I need that same outfit in a size 30," April said.

"No problem. Is that all?" the young man asked.

"Yeah, that'll be all" Heaven answered.

As soon as the boy disappeared into the back of the store April began to boost items from the rack.

"Girl, this shit is expensive as hell. You think I'm not finna get my bang for my buck."

Heaven giggled and looked at the back of the store where the man had disappeared and said, "Just put it back, I'll pay for your outfit"

"You ain't gotta tell me twice." April started returning the items quickly.

"I miss Stacy," Heaven said out of nowhere.

"Me, too, this would be her job if she was here." April placed the last shirt on the rack as the cashier returned from the back of the store holding what appears to be one large package. He stepped behind the counter and placed the outfits on top of it as he began to ring up the girls' total.

"$876.52 is your total."

"See un un that shit high as hell, let me see the tags," April grabbed one outfit and checked the price. "These outfits are only two seventy each."

"Correct," the cashier agreed.

"So how did our total come out to eight somethin'?"

"That includes the items you still have stuffed in yo' jacket." The cashier smiled.

April became embarrassed. She had been caught red handed. Heaven couldn't keep from laughing, her friend had been bashed. The funny thing is she had been held accountable without getting the police involved.

"That was a good one, Mr. Stalker," April said as she unloaded her stolen merch and placed it on the counter. The man smiled again.

"Now, I can be nice enough to use my discount," he cleared the register and rung up their total again. "Five eighty."

Heaven paid for the clothes with the money Blackboy had sent her.

"Thanks, Mr. Stalker," April rolled her eyes with a smile.

"J-Roc."

"Huh," April looked dumbfounded.

"My name is J-Roc and you're welcome sticky fingers." His smile widened.

"*Whatever*. Byeee!" April walked out of the store and busted out into laughter.

"Girl, he's kinda cute," April said as they walked towards Kids Footlocker.

"Well, next time try using your face to get what you want cause your hands ain't worth shit," Heaven joked.

Just like before, April wanted to rock the same shoes Heaven was interested in, but she had short change. Heaven bought her best friend the same Jordan 12s she purchased for herself.

Next they walked into the Victoria Secrets store. Heaven wanted to buy some sexy panties to wear for her man. Blackboy was set to hear his motion and come home next month. Heaven made up her mind to give him her virginity. Even though Blackboy seemed to outgrow her mentally they were on the same page emotionally. Heaven just hoped he had the same heart he's always had.

"Girl, what chu picking up lingerie for?" April asked, noticing the pink lingerie in Heaven's hand.

"Mind your business, bitch." Heaven placed her items on the counter.

"Blackboy finna tear that up, huh?" April teased.

Heaven was the only one who still had her v-card, her friends had lost theirs in grammar school. Heaven rolled her eyes at April. Since Stacy passed away, April had taken her place, annoying Heaven.

"Bitch hush," Heaven said as she paid her total and left the store.

She put all her underwear inside her Footlocker bag with her shoes and threw the Victoria Secret bag into a nearby trash can before taking the escalator down to the first floor of the mall where the food court was located.

Heaven bought her and her friend Chinese food while they waited for her mom to arrive. Marrissa had drove up the street to get a pedicure and massage while her daughter shopped.

"Watch my food, I'm 'bout to go use the bathroom before yo' mama pull up," April said as she rushed off to the lady's restroom. Heaven opened a pack of soy sauce and poured it on her shrimp fried rice.

She stirred the sauce around and took one bite. It felt like she hadn't eaten in weeks when the taste settled on her tongue. Heaven spotted a fortune cookie inside her bag. She grabbed it and cracked it open to read her fortune. *There's someone from your past waiting to ruin your future,* Heaven let the words she read sink in. She folded the piece of paper and threw it on the floor. The first person that came to her mind was Blackboy. *Will he break my heart?* she asked herself.

Blackboy had made her feel a way she never felt before. Every time he called her, she caught butterflies. They would spend hours on the phone talking about love. Heaven still thought like a twelve-year-old girl when it came to love.

Blackboy had thrown questions at her that she couldn't answer right away. His conversations had elevated to another level, and he knew Heaven would need time to understand the concept but he would wait as long as she needed him to. As long as their hearts were on the same page.

April clapped her hands, breaking Heaven from her daydream. "Girl, you ain't hear me calling yo' name? Yo mama here."

Heaven looked out the glass doors of the mall and spotted her mom van parked with her hazard lights blinking. Heaven grabbed her bags and walked out, leaving her food. April took hers and followed Heaven to her mom's van.

After taking April to her home in Maywood, Heaven sat back in silence the whole ride home. Once they pulled in front of their home her mom asked, "What's on your mind?"

"Am I that transparent?" Heaven asked.

"I'm your mom. It's my job to know when your mood changes."

Heaven sat back in her seat for a second, contemplating on venting to her mother before she finally said, "I read a fortune cookie today."

"And what did it say?" Marrissa asked.

Heaven recited the words to her mother, "There's someone from your past waiting to ruin your future,"

Marrissa let the words settle just as her daughter did moments earlier. "Do you think it's April?" she asked. Heaven was too busy thinking about Blackboy to give her best friend any thought.

"April?" Heaven repeated.

"Yeah April. She's not the April you used to know, Heaven."

Heaven began to think about her friends' new personality. The way she carried herself was much different from the April, Heaven used to know. "I didn't want to say anything but before we left home, I went to use the restroom and I could've sworn I saw April searching through my purse when I came out. I brushed it off, but when I went to pay for my pedicure my money was missing. I had to use my credit card."

Heaven listened to her mother's words as she sat in silence. *What has gotten into her?* she asked herself. April had become a whole new person since Heaven reunited with her. She had witnessed April stealing things on countless occasions. Pointless things. She always told April, *If you need anything let me know.* April had always turned down Heaven's offer just to steal the items she desperately wanted.

Still, that wouldn't be something that'll ruin my future,

Heaven thought. Her mother seemed to read her mind. "Unless there's someone else from your past you can see ruining your future, honey. Either way, protect your peace," Marrissa said. She witnessed her daughter go through a lot in life for a teenager. She, as a mother, had not endured half the pain her daughter felt, mentally, physically, and emotionally.

Heaven still had nightmares about Stacy that she started taking medication for. Heaven's mind went back to Blackboy as she and her mother exited their vehicle and made their way into their house. Marrissa needed to take a quick shower before leaving out for work. Heaven dropped her bags on the floor of her room and undressed before climbing into her bed. Her phone began to ring just as she pulled the cover over her body. She eagerly grabbed it and answered, "Hello", without looking at the caller ID.

"Damn, you must've been waiting by the phone," Blackboy joked.

"Maybe," Heaven replied.

Blackboy shared news about his upcoming motion, he wanted Heaven to be there to see him win.

"Dennis, do you love me?" Heaven asked softly. She wanted to make sure she was making the right decision.

"Of course I do. Why you ask?"

"I read a fortune cookie today," Heaven paused.

"Okay. What did it say?"

Heaven could sense that Blackboy didn't like where the conversation was going but she finished anyway. "It said there's someone from your past waiting to ruin your future"

"I guess you believe that someone is me." Blackboy felt offended by Heaven's words.

"I don't believe anything; I just don't want to be hurt by you or anyone else. You know what I've been through."

"Heaven, you're believing a cookie that anybody could have bought –"

"It was God that led me to the mall. I was in the right place at the right time," Heaven defended her beliefs.

Blackboy knew how spiritual Heaven could get so he left the argument alone. He just wanted to assure her that he was not the enemy. "You're right baby. But you don't have to question my love. I'll be the person from your past that builds your future, not tear it down." Blackboy's words soothed Heaven's heart, making her smile inside and out.

"That's all I needed to know because I love you Dennis."

"I love you more."

Heaven told Blackboy about her trip to the mall and the sexy lingerie she had purchased for the day he came home. After one straight hour of sweet-talking Blackboy had to end the call and hide his cell phone.

"Honey I'm going to work, call me if you need anything," Marrissa called out before walking out of the house.

Heaven put her phone on the charger and closed her eyes with Blackboy on her mind. She had the deepest thoughts of him pleasing her sexually. Her juice box became moist from her wild imagination. She wanted a future and a family with Blackboy. He was the light to her dark tunnel.

Heaven heard the front door open. She figured her mom must've left something like she had often done. That wouldn't stop her from fantasizing about her future with her man. Heaven kept her eyes closed and thought of all the things she would do with Blackboy when he came home. She could hear her room door being opened but she remained in a dream world. Heaven knew her mom would eventually leave if she pretended to be asleep. *'She probably just wants a hug anyway'* Heaven thought as she felt her mom's presence looming over her. She smiled on the inside at how sweet her mom was when it came to her. Suddenly she felt hands wrap around her neck, choking the life out of her as she tried to gulp for air. When she opened her eyes all she saw was a hospital mask and blonde hair. Heaven's vision went blurry just moments before she lost consciousness.

Chapter 45

Big Juan

Two weeks later

Big Juan had been making his rounds around the city, claiming his throne again. He had made a call to his drug connect which he was scheduled to meet the next morning. Big Juan had a busy schedule but first he had to go see an old friend about some serious business. His ex-wife was murdered and only one person knew what had went down. He looked at the photo in his hand of the house he was parked in front of and turned off his GPS. Then he deaded the engine on the blue F-150 truck that he had a friend rent for him before hopping out and approaching Tiffany's doorstep. As he raised his hand to knock, the door came open.

"Welcome home, daddy." Tiffany wrapped her hands around his neck and kissed his lips repeatedly. Big Juan pushed Tiffany inside her house and closed the door behind him. He whistled and the three pitbull's he purchased had come running full speed. He rubbed each one behind their ears before turning his attention back to Tiffany.

"So, everything's, everything?" Big Juan asked

"You're here ain't you?" Tiffany took Big Juan by the hand and led him to their master bedroom where she showed him a hidden safe. Tiffany pressed a few buttons and the safe popped open, revealing so much cash it made Big Juan knees buckle. He could smell the Benjamins. He grabbed a stack of hundreds and sniffed long and hard. It's been a long thirteen years since he touched the almighty dollar that made the world go around.

"And that other thing?" Tiffany knew what he was referring to.

"Chapo took care of Ci-Ci for you, she'll never be able to cross you again."

"That's my baby," Big Juan grabbed a handful of Tiffany's bare ass before sticking his tongue down her throat.

It was Big Juan's plan to have Ci-Ci date Chapo. He knew once Chapo found out he was being set up, Ci-Ci was dead as a doorknob. Tiffany told Juan all about the torture Chapo had taken her through. The plan he gave her to have Ci-Ci killed, had killed two birds with one stone.

She was able to rob Chapo blind and put her lover back on his feet. Tiffany could step down and be a housewife now while Big Juan ruled the city again. His only competition would be his stepson, Blackboy. Big Juan would have to accept sharing the pie in order to eat in peace.

Tiffany led Big Juan to the bed and gave him what he'd been missing. She pulled his pants to his ankles and dropped to her knees, taking him to the back of her throat inch by inch until he disappeared in her mouth. Big Juan's ten inches slid somewhere in Tiffany's chest before she pulled him out and deep throated him again without gagging. Big Juan squeezed his eyes closed, trying to fight back the feeling of exploding in just seconds. He knew he was out of luck when it came to Tiffany's head game, she was a boss with it.

She wrapped both hands around his dick and twisted as she sucked him off until he filled her throat with semen. Big Juan hadn't jacked off in two months so he nutted enough to fill a cup. Tiffany didn't let a drop go to waste as she cleaned up her mess before pushing Big Juan onto the king size bed. She climbed on top of him and rubbed his limp dick against her clit. She could feel it jumping back to life in her hand. When his dick stiffened up, she inserted it in her walls inch by inch. She slid up and down slowly until Big Juan became fully erect again. Then she pressed both her hands in his chest like she was performing CPR while she bounced on his dick.

Big Juan was in heaven. He hadn't felt a woman's insides in thirteen long years and Tiffany was outdoing herself with refreshing his memory. Her juices were flowing like water as she rode him to the end of the line before jumping off the train and letting him put it in her asshole. She bent over and put her face in the pillow as Juan slid inside her back door. Tiffany bit the pillow to stop from screaming out. She wanted to take the dick like a porn star. Next, she smacked her own ass to let Big Juan know she wanted him to kill it.

Big Juan smacked her ass so hard he left a handprint. Tiffany still threw her ass back. If he thought she was gonna run from it he had another thing coming. He wasn't aware that she had crack in her system. Big Juan thought this was the new Tiffany, ten times freakier. After ten straight minutes of rodding her asshole out he showered and grabbed the keys to the brand new Bentley she had leased for him and headed out. Big Juan had somewhere to be.

Chapter 46

Miracle

Miracle stared in the mirror at herself, she looked like she was getting married instead of going on prom. Tears came to her eyes as she began to think about everyone who matters. Her biological parents, Baby J, and Heaven. She hasn't talked to Heaven in two days. Marrissa said she was missing when she returned from work. Heaven's cell phone was still laying in her bed which raised a red flag, Miracle knew Heaven would leave her head at home before leaving her cell phone. April told Marrissa she hasn't heard from Heaven since they took her home. Miracle prayed for Heaven to return home safely. Her friend was supposed to be there to watch her act a fool. Tiffany had rented Miracle a Maserati for prom and purchased her a YSL purse to match her dress. She upgraded her prom shoes to Red Bottoms heels. Miracle looked like she stepped off the front page of a magazine.

Knock! Knock! Knock!

"Who is it?"

"It's me, baby. Your date is here," Miracle's foster mom answered.

Miracle caught butterflies instantly at the mention of Boozer's name. She'd been waiting to see him in his suit for months. He told her he was keeping his drip a surprise.

"I'm coming!" Miracle yelled through the door before checking out her hair and makeup. When she opened the door, Boozer was standing there looking sharp as a tac. He wore a silver Christian Dior suit with an aqua colored trimming. His vest and shoes were also aqua. Boozer waves looked like they belonged on a hair product commercial as they spun into a 360 style around his head. He had dark tinted shades to cover his eyes. Miracle smiled at her thug. 'He so fine' she said in her mind from the way he licked his lips she knew Boozer was thinking the same thing. She gave him a hug and grabbed his hand.

"Come on you two. The people are waiting to see y'all," her mom said as she went over and played the song Miracle requested

Turn on the light, I'm looking for her/I'm looking for her /I'm looking for her... Future's voice pumped through the speakers as Miracle and Boozer stepped into the doorway.

The crowd screamed and applauded. So many people came to see Orr's star basketball player. Miracle didn't recognize half of the faces she laid eyes on, but she kept her best smile on for the camera. Boozer put on a slight smile, but he was a little uncomfortable without his gun. Miracle told him they would be searching at the plaza, but Bizzy was in the cut with his Glock ready to pop off at the first sign of action.

Miracle and Boozer stepped down the stairs one step at a time as the crowd caught them from all angles. Once they reached the last step, Boozer grabbed Miracle by the waist and began to pose. They looked amazing together. Miracle was worried that Boozer's drug money wouldn't be long enough to keep him in the race, but her man came to play. The crowd grew quiet as a royal blue Bentley pulled up with dark tinted windows. Boozer located Bizzy who was already clutching his heat. Boozer smiled at his homie's instincts.

The engine went dead, and the driver's door opened slowly. Miracle looked to see who was stealing her show. Big Juan stepped out of the car and her heart dropped. She hiked up her dress and ran into the street with her heels on.

She hugged her father so tight he felt tears forming in his eyes. Miracle looked up to him with tears in her own
"You made it!" She smiled before burying her face in his chest.

"I told you I wouldn't miss this for the world," Big Juan said as he wrapped his arms around his daughter, one tear fell, and then another. Big Juan took no effort in trying to stop them from flowing. His baby girl was a young woman now. "I don't want to steal your show, baby girl. Go take pictures for a night you'll never forget."

"You got that right." Miracle smiled before turning around. "Take our picture."

Snap! Snap! Snap! The cameras started rolling again.

Miracle looked at Boozer and signaled for him to join them. He hesitated before finally joining her side. He looked Big Juan in his eyes like a man and spoke.

"Nice to meet you, I'm –"

"My daughter's future husband, right?" Big Juan winked as he and Boozer shook hands. He respected the love Boozer had for his daughter therefore he would save the lecture for later and support his daughter's decision.

"Right," Boozer agreed.

Big Juan leaned in and embraced him before whispering in his ear. "Don't worry, I'll have security watching you from here to there. Go have fun." He patted Boozer's back. *Who is this nigga?* Boozer asked himself. Big Juan's presence felt powerful. Big Juan slid Boozer a stack of money. "Make sure this night is everything she imagined." Boozer nodded. He liked Miracle's dad already.

"Okay we 'bout to get up out of here, I love you guys," Miracle yelled as she handed Boozer the keys to the Maserati. She gave her dad another hug and a kiss on the cheek. "Welcome home, Dad, I love you."

"I love you more, baby doll. Enjoy your night."

Miracle climbed into the passenger seat and put her seatbelt on. She looked in her rearview mirror to see Baby J climbing into the driver seat of their father's Bentley and she smiled. She had the three most important people of her life all on the same team. Boozer locked his hand into hers and drove off into the night. He noticed the same three cars that were parked outside Miracle's house, following him. He smiled

"What chu smiling at? What my daddy say to you?"

"He told me what I already knew," Boozer turned up the radio and let the radio express his feeling. *Even when your hustling days are gone/she'll be by your side still holding on/and even when yo' spinners stop spinning, and all those gold-digging women disappear/she'll still be here...*

Chapter 47

Heaven

Heaven woke up in a bedroom handcuffed to the bed. Since she had been kidnapped her captor had fed her three meals; three of her favorite meals. Heaven found that a little strange. She made a mental note that whoever had abducted her knew her very well. The bedroom she was being held hostage was pink just like hers.

Other than her being kidnapped, no harm was done. The person never revealed their face. Each time they came to feed her, but Heaven could tell that it was a woman. She smelled the perfume and every time the woman left the smell would linger for hours. Heaven started to play process of elimination in her head. Her first guess was Stacy's mother, Tiny. *She's too skinny to be Tiny. Tiny's thick as hell,* she thought. *Daddy's ex-wife. She's probably mad that my dad left her for my mom.* She didn't know how Karim's ex-wife looked but if anyone had a reason to kidnap her it would be a mad ex-wife. Heaven stopped thinking to focus on the room door that came open.

The lady walked in with a mask on with a plate of blueberry pancakes. This time Heaven wouldn't be so cooperative, she wanted answers. The lady chopped the pancakes in squares just how Heaven likes them. "Open wide."

Heaven shook her head. "Why are you doing this? What do you want from me?" The woman sat the plate down on the dresser and sat beside Heaven.

"You ruined my relationship and my life," the woman answered.

This has to be his ex-wife, Heaven thought as the lady kept talking. "Everything was just fine until you came into the picture. I thought you would've made us closer, but I was wrong, you caused me more pain."

"I'm not the reason you and my dad didn't work out. He's not good enough for you and he's not good enough for my mother. He'll always be a cheater."

"Your mother?" the woman repeated

"Yes, she left him. She must've caught him cheating. You're not the only person that hates him,"

"Do *you* hate him?"

Heaven sat back and thought about the question the woman asked her. "Not really. I haven't gotten the chance to know him as a father, I've always known him as a principal."

"How did he treat your mother?"

"He couldn't have been treating her too good; she left him. I know you're his wife. Just let me go; I'll call him and talk to him" Heaven tried to reason with the woman.

"I don't want him. He's nothing but a manipulator and a cheater"

"So, what do you want from me?" Heaven asked. *What else could she possibly want?* she asked herself.

"I came to take back what's mine," the woman said.

Heaven was confused. She had no idea what the lady was referring to. Finally, the woman pulled down her mask and removed her wig. Heaven couldn't believe her eyes. She was seeing a ghost, literally. *This has to be a dream*, she thought. "Mom?"

"In the flesh." The woman smiled. Heaven became puzzled, staring at her biological mother, Gabriella Guzman.

"How is this possible?" Heaven asked.

"God gets the last word."

To be continued…

COMING SOON

Until We Meet Again Part 2

Made in United States
Orlando, FL
30 May 2025